THE VALUATION OF SOCIAL COST

Other books by D. W. Pearce

Cost-Benefit Analysis (Macmillan, 1971)
Capital Investment Appraisal (with C. J. Hawkins) (Macmillan, 1971)
Cost-Benefit Analysis: Theory and Practice (with A. Dasgupta)
  (Macmillan, 1971)
The Economics of Natural Resource Depletion (ed.) (Macmillan, 1975)
Environmental Economics (Longman, 1976)

The Valuation of Social Cost

Edited by
DAVID W. PEARCE
Professor of Political Economy, University of Aberdeen

London
GEORGE ALLEN & UNWIN
Boston   Sydney

First published in 1978

GEORGE ALLEN & UNWIN LTD
40 Museum Street, London WC1A 1LU

© George Allen & Unwin (Publishers) Ltd, 1978

ISBN 0 04 330289 0 Hardback
   0 04 330290 4 Paperback

Typeset in 10 on 11 point Times
and printed in Great Britain by William Clowes and Sons Limited, Beccles

Contents

Notes on Contributors

DAVID W. PEARCE is Professor of Political Economy at the University of Aberdeen, Scotland.

CHRISTOPHER NASH is British Rail Lecturer in Transport Economics at the Institute for Transport Studies, University of Leeds.

JOHN GIBSON is Lecturer in the Department of Transportation and Environmental Planning, University of Birmingham.

R. KERRY TURNER is Lecturer in Environmental Economics, School of Environmental Sciences, University of East Anglia.

GAVIN MOONEY is Director of the Health Economics Research Unit, University of Aberdeen, Scotland.

JOHN K. STANLEY is Chief Economist, Premier's Department, Victorian Government, Victoria, Australia.

ALAN RATTRAY is Principal Planning Officer (Social Science), National Telecommunications Planning Branch, Telecom Australia, Melbourne, Australia

RICHARD LECOMBER is Reader in Economics at the University of Bristol.

Introduction

A basic tenet of what we might call 'conventional' economics – economics based on the neoclassical tradition and which still dominates teaching in both developed and less developed countries – is that the prices of goods and services are 'signals' reflecting consumer desires. The free interplay of market forces should therefore allocate resources to goods and goods to people in such a way as to secure the maximum welfare of society, where 'welfare' is equated with the satisfaction of wants. No modern economist seriously believes that any real world economy operates in such a way as to maximise welfare. Rather, the *idea* that there exists some configuration of prices which will achieve this optimum is used as a yardstick against which to measure the degree of imperfection in an economy and hence the extent to which policies should be directed towards correcting those deviations.

Without in any way sanctioning the view that consumer wants *should* dictate the allocation of all goods and services (indeed, several chapters in this volume explain why such an 'economic democracy' is undesirable for some sectors of the economy), we can take this yardstick concept and use it to focus on one of the imperfections in modern economies. This concerns the extent to which market prices deviate from 'socially desirable' prices – let us call them *social prices* – because some goods and 'disgoods' appear to be provided other than through a market mechanism. Indeed, the emphasis is on disgoods – nuisances such as noise, regrettable happenings such as injury or loss of home or neighbours – although one chapter is devoted to a positive good, the experience of recreational benefit. Hence the title, *The Valuation of Social Cost,* for what this book is concerned with is both the idea and the practical problems of placing a money value on these non-marketed goods and disgoods (or 'bads' as we might now call them).

Certain philosophical problems have to be overcome before such an investigation can take place. Not the least of these is the widespread feeling, not necessarily confined to non-economists, that at least some things in life are 'beyond money'. Such a view is often the result of an almost theological stance to the effect that money is the root of all evil, and hence to attempt a money evaluation of things which, perhaps for good reason, lie outside the market system is to be tainted with some of that evil. Yet if such a view is to be sustained it must encompass all goods, marketed or otherwise, for with few exceptions, non-marketed goods lie outside the market simply because of historical accident. For example, the fact that airspace is not generally owned by individuals has meant that 'peace and quiet' in respect of aircraft noise is not a good that is sold on the market. The establishment of property rights to such a good would bring it within the market sphere and a price would result. Thus, to object to the 'monetisation' of peace and quiet by indirect methods aimed at observing behaviour in response to this non-marketed good can only be philosophically sound if the same objection is made against the pricing of apples or TV sets.

Further, the opponents of monetisation often fail to see *why* the economist seeks to put money values on as many goods and bads as he can. Essentially, money is just a convenient measuring rod. It is designed to measure the extent to which individuals express a preference for or against the good or bad in question. If some other measure were available one doubts if the quasi-theological objection noted above would arise. Indeed, some of the current movement back to the measurement of preferences in terms of cardinal units ('utils') may reflect the desire to escape this misplaced criticism.

Nor does it seem that the opponents of monetisation object to the adding up of the costs of different inputs to arrive at a cost figure for, say, a motorway or an airport. (We abstract from that school of economic thought which objects to the aggregation of the money values of real capital inputs: for this debate, which will not be considered at all in this book, see Harcourt, 1972.) Yet, if costs are measured in monetary units, there are substantial gains to be had from measuring other costs and benefits in money units as well. The simple justification for this is that *without* such monetary measurement, we have little idea of *how much* of a good to provide or *how much* of a bad to remove. If we can measure everything in money terms we can adopt a simple rule:

Maximise (Benefits − Costs).

In conventional cost-benefit terms, allowing for the inclusion of a positive discount rate and for the fact that costs and benefits are distributed over time, the above formulation can be written more rigorously as:

$$\text{Max} \sum_{t}^{T} \frac{B_t - C_t}{(1+r)^t}$$

where B_t and C_t are benefits and costs in time period t, r is the discount rate and T is the 'time-horizon'. Obviously, if B_t and C_t are in different units, no such decision rule can be used. Indeed, when it proves practically impossible to secure monetary estimates of a project's outputs (whether cost or benefit), we are reduced to *cost-effectiveness analysis*. Cost-effectiveness is better than nothing: by expressing effects in terms of output per unit of cost we at least secure the best piece of information we can. But, by definition, a cost-effective picture will not tell us how much of a good to provide without judgement being exercised by someone as to what level the project should be cut off. The basic desire of economists to put monetary values on all costs and benefits is therefore understandable.

As a final justification we must consider the fact that, like it or not, *any* decision *implies* a monetary valuation. Given a project with known monetary costs and benefits, C and B respectively, and unknown costs of U, we have the following possibilities:

(i) $$B > (C + U)$$

(ii) $$B < (C + U)$$

(iii) $$B = (C + U)$$

They are exclusive possibilities simply because once a project is considered as a possibility, we can either accept or reject it. Doing nothing is equivalent to rejecting the project. But if accept or reject are in turn all-encompassing and exclusive decisions, then an acceptance implies that option (i) is the case and rejection that (ii) or (iii) are the case. If option (i) is chosen we have *implicitly* valued U at a monetary amount which must be *less* than $B - C$. If (ii) is chosen we have implicitly valued U at some amount greater than $B - C$. Notice that we do not secure *actual estimates,* merely upper bounds (case (i)) or lower bounds (case (ii)). *But the essential point is that the necessity to choose entails a monetary evaluation.*

How far implicit values should be used is a debatable question. There are practitioners who argue for the use of such implicit values even when valuations derived from the persons affected by the project might be available. The justification here might be that decision makers (a convenient phrase for a frequently unidentifiable class!) are in a better position to judge than are those affected. This may well be so for health-care, with major decisions such as investment in nuclear energy where the technological knowledge required is complex, and so on. All too often, however, one suspects that such arguments understate the ability of individuals to understand information if it is presented to them, and reflect a desire to avoid public participation so that the civil servant can secure a 'quiet life'. The approach certainly does nothing to further the concept of an open government. However, it must be conceded that there will be situations in which individuals' preferences will not be obtainable *in principle*. As a rule, however, we might advance the idea that 'implicit' valuations should be sought only *after* we are fully satisfied that we can do no better. Moreover, the use of implied values raises a question not often asked, namely whether it is ever legitimate to *add* implied values to other valuations derived from observations of consumer preferences. For example, if all benefits are measured by implied values but costs are measured at market prices, the practitioner has effectively used two entirely different bases for securing monetisation: benefits are measured at what decision makers think they are worth and costs are measured at what individuals are prepared to pay for resources.

It is also worth noting that monetary estimates of social costs are essential for the application of social cost pricing. The idea that prices in an economy should be equal not to marginal *private* cost but marginal social cost is a well-established requirement for optimality in the neoclassical sense (for a proof, see Pearce, 1976, Chapter 1). But for such a principle to be applied it is necessary to know the marginal social cost at the point of optimality and this can only be identified with knowledge of the marginal external cost *function* (where marginal external cost is the difference between marginal social cost and marginal private cost). That is, it is necessary to know how external cost varies with the output of the externality creating good. The extent to which *functions* as opposed to *point estimates* are known is discussed later. For the moment, we simply observe that marginal social cost pricing requires us to value social cost in money terms.

All this said, the philosophical desirability of securing money estimates of costs and benefits is something quite different from the practical possibilities of securing such estimates. And it is mainly to the latter question that this book is devoted, although the fundamental theoretical issues are raised several times in different contexts. The overall conclusion must be that the current 'state of the art' is not encouraging for those who think that social cost and benefit can be measured. One may draw various conclusions from this outcome. Perhaps the state of the art can be improved. Several chapters in this book indicate areas where more research might generate 'acceptable' valuations. Or perhaps we have gone as far as we can and the intrinsic difficulties of extracting values from non-market situations might be such as to make it impossible for us to go any further. The reader is left to judge for himself. In the meantime it is useful to outline what *can* be said if various states of knowledge are available to us.

Consider the case of pollution control. Figure I.1 shows the benefit and cost functions for various degrees of pollution control. CC is the total cost of controlling pollution, and CB the benefits from control. The optimum level of pollution control is then X, where the benefits minus costs are maximised in accordance with the rules stated earlier. Figure I.1 represents the most hoped for state of knowledge. It enables us to identify the optimal degree of pollution control (and hence the optimal level of externality which, in this case, is the amount of pollution associated with points to the right of X^* in Figure I.1) and it requires us to estimate an entire benefit (cost) *function* such as CB in Figure I.1.

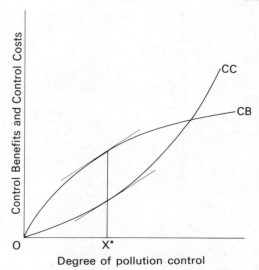

Figure I.1   *Costs and benefits of pollution control*

Figure I.2 illustrates the situation for remaining states of knowledge. In Figure I.2 we assume that the benefit function is not known. In the case of Figure I.1 the benefit function was in fact the pollution damage function seen from the standpoint of pollution control – increased benefits mean reduced damages. Now, assume someone 'in authority' chooses a pollution control level, say X_1 in Figure I.2. The argument is that, in so doing, they 'imply' that benefits exceed X_1. But this is all, for we have no particular reason to say that benefits are equal to B_1, B_2 or whatever. The most that can be said is that the relevant part of the benefit function, as perceived by the decision-maker, lies in the area above CC in Figure I.2. (Strictly, a little more than this is implied. The area has CC as a boundary, implying that B could be equal to B_0. But this is inconsistent with the implied value approach because such a belief would lead the decision maker to reduce control below X_1 since, assuming reasonable shapes for the unknown benefit function, he would know that net benefits would be greater than zero to the left of X_1. Thus the lower boundary of the shaded area becomes indeterminate.) This is an important point. If the decision maker were continually to change the pollution control level because of, say, altered standard setting requirements, he would effectively trace out the CC function up to some point which might perhaps be the point of maximum net benefits (if his beliefs were very accurate) or the point at which benefits equalled costs. The 'implied' valuation approach therefore adds slightly to our knowledge, but it does *not* trace out a benefit function.

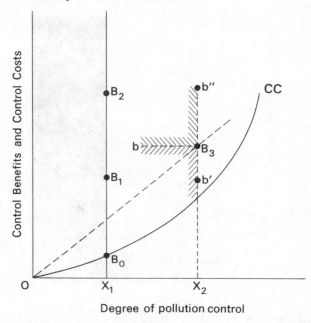

Figure I.2   *Optimal control with unknown benefit function*

Now suppose we have some information about one *point* on the benefit function, say, B_3. This improves our knowledge to some extent. We cannot assume that the decision maker has knowledge of the curvature of the benefit function, although where benefits are related to 'threshold' values of environmental quality (e.g. water quality related to potability, fish species present, swimming, etc.) he may have some idea. As a first approximation, he might draw the line OB_3 on the assumption that benefits are linearly related to pollution control (there is some evidence on this for noise, for example). Then, B_3 would be revealed as lying to the right of the optimum and control levels could be set accordingly. Of course this is a considerable jump to make from such limited knowledge, but if nothing else is known it might serve as an approximation.

Perhaps more important is some assessment of whether B_3 is likely to be a maximum estimate or a minimum estimate. If it is thought to be a maximum, the implication will be that the benefit function lies in the quadrant the corner of which is represented by bB_3b' in Figure I.2. Again, we see that this would help us locate the optimum to the left of B_3 if CC has the shape shown in Figure I.2. If, however, B_3 is a minimum the benefit function lies in the quadrant the corner of which is bB_3b''. We now have no real ideas as to whether B_3 is above or below the optimum. Hence it is useful to have some statement concerning the belief about whether a point estimate is a minimum or maximum. A maximum estimate is more useful if we are seeking the optimum standard. Remember, however, that a minimum estimate still enables us to exclude some options: thus if B_3 is a minimum it nonetheless lies above the CC curve thus showing that a move from O to control level X_2 is worthwhile. Of course, a minimum estimate that lies below AC would have little value since the true value could then lie above AC.

The general point is that some *knowledge* of social cost valuations is better than none, whether it be for designing taxes to secure marginal social cost pricing, for setting standards to regulate output, for determining the optimum size of projects, and so on. There are then forceful reasons for searching for monetary estimates of social cost. Whether the practical experience in valuing social cost gives cause for comfort or dismay in this respect is another matter and one which this book is concerned with. It is perhaps fitting to note that the strongest advocates of measuring social cost have often been those who have never engaged in the actual practice of trying to measure it. All the authors in this book have extensive experience of making that effort.

REFERENCES

Harcourt, G. C., *Some Cambridge Controversies in the Theory of Capital* (Cambridge: CUP, 1972).
Pearce, D. W., *Environmental Economics* (London: Longman, 1976).

Chapter 1

The Theory of Social Cost Measurement[*]

INTRODUCTION

Whilst attempts to measure the social costs of alternative courses of action, and to use the results in a policy context, are of relatively recent origin, the theory of social cost measurement has been the centre of academic controversy ever since the publication of Pigou's classic work *The Economics of Welfare* in 1920 (Pigou, 1920). The debate has centred on two broad areas:

(1) The significance of divergences between private and social cost and their implications for the role of the state in a market economy.
(2) The principles upon which the measurement of social cost is to be based.

In the first place, acceptance of the notion that social costs and private costs differ implies acceptance that individuals seeking their own utility and firms seeking to make profits will ignore certain costs to society of the decisions they make. An *a priori* case is therefore created for some form of state intervention in the workings of a market economy. This could take the form of direct controls, outright ownership of the sector in question, or a system of taxes and subsidies to bring about equality between private and social cost. Clearly the latter will require a money measure of social costs, but it has been the growing popularity of the use of cost-benefit analysis as an aid to decision taking in the first two cases that has led to the tremendous growth in effort to measure social costs in money terms in recent years. On the other hand, some economists have argued that the market is well able to cope with most of the apparent divergences between private and social cost in a modern economy, and that the preoccupation with the measurement of social cost is unnecessary and fruitless. The first part of this chapter will look at these debates, and consider the desirability and importance of obtaining money measures of social cost.

[*] I am indebted to Peter Mackie of the University of Leeds and David Pearce of Aberdeen University for comments on a previous draft of this chapter.

If it is considered that such measures are needed, the problem must be faced as to how to obtain them. When the concept was first introduced, before the rise of ordinalism, the principle seemed obvious: measure the total disutility caused to all members of society. Measurement in practice remained a problem, however, even where costs could be expressed in money terms. Aggregation required knowledge of how the marginal utility of income varied between members of society. With the rise of ordinalism, even the principles appeared threatened. If utility is regarded solely as an ordinal concept, how – even in principle – can the disutility caused to different members of society be aggregated? The solution which has been most commonly adopted by modern practitioners has resort to the 'compensation principle', usually associated with the names of Hicks (1939) and Kaldor (1939). By this, the social cost of a given output is defined as the sum of money which is just adequate when paid as compensation to restore to their previous level of utility all who lose as a result of production of the output in question. The second half of this chapter will take a critical look at the way in which the compensation principle is used in practice in the measurement of social cost.

DO PRIVATE AND SOCIAL COSTS DIFFER?

An implication of the above definition of social cost is that in the perfectly functioning competitive economy of elementary text book fame, in which individuals' utility depends solely on the consumption of goods, private and social cost are always equal. In order to produce a good, producers will have to pay for factors of production a sum just adequate to compensate their owners for diverting them from the next best use. If that use were the production of alternative goods, the value of the goods forgone by the diversion of the resources in question is exactly equal to the value produced. This is achieved by the universal pricing of goods at marginal cost and factors of production at marginal value product. (See any text on welfare economics, e.g. Bohm, 1973.)

In looking for divergences between private and social cost, then, we must look for cases of what is often termed 'market failure' (Bator, 1958). The most obvious of these is the presence of imperfect competition in either the commodity or the factor markets. For instance, suppose that the price of a factor exceeds the value of its marginal product, or the price of an intermediate good exceeds its marginal cost. Then the private cost of any production which uses these inputs will include an element of economic rent or profit over and above the necessary compensation. In this case private costs would exceed social cost. If the prices of inputs were held below their competitive level by monopsony power, private cost would understate social cost.

Although such market imperfections have long been central to the theory of resource allocation, comparatively little of the recent effort on the measurement of social cost in developed economies has been devoted to them. Studies have estimated shadow prices for particular categories of labour (for instance, specialised workers in declining industries who would be unlikely to obtain alternative employment if they were made redundant) and for foreign exchange, but no attempts have been made to assemble comprehensive and internally consistent sets of shadow prices for developed countries in the way in which this has been undertaken for developing economies (Little and Mirlees, 1974). For most purposes, market prices have generally been treated as being adequate.

The bulk of the effort in developed economies surrounds that far-flung group of phenomena generally lumped together in economic jargon as 'externalities'. A standard definition of an externality is 'any interdependency between production and/or consumption functions that is not traded in the market'. It thus encompasses the disbenefits imposed by the production or consumption of goods in the form of noise, air and water pollution, danger to health or safety, and social disruption. The effect may be on consumers, as when water pollution spoils recreational facilities, or on producers, or when it damages fisheries or inflicts costs on those using the water in industrial processes. When the divergence between private and social cost is of the form of an externality, it is termed the 'external' cost of the output in question.

The importance of such divergences will be obvious to any student of welfare economics. In the first place, in a competitive market output will be expanded up to the point at which price equals marginal private cost. But if there exist external costs at the margin, this means that output is being produced at the margin for which consumers are willing to pay less than the total compensation required for its production. A reduction in output to the point at which price equals marginal social cost will achieve a potential Pareto improvement in welfare, in that those gaining from the cutback could in principle more than compensate the losers for their loss of output. In Figure 1.1 let MPC_1 be marginal private cost, MSC_1 be marginal social cost and D be the demand curve. A cutback in output from Q_2 to Q_1 would save social costs of S, whilst leading to disbenefits of only B. That is, there are net gains equal to area S – area B. Note that external costs equal to area E remain even when price is set equal to MSC_1. E is the 'optimal externality'.

As well as leading to non-Pareto optimal levels of production of certain goods, the existence of external costs may mean that the production technique chosen by the producer as minimising private costs does not minimise social cost. An alternative technique, or the installation of equipment to eliminate or reduce the external cost, may

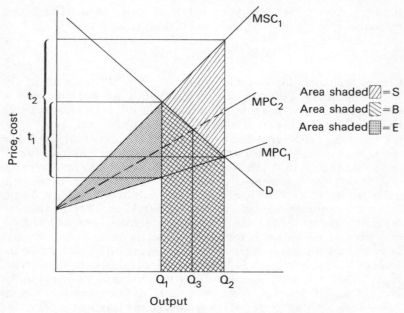

Figure 1.1 *Optimal externality in the context of the firm*

reduce social costs. For instance, in Figure 1.1, suppose an alternative process involving no external costs but private costs given by MPC_2 is available. In this case, the problem is to ensure that this production process is the one used; market forces will then suffice to drive output down to Q_3.

The widespread evidence of discontent with all the forms of externality discussed in this book might be thought to be sufficient proof of the importance of these problems. But a number of economists have argued otherwise (Coase, 1960). For if those suffering from the external cost really value it highly, surely they could come together and pay the firms or individuals in question the difference between marginal social cost and marginal private cost as a bribe to cut production, or to change production methods? Thus, the market mechanism itself would lead to production being at the optimal level by the establishment of what is, in effect, a market in the externalities concerned. The requirement for such 'trade' to take place can be simply stated in terms of Figure 1.1 (ignoring MPC_2). The external cost suffered per unit output is equal to $MSC_1 - MPC_1$, while the net benefits enjoyed by the creator of the external cost are equal to $D - MPC_1$. Hence if

$$MSC_1 - MPC_1 \text{ is greater than } D - MPC_1$$

sufferers can 'bribe' others to cut back production. The above inequality is easily restated: the condition for trade is that

$$MSC_1 \text{ is greater than } D.$$

Clearly the possibility of trade will cease when MSC_1 equals D, the Pareto optimum. Certainly some externalities are still produced at this level, and those suffering from them will still complain, and seek to have them eliminated at someone else's expense. But that they do not bribe the producer to reduce them further proves that they value the externalities at less than the net benefit obtained by production of the good in question. Therefore, there is no case for state intervention.

Although the argument is theoretically correct, there seems great cause for doubt as to its widespread applicability in practice. In the first place, groups of individuals may lack the organisation or leadership to undertake the type of negotiation involved. Indeed, many would say that it is for exactly this type of task that we elect local and central government. Moreover, many externalities take the form of local public goods (or bads). One individual cannot buy relief from pollution without simultaneously conferring it on others in the area. Thus, if left to voluntary action, a free-rider problem of individuals wishing to see pollution reduced but leaving the effort and expense of its accomplishment to others would emerge.

Perhaps there is more chance of such voluntary negotiation taking place where those involved are other producers rather than consumers (the payments made by railway companies to coal mines as compensation for not mining coal in locations where it would lead to serious subsidence of railway lines would appear to fall into this category). In the private sector, one obvious way of dealing with an externality producer is to take it over. In this way the externality is internalised, and becomes part of the private costs of the merged firm. Even so, such situations typically involve negotiation between small numbers of firms, and the possibility of bargaining leading to a solution other than an output of Q_1 (for instance, the producer of the externality holding out for more compensation than he strictly requires) should not be overlooked. It is a long way from saying that, to a limited extent, markets may exist in supposed externalities to saying that they are a reasonable approximation to perfect competition!

The opponents of state intervention have other arguments. For instance, it is argued that where externalities produce purely local disbenefits, those suffering them have the option of changing location. (Those who choose to remain in the locality will be those who are compensated for the disbenefit by the lower property prices which will pertain in the area.) Again, subject to the rigidities and imperfections of the property market, this is a valid possibility, but it does not necessarily follow that the best way of dealing with a localised pollution problem is to move those who object to it away! Another argument is that those harmed by externalities can seek damages in a court of law. Whilst this may be true in some cases, in others it has been judged that the producer of the externality has the legal right to continue to produce the effect and sometimes bodies have been specifically given immunity from legal action in respect of certain effects (e.g. airlines in the case of noise nuisance). If this were the only problem, it might be solved by a redefinition of legal rights in this respect, but the other problem is that legal proceedings are costly, and few private individuals are willing to bear the risks attached to bringing them. Moreover, their outcome does not necessarily deal with the problem in the best way; injunctions to desist, for example, may prevent a negotiated solution rather than bringing it about (Burrows, 1970).

The distribution of legal rights has been recognised as being important even in cases where court action is not involved, in that it influences the outcome, for instance, of a negotiated solution. Consider the case of a factory which pollutes the neighbourhood in which it is situated. If it has the legal right to pollute, it will be up to the residents to bribe it to reduce pollution. In this case, it will be their willingness to pay for the benefit of a clean environment (in Hicksian terms, their compensating variation, or the sum of money which when removed from the consumer leaves him on the same indifference curve as he was in the presence of the pollution) that determines the outcome. On the other hand, if the factory owner is legally obliged to pay full compensation for any externalities he produces, it will be the equivalent variation, the sum of money necessary to restore the consumer to the same indifference curve as he was on in the absence of the pollution. For a normal good, the equivalent variation exceeds the compensating variation. Thus the outcome is influenced by the initial distribution of legal rights (Mishan, 1971).

The point is illustrated in Figure 1.2. The vertical axis shows income; the horizontal axis shows environmental quality, and I_1 and I_2 are indifference curves. Suppose that we are considering an improvement in environmental quality from E_1 to E_2. The consumer's initial income is Y. In order to obtain an increase in E from E_1 to E_2 he would be willing to pay at most $Y_1 - Y_2$, as this would just leave him on the same indifference curve (I_1). On the other hand, if he started at E_2 with income Y_1, he would require compensation of $Y_3 - Y_1$ to keep him on indifference curve I_2. For a normal good, the marginal rate of substitution for income of which rises as income rises, $Y_3 - Y_1$ is greater than $Y_1 - Y_2$.

The result of calculating these two variations for all possible levels of pollution would be to produce two separate marginal social cost curves (Figure 1.3). MSC_1 represents MSC when the polluter has the right to pollute freely, whereas MSC_2 represents MSC where residents

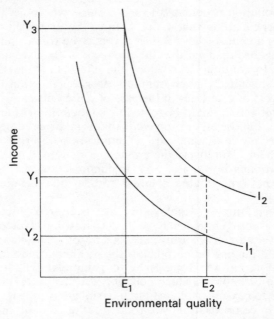

Figure 1.2 *Alternative property rights and the value of environmental quality*

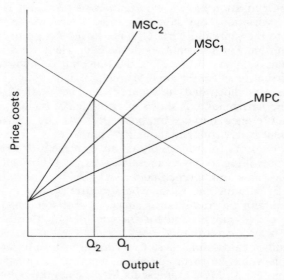

Figure 1.3 *The effects of valuations based on differing property rights*

are automatically entitled to full compensation. We now have two alternative Pareto optimal situations to choose from (Q_1 and Q_2). This should come as no surprise; a redistribution of legal rights is equivalent to a redistribution of real income; and it is well known that there may be a different Pareto optimal set of outputs corresponding to every possible distribution of real income. It is a special case of a topic we return to below, namely, the dependence of the valuation of marginal social cost on the distribution of real income.

Finally, suppose that the *a priori* case for believing that appropriate state intervention would be beneficial is established. It has been argued that there is still no reason to suppose that the state itself will be any more inclined to take into account social costs than are private firms (Buchanan, 1962). Evidence for this may be cited in that many of the most hotly debated social costs are in fact inflicted by state-owned bodies (e.g. authorities responsible for the provision of transport facilities or urban redevelopment). This point will be returned to in the next section.

It is the author's belief that, despite these counter-arguments, the existence of external costs is an important source of resource misallocation in modern economies. Indeed, some recent writers on the subject, reasoning from a 'materials balance' approach which recognises that the entire mass of resources used as inputs in the production process must, sooner or later, re-emerge as wastes, either at the production stages or as the products are consumed, have argued that 'technological external diseconomies are not freakish anomalies in the processes of production and consumption but inherent and normal parts of them' (Kneese, Ayres and D'Arge, 1970).

ALTERNATIVE CORRECTIVE MECHANISMS AND THE NEED TO MEASURE SOCIAL COST

Suppose that the costs of producing a particular product are as given by MPC_1 and MSC_1 in Figure 1.1 and none of the above suggested market solutions has come into play. A number of alternative corrective mechanisms to allow for this divergence immediately come to mind.

1 *Nationalise the Industry Concerned*
This may appear to be the large-scale equivalent of internalising externalities; if the producer is the state, then surely all social costs are internalised. Unfortunately, the argument is too simplistic. Just as when two firms merge, externalities between them will only be effectively internalised if henceforth they are managed as a single unit rather than as decentralised and independent ones, so the fact of ownership by the state is not in itself sufficient to ensure that social costs are adequately taken into account. In certain cases, as where

publicly owned sewage works pollute rivers and inflict costs upon water supply organisations, it may be possible to define units of management (regional water authorities) such that the externalities in question are effectively internalised. But in the majority of cases, the problem remains of how to set objectives and monitor performance for the state-owned industry.

State-owned industries are usually, possessed of some degree of monopoly power. At the same time, just as with private firms, the private interests of their managers and their owners may not always coincide. In particular, their managers are likely to gain in prestige, if not financially, from increasing the size of their organisation, its staff, output and sales (Williamson, 1964). In order to ensure that the industry in question is internally efficient and producing at the desired level of output, it is usual to set and monitor financial targets on the levels of profit earned. If, in measuring this profit, only financial costs are measured, then the state-owned producer will be given exactly the same incentive as the private producer to ignore the difference between private and social cost.

It is this dilemma that has led to the growth in the user of cost-benefit analysis for assessment of public sector projects in recent years. By measuring social costs and benefits in money terms, targets may be set and performance may be monitored in terms of social rather than private profitability. But if this step is taken, could not the same approach be taken with a privately owned industry, by imposing taxes and subsidies equal to the divergence between private and social cost? Thus it may be argued that state ownership is neither a necessary nor a sufficient condition for the solution of this problem.

2   The Tax Solution

If the output of the industry concerned is determined competitively, then, in terms of Figure 1.1, it may be reduced from Q_2 to Q_1, by the imposition of a tax per unit of output of t_1. The effect of this would be to cause a parallel upward shift in the marginal private cost schedule such that it intersected the demand curve (and marginal social cost) at output Q_1.

Notice that to implement this approach requires advance knowledge of the level of external cost at the optimum output level. That is, the tax, t_1, is determined by the actual magnitude of the divergence between MPC_1 and MSC_1 *at the optimum*. In the presence of non-linearities and non-separabilities in the cost function, calculation of this will be extremely difficult (Davis and Whinston, 1962). An alternative approach that is sometimes suggested is an iterative one. First, measure the difference between MSC and MPC at the current level of output, and implement a tax equal to this (t_2). The effect of this will be to reduce output below Q_1. The tax will then be revised to the new MSC/MPC divergence (which is less than t_1). Output will expand again to above Q_1. Eventually, hopefully, the procedure will converge on the new equilibrium output, Q_2. But even if such convergence could be guaranteed (which it cannot, particularly if the procedure were simultaneously taking place for a number of related products), the adjustment costs involved in such repeated changes in tax and output levels should be borne in mind.

If there were complete knowledge of the marginal social cost curve, but not of the demand curve, it would again be impossible to calculate in advance the optimum output level. In this case, an alternative to the iterative adjustment of taxation would be to implement a non-linear tax to equate MSC and MPC over the whole range of outputs. The complication of this situation, where the tax levied on each firm depends on the output of the industry as a whole, and the unclear incentives it would produce, may readily be imagined. Only if marginal external cost is approximately constant over a wide range of output does the tax solution appear simple to implement.

In any event, all of these solutions fall to the ground as soon as alternative methods of production are taken into account. For in taxing output, we have been really only using output as a proxy for the level of externality produced. If alternative methods of production exist, then the relationship between outputs and externalities is no longer unique. Sometimes it may be that the externalities are directly associated with the use of a certain input (e.g. coal rather than natural gas). In this case, it may be appropriate to tax the input rather than the output (for instance, petrol rather than car-miles travelled). But in general the same input is used in the production of many different goods by many different processes; to tax it at a different rate in each of these cases would not be feasible. Ultimately, there may be no alternative for the tax solution but to try to measure the amount of externality and the person or firm causing it in order to tax them directly. The complexity of this in most circumstances will be readily apparent, and is the subject of the remaining chapters in this book. Finally, it is worth mentioning that the level of external cost produced by a particular production process often depends on the geographical characteristics of the area in which production takes place – for instance, the number of households within a given range; prevailing winds; speed and volume of water flow. To vary tax rates according to such factors would again be complex.

3 *The Imposition of Direct Controls*

Given these administrative problems in implementing a system of Pigovian taxes, it is not surprising that, in practice, the simpler system of imposing direct controls on the level of externalities produced is often preferred. Such controls may often be administered by local bodies in accordance with the particular circumstances in their area, and whilst obviously some degree of monitoring will be needed, continuous monitoring can be replaced by periodic sampling, provided that the penalties for infringement are high enough to counteract the effect of a reduced probability of detection. (It should be noted, however, that the same enforcement system may be combined with a tax solution by, instead of taxing externalities directly, selling licences to produce given amounts of externality, and then monitoring results to ensure compliance.)

A further attraction of direct controls is that it no longer appears so essential to be able to measure social cost in money terms as with a tax solution. To a large extent this is a delusion, however. If the way of choosing an optimal output level outlined above is still regarded as appropriate, then it will be necessary to measure social cost in money terms in order to select the best level at which to impose the control. Only if that level is readily identifiable without precise quantification, as may be the case with certain pollutants where a moderate dose is believed to be relatively harmless, whereas exceeding a certain limit would have very serious consequences (in other words, there is a sharp discontinuity in the marginal social cost curve) will this problem be avoided. On the other hand, once a target level for the externality has been chosen, by this or any other means, implementation may be via taxes or controls.

Suppose that the overall level of a particular externality to be permitted has been chosen. Somehow the regulatory body then has to allocate this amongst the relevant industries and firms. This may take the form of a regulation requiring an equal proportionate reduction in emissions from all firms. For some firms, this may require relatively minor expenditure on new equipment; for others (including perhaps some who have already implemented the cheaper methods of amelioration on a voluntary basis) it may spell bankruptcy. It is difficult to see how such an approach is either efficient or equitable. When new firms wish to enter the area, they may be refused an allocation of any part of the permitted emission level on the grounds that this would mean reallocation from existing firms. Whilst some degree of protection for existing employment would seem reasonable, the inhibiting effect of such a situation on any economic change is obvious. However, to allocate quotas on a more rational basis, the regulatory authority would need to know in detail the costs of reducing emissions by amelioration, changing production processes or cutting output, for all firms under its authority.

The difficulty and expense of this has caused some economists to espouse a solution involving elements of both direct controls and of taxation (Baumol and Oates, 1971). First, the regulatory body would choose the overall level of externality permitted. Then it would set taxes or sell licences such that this level was achieved. The result would be that each firm would pay the price to expand its right to pollute only as long as doing so was a cheaper option than achieving marginal reductions in pollution in any other way. Thus the desired level of pollution would be achieved at minimum social cost.

4 Cost-benefit Analysis on a Case-by-Case Approach

A final method of taking social costs into account which is much used in practice must be considered before we close this section. This is the cost-benefit analysis of individual proposals on a case-by-case basis. It is the method used most often for examining single major projects which are considered too radical in effect to be left to the market for a decision; for evaluating proposals from government departments or nationalised industries which have widely varying external effects from case to case (e.g. road schemes) and for which single shadow prices are therefore inadequate; and for considering schemes where the only influence the relevant authority has is the negative one of being able to withhold planning permission.

In certain respects, such an *ad hoc* approach may seem to involve grave disadvantages in comparison with that previously considered. No clear-cut targets for externalities are set, not is there any mechanism for the automatic comparison of all methods of achieving them. On the other hand, it may be argued that the target level of externality should be reviewed in the light of each new proposal, as the opportunity cost of achieving it changes as new alternatives are proposed. Moreover, it is unlikely that the cost of administering a tax/subsidy scheme or direct controls for every form of divergence between social and private cost would ever be thought worthwhile. Thus, for instance, if licences to emit waste into rivers are sold to the highest bidders, it is not necessarily the case that this will minimise the social costs of enforcement if other divergences between social and private cost exist. New firms entering the area may bid the quota away from existing firms regardless of the social cost of unemployment, levels of air pollution produced, etc.

For certain intangible external effects, even measurement in purely physical terms is difficult or impossible. The aesthetic qualities of a new building and the loss of existing views are prime examples. Whilst guidelines may be laid down, it is difficult to see how such factors could ever be judged on anything but a case-by-case basis.

The conclusion of this section must be that there are many different ways of introducing considerations of social cost into decision taking, and the choice between them rests far more on organisational considerations and on administrative costs than on theoretical grounds. If the framework for determining the acceptable level of an externality outlined above is accepted, namely, whether what the beneficiaries are willing to pay for the product exceeds the monetary compensation required by the losers for them to be no worse off, then any of these approaches requires that social costs be measured in money terms. On the other hand, if such decisions are based on other grounds, any of these methods of implementation can be adopted. For instance, taxes can be set to achieve a level of externality defined by what politicians regard as acceptable. The important question in considering the need for money measures of social cost is not, therefore, the method of implementation to be adopted but the desirability of the compensation principle itself. It is to this that we turn in the next section.

USE OF THE COMPENSATION PRINCIPLE FOR MEASURING SOCIAL COST

So many attacks have been made on the compensation principle since it was first formulated that the economic theorist may be excused for thinking the issue a closed book. Amongst the more important contributions to the debate are those of Scitovsky (1941) who first noted the possibility that the undertaking of a project without the payment of compensation may redistribute income in such a way that an *ex post* application of the compensation test yields a different answer from an *ex ante* one, and Little (1950) who stressed the value content of the approach and the need to take distributional factors into account. Yet the compensation principle remains the basis on which most studies of social cost depend, and it is necessary to review once more its appropriateness for this role.

Suppose that a particular project has its supporters, whom we shall label the growth lobby, and its opponents, the environment lobby. How should one decide whether it is to go ahead? One method might be to hold a referendum. Apart from the obvious expense of subjecting a large number of decisions to this procedure, it has the obvious drawbacks that first, it provides no information on strength of preferences (a slight preference for the scheme on the part of the majority being sufficient to outvote those who regard its rejection as a matter of life and death) and secondly, a large proportion of the population may be unaware of the expected effects of the scheme. The result is that the referendum is usually used sparingly, and decisions are taken instead by the elected representatives of the people rather than the people themselves. These in turn require information on individual's preferences, and whilst much can be gained from canvassing and political meetings, a more scientific source of information might be welcomed. Moreover, it is unrealistic to expect politicians to be able to consider the details of every scheme individually. The normal practice is to set guidelines for action by the officers of the authority in question, with exceptional or particularly controversial cases being examined by the politicians themselves. The compensation test is, therefore, to be examined in the latter two respects:

(1) as a guideline for the taking of routine decisions;

(2) as a source of information on more important matters.

The case for using the compensation test in the former context may be expressed as follows. Repeated application of the compensation test will ensure that decisions are taken which move the economy towards the utility possibility frontier (i.e. to a position where there is no further possibility, even with payment of compensation, for making one person better off without harming another), whilst the government can use taxation and income supplementation to shift the economy to its most favoured position along the utility possibility frontier (i.e. to redistribute income). A clear statement of this view is given by Musgrave (1969).

Against this, a number of criticisms may be cited.

1 The Projects which are Selected Depend on the Current Distribution of Income

The amount one is willing to pay for certain benefits, and the compensation one requires to endure certain costs, both depend on one's level of income. Examine Figure 1.4. The frontier labelled 'Yes' represents the alternative distributions of utility that it will be possible to achieve if the project goes ahead. That labelled 'No' represents the possibilities if it is rejected. If the frontier representing one project is always above and to the right of the other, then that project will be selected whatever the distribution of income (Samuelson, 1950). But it is perfectly possible for the frontiers to cross (perhaps more than

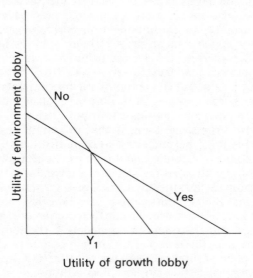

Figure 1.4　*Compensation tests and the distribution of income*

once). In the case illustrated, if the growth lobby has a level of real income higher than Y_1 it will be able to pay adequate compensation to the environmental lobby for implementation of the project. If the distribution of real income is more favourable to the environmental lobby, however, this will not be possible. (The Scitovsky paradox arises in the, perhaps rare, case where the project itself redistributes real income in such a way that this intersection is crossed.) In other words, the compensation test weights individual preferences according to their current level of income.

The upshot of this is that if people believe the distribution of real income to be unfair, then they will campaign both for fiscal changes and for projects to be evaluated as though the distribution of income were different from its current level. The latter may be approximated if the income elasticity of demand for the goods and bads produced is known. For then, current measures of willingness to pay and compensation required may be weighted by the ratio of the existing to the desired level of real income of those affected, raised to the power of the relevant elasticity (Nash, Pearce and Stanley, 1975).

2   *The Impossibility of Achieving an Optimal Distribution of Income*
Even if there were universal agreement on the desired distribution of income it does not follow that the government would necessarily be able to achieve it. First, all forms of taxation and income supplementation have potential harmful side-effects on the economy, and governments may be constrained, for instance, from raising income tax for that reason alone. Secondly, what we are discussing here is the distribution of real income; money income may be an inadequate proxy. For instance, in considering transport projects it should be borne in mind that the inhabitants of inner suburbs have in recent years suffered both from the decline in public transport – on which they have a greater tendency to rely – and from the external costs brought about by the use of the motor car by commuters from outer areas. Neither effect shows up in income tax returns, but they may be taken into account when choosing a transport policy.

What we are suggesting, then, is that in certain circumstances it may be sensible to go beyond simply taking decisions in the light of the desired income distribution, and to use such decisions as a way of influencing income distribution. The actual payment of compensation, rather than using the test hypothetically, may go part way to resolving the latter point. But of course there may be other cases where the payment of compensation worsens the distribution of real income.

Before proceeding, two counter-arguments to the above suggestions should be noted. In the first place, it may be argued that it infringes the principle of horizontal equity to use the effects of projects as a way of redistribution, since they do not affect all those at a given level of income equally. Unfortunately, even if compensation is paid, project selection still effects the distribution of real income in giving more benefits to some than to others. There is no way of avoiding this. The second point is more serious. Suppose we evaluate projects as though the distribution of income were what we should like it to be, rather than what it is. We run the danger of providing the poor with luxuries in those sectors in which decisions are taken publicly, whilst neglecting their basic needs in other directions. This is a natural outcome of piecemeal policy operating under the type of constraints we have postulated, and stresses the need to seek far more effective ways of circumventing these constraints.

3 The Use of Market Preferences

The use in the compensation test of evidence derived from the behaviour of individuals in the market place is based on the value judgement that the individual's view of what constitutes his own, or his family's, welfare is to be adopted, and that it is preferences revealed in the market rather than any other form of preference that is to count. Many people are observed simultaneously to hold one view of what constitutes socially desirable behaviour, but to behave quite differently in the market place. Harsanyi (1955) terms these 'ethical preferences' and 'subjective preferences' respectively. The co-existence of both sets of preferences may be rationalised in as much as the behaviour of one individual does not determine that of society as a whole (Marglin, 1963). One may believe it desirable to have speed limits but still exceed them oneself; and even murderers may regard it as socially desirable for murder to be illegal!

It is clear that also the individual's market behaviour can only reflect his true preferences if he is aware of the consequences of what he is doing. The purchase of a brand of car with a poor safety record, for instance, could only be regarded as evidence of high risk preference if the consumer in question was aware of the different standards achieved by this and competing models. Now there may be some merit in allowing people to make their own mistakes, although this merit derives from seeing freedom as of value in itself rather than from pursuit of the Pareto optimality goal of the compensation test. But most people accept some degree of paternalism and exhibit some willingness to be guided by expert opinion. This argument is particularly important when considering pollution and resource depletion; the long-run effects of decisions in this area are poorly understood; and many serious forms of pollution (e.g. carbon monoxide, lead) may be completely invisible to the public at large.

4 Whose Preferences Should Count?

Closely related to the issues raised in the last section is that of whose preferences should count. For if we adopt market preferences, then it is likely that within households it will be those who – singly or collectively – control the allocation of the household's budget that will be taken as representing the household's views on social decision taking too. Any attempt to give extra weight to those who, for reasons of age, sex or character, play a lesser role in household budgeting will founder for lack of data. Similarly, it is likely that we shall restrict our range of relevant households to those directly affected by the decision in question, although it is clear that many people do care about effects they are never likely to experience – the suffering of others, the destruction of wildlife and the countryside in places they are never likely to visit, and so forth. To some extent, market evidence is available on these preferences, but in the highly approximate form of voluntary donations, which suffer from the usual problem that such charities are of the nature of public goods. Indeed, the main reason such donations take place at all is that consumers have moral as well as purely selfish motives at heart.

One particular problem concerns the interests of future generations. It is clearly the case that these may be radically affected by current decisions, particularly when these involve long-term or irreversible changes in the environment, for instance by depleting stocks of natural resources. Obviously, the views of the unborn cannot be directly taken into account, but surely it can hardly be disputed that those who have made a special study of long-run economic, social and environmental prospects are in a better position to represent their interests (for instance, to argue which resources are in particular need of conservation) than is the man in the street.

The importance of the above arguments is that they provide good reason for doubting whether the compensation principle provides an appropriate general method for measuring social cost in routine decision taking. Instead, each case needs taking on its merits, to decide whether distributional factors matter (in which case some form of income-related weighting might be appropriate), whether it is a subject on which ethical preferences rather than market preferences should be sought, whether consumers are sufficiently well informed for their market decisions to reflect their true preferences and whether it is a matter for general rather than restricted concern. Obviously, in practice, it will be politicians who will have to take such decisions, acting on the advice of relevant specialists. Some writers (e.g. Williams, 1972) have suggested that it is helpful if they express such decisions in money terms; for instance, if it is decided that the value to be attached to saving human life is not appropriately determined in the market place, the politician could be asked to attach a money value to this objective. The advantage of this is that it enables such factors to be introduced readily into an objective function expressed in money units. It should always be remembered, however, that such politically determined social cost estimates have a totally different value basis from market-determined social costs, and that their relationship to individual preferences is much less direct. In any event, there is no necessary reason why a politician should treat such factors in this way; he may, for instance, believe it appropriate to specify a constraint – for instance on the maximum noise level to which any home should be subjected, or on the proportion of open space built upon in a given area.

Such constraints are the natural way of taking into account factors which are regarded as preconditions for the pursuit of economic welfare, whether in terms of the health of existing human beings or the long-term prospects for survival of the species. One of the most important current controversies concerning the environment is that between those who believe that levels of pollution and resource depletion should be set in such a way as to bring about a steady-state solution that would be sustainable in the long run, and those who believe that these levels should be determined with reference to the compensation test (Pearce, 1976). Such physical constraints obviate the need to measure social cost in money terms at all. (Although economists will no doubt wish to calculate, for the information of the politician, the costs of achieving the standard he has set up. Moreover, decentralisation of decision taking will probably require estimation of shadow prices representing the opportunity cost of putting the resource to any particular use, given the level of the constraint.)

Suppose that the measurement of social cost is being undertaken not to use in a decision rule as such, but simply as a relevant piece of information to help those responsible for the decision to make up their minds. In this case, again, money measures based on the compensation principle or otherwise weighted may be relevant. On the other hand, where there is reason to think that the above listed factors apply, or where there is doubt about the accuracy of the figures, it will be better to present evidence on the relevant effects in physical terms and to leave it at that. If public opinion is to be investigated directly, by consultation or public participation, physical measures will be more comprehensible than money measures.

SOCIAL COST MEASUREMENT IN PRACTICE

The measurement of social cost is sometimes portrayed as being directly analogous to that of private cost except that it examines costs imposed on all members of society rather than on the decision taker alone. Such an approach is potentially misleading on two grounds.

1 *It Confuses Pecuniary and Real Externalities*
In addition to creating externalities as we have defined them above, many decisions will lead to widespread price changes, resulting in some consumers paying more for goods they purchase, others less.

Scitovsky has termed such effects 'pecuniary externalities' (Scitovsky, 1954). The analogy with private cost would suggest that such factors are to be counted as part of the social cost of the decision. However, price changes themselves redistribute income; for every consumer who pays more, a producer receives more, and vice versa. Therefore, if we are adopting the compensation principle, such changes are to be ignored, except in as much as they cause 'second-round' changes in other real externalities or in the degree of distortion due to imperfect competition. Once again, it is necessary to stress the lack of concern for distributional questions embodied in this way of measuring social cost. If distributional effects were to be taken into account, for instance by means of a weighting procedure, then it would be necessary to trace out all pecuniary externalities.

2   It Places Undue Emphasis on Money Costs

Certain externalities manifest themselves in the form of increased money expenditure on the part of those affected. Water pollution may lead to increased expenditure on purification; air pollution to increased expenditure on laundries, cleaning, painting and renovating buildings. But many important effects are not of this type. Particularly significant here are so-called 'disamenity' effects – the simple fact that people do not like living in dirty areas, walking through filthy streets or passing their leisure time on the banks of smelly, polluted rivers. Of course, the private costs of decisions may include such factors; the decision taker himself may suffer discomfort and inconvenience as a result of the decisions he takes. The accountant measuring private cost makes no attempt to value these items. But when we come to social cost measurement, if we are to apply the compensation principle, then such items must be valued.

Basically, three approaches have been taken to the measurement of social cost in such circumstances.

The Surrogate Market Approach

This approach relies on finding situations in which consumers do have a choice between incurring money expenditure and suffering the ill effect in question. The most successful application of the technique has probably been to the valuation of journey time in transport studies (Harrison and Quarmby, 1972). The choice between a fast journey at a high price and a slower journey at a lower one occurs moderately frequently in practice. Even so, the example should be enough to warn of the possible dangers. It is necessary to assume that choices observed in one context can be transferred to the case at hand, where certain circumstances (time of day, journey length, relative comfort, etc.) may be completely different. For many other effects, surrogate markets are more difficult to find, although it will be clear from succeeding chapters that the housing market has been a favourite one for investigation, since it is clearly one in which a host of environmental, spatial and amenity factors play some part in determining relative prices.

The Alternative Cost Approach

Where a surrogate market cannot be found, analysts have often asked the question, 'What would be the minimum money expenditure necessary to remove the ill effect in question?' This is often presented as an upper limit on the social cost in question, since it will represent the true social cost only in cases in which the expenditure is actually worthwhile rather than accepting a smaller amount of compensation simply to continue to suffer the effect in question. All too often, however, the effect is only one of partial amelioration, and may in itself cause discomfort or inconvenience; for instance, double glazing as sound insulation only gives protection whilst inside the building, and many people like to be able to have a window open. In such cases, it is not at all clear whether the estimate is to be regarded as an upper limit, a lower limit or neither. As a result, this method of valuation often spreads more confusion than understanding.

Survey Techniques

In general, economists working in this field have been highly suspicious of the use of survey techniques, regarding what people do as being better evidence of their preferences than what they say, even though they may be acting on faulty knowledge and perception of the alternatives, habits or motives quite different from those imputed by the researcher. Colleagues working in the closely related field of market research have suffered no such inhibitions, and it is generally accepted that survey techniques have a major role to play in assessing the potential demand for alternative product specifications under consideration.

The traditional attitude survey may provide valuable information on what people perceive as disbenefits and their relative importance, but it cannot provide money measures of social cost. More recently, a number of techniques have been devised for placing respondents in a hypothetical trade-off situation between incurring higher external costs and higher money expenditure. For instance, respondents may be given points to allocate with which they can 'buy' reductions in noise, air pollution or taxation at predetermined prices. Responses to a variety of prices may be tested, and the extent to which respondents would be willing to spend money to reduce externalities observed (Hoinville, 1971). Obviously, the reliability of the results depends on how seriously respondents take the game and how accurately they perceive the alternatives postulated (it is helpful if these can be limited to situations with which they are familiar, or small deviations from them, and back-up facilities such as films, recordings, models and photographs may be used). There is evidence from studies of transport mode choice, where results can be checked against actual behaviour, that a careful survey can produce reasonably reliable results (Hensher, Stanley and McLeod, 1975).

CONCLUSION

Before we set about measuring social cost, we ought to be clear as to why we want to measure it and whether the measure has to be in money terms. If it is to be used in levying Pigovian taxes, or in assessing monetary compensation, then clearly the measure must be expressed in money terms. It may be convenient, if the measure is to be used in routine decision taking by means of cost-benefit analysis, that the measure should be in money terms so that it may readily be added to other costs which are so expressed, but this is not essential and for certain aspects of social cost – especially where these affect health or survival – it may be more appropriate to take them into account in the form of physical constraints. Where the aim of the exercise is to spread information amongst politicians or the public at large there appears to be no good reason for preferring money measures to physical data. If reliable money measures can be obtained, they add information on consumer preference to that contained in purely physical data and may be worth reporting as well as the data themselves. If reliable measures cannot be obtained, then it is better by far to report accurate physical measurements than wild monetary guesses. This needs emphasising, given the growing habit in some quarters of plucking money values out of mid-air, whether they are relevant or not.

But this raises the issue of what is to be regarded as an accurate money measure. In the first place, it should be clear from the above that there is no single figure for the social cost of any item that can be proved to be correct. This is because the concept of social cost is grounded in ethical judgements. The much-used 'compensation principle' is derived from just one such set of judgements, namely, that individual preferences as revealed in the market are to count, and that these are to be weighted by current market power (i.e. income). Just as there are no objective rules whereby one set of ethical judgements can be proved to be superior to another, so it is open to any individual to measure social cost according to some other distribution of market power, to place extra weight on costs imposed on certain groups by an explicit weighting system, or indeed to reject the whole market preference approach in favour of some other way of measuring social cost.

Given this proviso, we can outline some of the criteria by which we would like to see the relevance of money measures of social cost derived from market preferences judged.

(1) Are the valuations based on the free choice of individuals, unhampered by constraints (other than the budget constraint), in adequate knowledge and perception of the alternatives available?
(2) Is the subject one on which people hold no strong moral views – i.e. ethical preferences do not deviate substantially from subjective preferences?

Clearly, this is not providing a simple, unambiguous answer to the problem of measuring social cost. Nor were we able, on *a priori* grounds, to resolve the issue of the best way of dealing with divergences between private and social cost (comparisons of organisational factors and administrative costs were found to be more important than theoretical arguments), nor even to reach any very clear conclusions on the significance of such divergences at the present time. In each case, it appeared that a mixture of value judgement and empirical research would be needed to resolve the issue, there being no alternative but a case-by-case approach. As a previous writer on the subject concluded, this is a problem on which 'the theorist should be silent, and call in the applied economist' (Turvey, 1963). That, in succeeding chapters, is what we do.

REFERENCES

Bator, F. M., 'The anatomy of market failure', *Quarterly Journal of Economics*, vol. 72, 1958
Baumol, W. J. and Oates, W. E., 'The use of standards and prices for the protection of the environment', *Swedish Journal of Economics*, vol. 73, 1971.
Bohm, P., *Social Efficiency, A Concise Introduction to Welfare Economics* (London: Macmillan, 1973).
Buchanan, J. M., 'Politics, policy and the Pigovian margins', *Economica*, vol. 29, 1962.
Burrows, P., 'On external costs and the visible arm of the law', *Oxford Economic Papers*, vol. 22, 1970.
Coase, R. H., 'The problem of social cost', *Journal of Law and Economics*, vol. 3, 1960.
Davis, O. and Whinston, A. B., 'Externalities, welfare and the theory of games', *Journal of Political Economy*, vol. 66, 1962.
Harrison, A. J. and Quarmby, D. A., 'The value of time', in *Cost-Benefit Analysis*, ed. R. Layard (Harmondsworth: Penguin Books, 1972).
Harsanyi, J. C., 'Cardinal welfare, individualistic ethics and interpersonal comparisons of utility', *Journal of Political Economy*, vol. 59, 1955.
Hensher, D. A., Stanley, J. K. and McLeod, P., 'Usefulness of attitudinal measures in investigating the choice of travel mode', *International Journal of Transport Economics*, vol. 1, 1975.
Hicks, J. R., 'The foundations of welfare economics', *Economic Journal*, vol. 49, 1939.
Hoinville, G., 'Evaluating community preferences', *Environment & Planning*, vol. 3, 1971.
Kaldor, N., 'Welfare comparisons of economics and interpersonal comparisons of utility', *Economic Journal*, vol. 49, 1939.
Kneese, A. V., Ayres, R. U. and D'Arge, R. C., *Economics and the Environment, Resources for the Future* (Baltimore: Johns Hopkins Press, 1970).
Little, I. M. D., *A Critique of Welfare Economics* (Oxford: OUP, 1950).
Little, I. M. D. and Mirrlees, J. A., *Project Appraisal and Planning for Developing Countries*, (London: Heinemann, 1974).

Marglin, S. A., 'The social rate of discount and the optimal rate of investment'. *Quarterly Journal of Economics*, vol. 77, 1963.

Mishan, E. J., 'Pangloss on pollution', *Swedish Journal of Economics*, vol. 73, 1971.

Musgrave, R. A., 'Cost-benefit analysis and the theory of public finance', *Journal of Economic Literature*, vol. 7, 1969.

Nash, C. A., Pearce, D. W. and Stanley, J. K., 'An evaluation of cost-benefit analysis criteria', *Scottish Journal of Political Economy*, vol. 22, 1975.

Pearce, D. W., 'The limits of cost-benefit analysis as a guide to environmental policy', *Kyklos*, Fasch. 1, 1976.

Pigou, A. C., *The Economics of Welfare* (London: Macmillan, 1920).

Samuelson, P. A., 'The evaluation of real national income', *Oxford Economic Papers*, N.S., vol. 2, 1950.

Scitovsky, T., 'A note on welfare propositions in economics', *Review of Economic Studies*, vol. 9, 1941.

Scitovsky, T., 'Two concepts of external economies', *Journal of Political Economy*, vol. 58, 1954.

Turvey, R., 'On divergences between social cost and private cost', *Economica*, vol. 30, 1963.

Williams, A., 'Cost-benefit analysis: bastard science? And/or insidious poison in the body politick!' *Journal of Public Economics*, vol. 1, 1972.

Williamson, O. E., *The Economics of Discretionary Behaviour: Managerial Objectives in a Theory of the Firm* (New York: Prentice-Hall, 1964).

Chapter 2

Noise Nuisance

INTRODUCTION

There can be little question that some of the most marked advances in both the theory and practice of social cost measurement have occurred in the field of noise nuisance. Noise is a readily identifiable and perceived form of pollution. As such, approaches based on an assessment of the response by individuals to noise exposure have been possible. We can expect a similar basis for the more marked forms of air pollution, those that are visible in the form of either smoke or smog or which exhibit some smell. As such, much of the methodology that has been developed for noise nuisance valuation has also been applied to air pollution. Rather than repeat material unnecessarily, this chapter discusses the general methodologies common to both fields of study and hence a reading of this chapter is a necessary precursor to a reading of Chapter 3.

In other respects, noise and air pollution are dissimilar. No one can really be in doubt as to whether they are annoyed by noise or not and their annoyance is highly correlated with measures of *actual* noise exposure: that is, perceived noise and actual noise are very closely linked. With air pollution, however, it is not always clear that individuals are aware of what they are suffering. Unless some olfactory or visual sense is offended, the individual will often not perceive physical levels of air pollution. Of course, to the conventionally minded economist this simply means that 'pollution' does not exist, for pollution damage is, as has already been explained, defined in terms of what affects an individual's utility level. None the less, uncertainty about the effects of 'unperceived' air pollutants – especially tiny particles of the heavier metals (e.g. cadmium) – should not be allowed to dictate a 'do nothing' policy. Rather, the potential for heavy negative damage should be used as an argument for caution. Second, while noise nuisance is unquestionably linked to bad health, particularly in respect of noise inside factories (Taylor, 1970, pp. 74–81), less appears to be known about the damage to mental health from exterior noise induced by road and air traffic. In contrast, serious attempts have been made, interestingly by economists in the main, to estimate the effect of air pollution on morbidity and mortality (see Chapter 3).

This chapter surveys the various methodologies used in measuring the money cost of noise nuisance and indicates where the same methodologies have been applied to air pollution. The most sophisticated attempts to measure social costs in both respects have centred on the 'property value' approach. In essence, this approach is based on the hypothesis that noisy (polluted) areas will exhibit house prices lower than those in quiet (unpolluted) areas, *all other things being held equal*. The translation of this simple idea into practice, however, has resulted in some fairly sophisticated economic models. No attempt is made here to look at all the aspects of such models and it is important to remember that many of the issues, both at the model specification end and at the empirical stage, are still hotly debated in the literature. Rather, the aim is to survey the essentials of each approach and to appraise the validity of such approaches and the accuracy of the resulting empirical estimates.

PROPERTY PRICE APPROACHES: THEORY

The essence of the property price approach to noise nuisance evaluation is that individuals can 'buy' peace and quiet by choosing to locate their homes in peaceful areas and by choosing to work only for employers who locate their activities in such areas. Accordingly, observation of the behaviour of people who vary in their sensitivity to noise should enable us to estimate their implicit (positive) evaluations of quiet and hence their implicit (negative) valuations of noise. If, to take an extreme example, an individual is able to choose between two houses, identical in every respect except that house A has a peaceful location and house B a noisy location, then the existence of noise-sensitive people should mean that the price of A (P_A) exceeds the price of B (P_B). The differential $P_A - P_B$ would provide a *prima facie* measure of the extra value of peace and quiet attached to house A.

This generalised approach requires us to accept: (a) that individuals are free to choose in the manner supposed; (b) that noise is not a ubiquitous 'public bad' but a localised one; (c) that noise, or 'quiet', can be measured quantitatively in a fashion similar to that for amounts of other commodities; (d) that the effects of noise on house prices can be disentangled from the many other effects of house prices.

We may briefly comment on these important assumptions. As far as assumption (a) is concerned, it is evident that many people will not be able to move house with the comparative ease required by property price models. We need therefore to investigate the effects of limited mobility on this approach and this is discussed later. Assumption (b) is necessary because price models would not reveal significant or meaningful house price differentials if individuals who are averse to noise are unable to find quiet areas. That is, if noise is everywhere, house prices will not differ even though actual noise nuisance is suffered. This point has been made forcefully by Mishan (1970). Walters (1975, p. 2) asserts, however, that 'aircraft noise is a local and not a ubiquitous phenomenon'. However, the United Kingdom Royal Commission on Pollution has estimated that some 10 million people are exposed to 'unacceptable' noise and that this figure could rise to 30 million in 1980. If this is true, then the housing market would have to be in a remarkable state of flux to accommodate the avertive behaviour of such large numbers of noise-sensitive persons.

Assumption (c) is an important one. For an individual without monopsony power, the price of any commodity is the same however many he buys. If apples in the market are priced at *x* pence each, the amount spent is a simple multiple of the quantity bought and the constant unit price paid. But, given the way noise measures are constructed,[1] one would expect units of noise to differ according to how many of them one already has. That is, the (negative) price of 1 unit of noise added to an existing 50 units of noise should be higher than the (negative) price attached to an additional unit on top of 40 units. In this respect we would expect the price-noise relationship to be non-linear. But Walters (1975) argues that the evidence from the information collected in the investigation of London's third airport supports the assumption of linearity – i.e. a constant price per unit of noise measure. Other studies have either made similar claims or have assumed such a relationship.

While assumption (d) has often been thought to be an insuperable difficulty in noise nuisance studies, a fairly substantial part of the literature does report a successful 'separating out' of the effects of noise on house prices through statistical technique. Where studies have failed to separate out such effects various conclusions are possible. Firstly, it is always possible that the methodology has been incorrect. Secondly, it is possible that the absence of an effect of noise on house prices means that noise simply does not affect house prices. This conclusion is consistent with two further views: (a) that noise is not considered to have a (negative) monetary value in that particular study, or (b) that noise has a negative value but that this value is not 'picked up' by house price changes or differentials. By and large, researchers have adopted the views that the *absence* of correlation means that noise has not been regarded as a diseconomy or that the technique has somehow failed to pick up what is surely an existing relationship. In the latter case, researchers have then resorted to professional (estate agent) valuations of what houses *would* be worth in the absence of noise. These latter approaches are suspect for reasons we shall consider later.

Studies finding significant statistical relationships between noise and house prices have primarily been confined to North America. While the studies vary in detail the consensus now appears to be moving towards the type of 'hedonic price' model described below.

A house may be considered as a composite entity comprising a bundle of 'characteristics'. These characteristics might consist of features such as size, number of bathrooms, age of the property, nature of the heating system, nature of the area surrounding the property, and so on. From each of these characteristics there comes a flow of services, so that the total consumption of housing services can be written:

$$C_h = F(c_1, c_2, \ldots, c_n), \tag{1}$$

where C_h is consumption of housing services, and $c_1, \ldots, c_n$ are the characteristics of the house (the selection of characteristics is something not discussed here, but tends to be reasonably uniform in practice).

Each individual or household is assumed to have a utility function of the form:

$$U = F_1(X, C_h, D), \tag{2}$$

where U is utility, X is the expenditure of the household on all goods other than housing and travelling to work and D is the distance to place of work (see Muth, 1969, for this type of function).

Finally, the consumer is faced with a budget constraint set by his income, such that:

$$Y = X + P_h(D) \cdot C_h + C_T, \tag{3}$$

where Y is income, P_h is the price per unit of housing service and is presented here as being a function of distance, although only some of these prices will in fact be related to distance: we expand on this shortly. C_T is cost of travelling to work.

The item $P_h(D) \cdot C_h$ in Equation 2 may be split up to indicate which services are dependent on distance to work and which are not. Thus the consumption of land will be distance dependent. In some models the attribute we are interested in, peace and quiet, is also treated as being distance dependent: that is, the 'place of work' may coincide with the source of noise pollution (traffic noise in the city, airport noise if employment is in the commercial centres surrounding airports). We follow Nelson (1976) in making noise independent of distance along with all other characteristics other than land services. Equations 1, 2 and 3 (with 3 suitably modified) enable us to present the problem as:

$$\text{Maximise } U = F_1(X, c_1, \ldots, c_m, c_n, D), \tag{4}$$

subject to

$$Y = X + \sum_{i=1}^{i=m} P_i \cdot c_i + P_n(D) \cdot c_n + T_D, \tag{5}$$

where services $i = 1$ to $i = m$ cover all services other than those from land, and the nth characteristic is the service of land. P_i is the price of the ith service and this price is known as the *implicit* or *hedonic* price. That is, hedonic prices are the implicit prices of the characteristics comprising a commodity, in this case a house. (For further extensive discussion of hedonic-price theory, see Griliches, 1971.)

Now, the model above establishes the basis for empirical estimation. To introduce noise (or air pollution) we simply regard it as another characteristic, so that c_m, for example, might be the characteristic 'noise', or we may think of c_m as the negative of this, i.e. as peace and quiet. We next need to allow for the fact that the above equations are presented in terms of annual values, whereas a house price is the present value of the future flow of services from that house. Hence, annual expenditure on *housing services alone* will be (from Equation 5):

$$H = Y - X - T_D = \sum_{i=1}^{i=m} P_i \cdot c_i + P_n(D) \cdot c_n. \tag{6}$$

Equation 6 requires conversion to present value terms. If the time horizon is infinite we simply divide by r, the rate of discount prevailing among householders, so that:

$$PV(H) = \text{House Price} = \frac{1}{r} \left[\sum_{i=1}^{i=m} P_i \cdot c_i + P_n(D) \cdot c_n \right]. \tag{7}$$

The empirical formulation of Equation 7 will therefore appear as a multiple regression equation with house price as the dependent variable and with the various characteristics as the independent variables. The coefficients that relate to each characteristic will be hedonic prices of those characteristics. This is all we need to identify the marginal price of each characteristic and hence the marginal price of peace and quiet: in short, it is all we need to secure the 'value' of peace and quiet. Thus the formulation of the problem in these terms gives us a theoretical rationale for multiple regression studies. It is perhaps worth noting that this rationale has only been provided recently in the literature: multiple regression studies tended to take place in practice without a proper theoretical underpinning. The latter has been provided by such works as Walters (1975) and Nelson (1976) for noise and by Polinsky and Shavell (1975) for air pollution. As it happens, a problem remains in that hedonic prices identified in Equation 7 above are really the result of supply and demand interaction. They do not therefore give us a locus of prices in terms of willingness to pay, which is what we require (see Chapter 3). Rather, they give us marginal willingness to pay if the market is in equilibrium.

Before looking at empirical applications, the reader may wonder why it was necessary to set out the seven equations when, in practice, Equation 7 seems to have been derived from Equation 5 – the income constraint – only. In fact, Equation 4 is there to remind us that the fundamental assumption of hedonic price models is that *householders are both free to move around and do so in response to changes in household characteristics, including noise.* We noted this assumption at the outset and the model has served to reinforce it. As we shall see, if this hypothesised world of perfect adaptation to change does not exist in which hedonic price models have limited value, at least in the form in which they have so far been presented.

One technical point deserves mention before looking at the way in which hedonic models of the above kind are used. Smith (1977) makes a particularly important point when he argues that hedonic prices indices may not, after all, be construed as marginal valuations in the sense that we require. Taking the Nelson (1976) model (which is, in turn, derived from the work of Rosen, 1974), Smith shows that the implicit (hedonic) prices obtained take the form:

$$a_i = \frac{m \cdot \dfrac{\partial P}{\partial Z_i}}{\dfrac{\partial U}{\partial q} \cdot P(D, Z_1, Z_2) - m},$$

where a_i is the derived coefficient from the regression analysis, m is the marginal utility of money, U is utility, q is the quantity of the housing services, P is the hedonic price, D is distance to work and Z_1 and Z_2 are attributes (two only are assumed). What is required for a marginal valuation by the consumer of noise is:

$$MV = \frac{\partial U}{\partial q} \cdot \frac{\partial q}{\partial Z_i}.$$

That is, what we require, the marginal valuation, cannot be identified from the regression coefficient we obtain. Smith concludes that 'our ability to identify the marginal valuations of particular attributes of a site, such as pollution, from appropriately defined hedonic equations seems questionable' (Smith, 1977).

PROPERTY PRICE APPROACHES: EMPIRICAL FINDINGS

According to Nelson (1976), the appropriate form of multiple regression equation to be tested in light of the preceding hedonic approach has the form:

$$PV(H) = b_0 . X^{b_1} N^{b_2} u_1,$$

where b_0, b_1 and b_2 are constants, X is the set of characteristics other than noise, N is noise and U_1 is an error term. Nelson's function is then multiplicative, or, if logarithms are taken in both sides, additive in logarithms. Further, Nelson measures N in semi-logarithmic form as follows:

$$N = c_0 . e^{c_1(\text{NEF})} . u_2,$$

where c_0 and c_1 are again constants e is the natural logarithm and u_2 is a random error term. NEF is the measure of noise known as 'noise exposure forecast'.[2] Substituting the expression for N in the multiple regression equation gives

$$PV(H) = d_0 . X^{d_1} . e^{d_2(\text{NEF})} . u_3,$$

where $d_0 = a_0 c_0^{b_2}$, $d_1 = b_1$, $d_2 = c_1 b_2$ and $u_3 = u_1 u_2^{b_2}$.

By formulating the multiple regression equation in this way, Nelson (1976) argues that we are able to interpret d_2 as the *constant percentage marginal damage cost per unit NEF*. The marginal damage cost is the partial differential of $PV(H)$ with respect to NEF and this is equal to $d_2(V)$, so that the model makes marginal damage cost rise proportionately with property value. It is worth noting that this result occurs because of the way the model is specified. However, as we shall see, there is some independent evidence to support this hypothesis. Note also that the formulation means that the price of a unit of noise is the same *no matter what the level of noise* – i.e. for a given house price the price of noise will be the same whether we move from 30 NEF to 31 NEF or from 40 to 41 NEF. This effectively 'cardinalises' the noise scale in economic terms and we saw earlier that was an assumption also made by Walters (1975). The empirical base for this will be discussed later.

Nelson's own study (1975, 1976) used the following characteristics: X_1 = percentage of housing built before 1930 (an 'age' characteristic); X_2 = percentage with air conditioning; X_3 = number of rooms per house; X_4 = the average 'lot' area – i.e. size of plot in which the house stands; X_5 = a dummy variable (i.e. entered as 0 or 1) according to whether houses had (desirable) riverside locations or not; X_6 = time to reach source of employment, and NEF = the (aircraft) noise variable. Houses were grouped into census tracts (the study area was Washington DC) so that each characteristic above tended to be an average of some sort across houses within the tract. For illustration we report the actual regression:

$$\text{Logarithm } \overline{PV(H)} = 1 \cdot 564 + 0 \cdot 027(\log X_1) + 0 \cdot 196(\log X_2)$$
$$+ 1 \cdot 350(\log X_3) + 0 \cdot 019(\log X_4)$$
$$+ 0 \cdot 073(\log X_5) - 0 \cdot 332(\log X_6)$$
$$- 0 \cdot 010(\text{NEF}).$$

$$R^2 = 0 \cdot 863.$$

From the equation we see that the coefficient for NEF is $-0 \cdot 01$ (all the reported coefficients above are statistically significant). Since it is the *logarithm* of median property value (the bar above $PV(H)$ indicates some average has been used) that is the dependent variable, we can immediately interpret the result as saying that a one unit increase in NEF will depreciate the house price ($PV(H)$) by 1 per cent.

We have taken some time to explain in reasonable detail how one major study has been carried out in order to see how a theory of locational adjustment can be allied to the theory of hedonic prices to secure empirical estimates of noise damage at the margin. Walters (1975) uses a similar model except that no multiple regressions are run. Rather, he attempts to show that a consumer maximising a utility function of the form:

$$U = X^{1-b} \cdot Q^b,$$

where U is utility, X is all goods other than quiet, Q is quiet and b is a constant less than unity, has his marginal willingness to pay for peace and quiet measured by the exponent b and that, in turn, b is measured by house price depreciation due to noise. Thus, rather than produce his own study, Walters surveys the literature to see what estimates of D have been obtained. Like Nelson (1976) he then 'standardises' the various results to see if there is similarity in outcomes. We consider these various studies in a moment. For now we may note that Walters's use of a 'constant returns' utility function (the exponents add to unity) is unduly restrictive, not least because it constrains the model to produce results which imply that the income elasticity of demand for peace and quiet is always unity. Exactly what the income elasticity is for peace and quiet is quite another matter since the various studies seem at odds with each other in some respects and other studies are formulated in such a way that a rising income elasticity is a necessary result of the model specification. As such, it is difficult to reach any general conclusions, conclusions that might otherwise be rather useful in deciding whether or not environmental quality in the form of peace and quiet is or is not an 'elitist' good.

The surveys by Nelson (1976) and Walters (1975) cover some common literature but with other differences. We take the common literature first. Both Walters and Nelson try to express the results of the various studies in terms of a 'noise depreciation index' (in Walters's case it is a 'noise depreciation sensitivity index') measured as the percentage change in house price per unit of noise nuisance. Walters works in terms of an index related to NNI and Nelson uses NEF, but it is possible to translate one to the other since 1 NEF equals approximately 2·25 NNI.[3] In their assessment of Emerson's study (1969a, 1969b), Nelson secures a noise depreciation index of 0·4 per cent for a unit change in NEF. However, Walters reports the same percentage for NNI when looking at the same study which would in fact mean less than 0·2 per cent when converted to NEF units. It is unclear why the difference in interpretation comes about. Similarly, both look at the study by Paik (1972). Nelson's NEF related index is 2·0 and Walters' NNI related index is 0·7, so that bringing them down to common NNI terms the index is 0·9 which is perhaps fairly in agreement.

Table 2.1 shows the results of the various studies reported in Nelson and Walters.

It should be emphasised that the results in Table 2.1 are taken from multiple regression studies *only*. The heavily lined area of the table shows those results which may be considered directly comparable. As far as possible they relate to similarly priced houses in the USA or Canada and cover a fairly limited period of time so that house price inflation should not seriously distort the results (although a very detailed analysis is needed if further accuracy is required). Walters (1975, p. 105) concludes that the USA date surveyed by him indicate that 'for a $25,000 house one pays between 0·4 and 0·7% ($100 to $175) for a unit NNI increase in quiet in the United States'. Nelson's own study also lies in this range, but there are some difficulties in accepting Walters's conclusion. First, it is based on only *five* studies. For three of those studies, the ones by Paik, Emerson and Dygert, Nelson's own interpretation gives depreciation indices outside the 0·4–0·7 per cent range quoted by Walters. That is, the range would appear to be about 0·2–0·9 per cent. The lower end of the range is supported by Price's study, while Nelson's own study lies within Walters's range. Mieszowski and Saper's study confirms the extension of the range downwards to 0·2 per cent while the rest of their values lie in the Walters range. The studies by Vaughan and Huckins and by Gamble *et al.* are difficult to evaluate in the terms we require since they use dBA and NPL respectively. There would therefore appear to be greater need for caution than is suggested by Walters, even on the basis of so few regression studies. Indeed, referring to his NEF related estimates Nelson (1976) states: 'Thus, for 1970, the empirical studies suggest a noise depreciation index of at least 0·5% and no greater than 1·0%. This is as strong a conclusion as can be obtained from the presently available empirical evidence.' In terms of NNI, Nelson's cautious statement translates to saying that the range is 0·22 per cent to 0·44 per cent,

Table 2.1   *Noise Depreciation Index*
(% change in house price with respect to unit increase in noise)

Study	Nelson (NEF)	Nelson[d] (NNI)	Walters[e] (NNI)
McClure (1969)	—	—	0·7
Colman (1972)	—	—	0·7
Paik (1970)	2·0	0·89	0·7
Emerson (1969)	0·4	0·18	0·55
Dygert and Sanders (1972)	—	—	0·4–0·8
Dygert (1975)	0·4–2·0	0·18–0·89	—
Price (1974)	0·4	0·18	—
Nelson (1975, 1976)	1·0	0·44	—

Regression studies not covered by Walters and Nelson

Study	Original result	Converted to NNI[c]
Mieszkowski and [a] Saper [b] (1976)	0·3–0·5 (CNR) 0·8–1·0	0·20–0·34 0·54–0·67
Vaughan and Huckins[f] (1975)	0·66–0·76 (dBA)	—
Gamble *et al.* (1974)	0·24–2·20 (NPL)[g]	

Notes: [a] Relates to Etobicoke for GNR = 95–105, house price of $35,000, apartment price of $25,000.
  [b] Relates to Mississauga for CNR = 95–105.
  [c] 1 CNR = 1·5 NNI.
  [d] Nelson uses an average house price of $28,000. 1 NEF = 2·25 NNI.
  [e] Walters uses an average house price of $25,000.
  [f] For $25,000 house.
  [g] Noise pollution level – see D. W. Robinson, 'Towards a unified system of noise abatement', *Journal of Sound and Vibration*, vol. 14 (1971). For current purposes we have taken the values for properties with average values of $25,100 (Rosedale) and $29,100. For all areas sampled by Gamble *et al.* the average property price was $31,100 and the average depreciation was 0·26 per cent per unit.

placing his estimate of the likely depreciation almost systematically *below* the range quoted by Walters.

Are hedonic price/multiple regression approaches useful? In the first place we must be clear that far too few studies have been done to place any degree of reliance on the various ranges suggested above. This may therefore amount to a call for further research. On the other hand, and the second point, the question must seriously be asked as to whether the mobility assumptions which are necessarily built into hedonic models actually hold. The importance of this assumption cannot be underestimated. If people *wish* to move but *cannot,* then the price of houses, being determined by the marginal turnover of sales in any one time period, will be higher in noisy areas than would be the case if everyone was free to react to house characteristics in the manner suggested. In short, there will be a large element of 'stayers' who suffer noise. According to the hedonic type models, they stay only if they value the costs of moving more than the noise costs they suffer. If there are constraints to moving, however, then noise sufferers will not be mobile.

Such evidence as there is suggests that precisely this phenomenon – sufferers *not* moving according to our expectations – occurs. Starkie and Johnson (1975) show that mobility around the London Heathrow airport area is not significantly different between noise bands. If they are correct, models such as we have been discussing have failed to capture one of the major constraints. What could this constraint be?

In the kinds of model we have discussed, people are assumed to weigh up costs and benefits. This, as we know, is the standard assumption of economic rationality. However, in the current context there is an oddity. Suppose a noise source emerges and house prices depreciate as some people move out. Others wish to move, placing a subjective evaluation on the noise (i.e. on securing peace and quiet) in excess of the costs of leaving the area. However, even if we suppose that the quiet area to which they wish to go has employment for the household's members, a *financial loss* has been sustained. To this must be added the actual cost of moving. If we consider a house priced at £20,000 and a depreciation rate due to newly introduced noise of 10 per cent (well within the range recorded by regression studies and other work), then £2,000 is immediately lost. Selling and buying fees for legal and estate agent (realtor) activities are typically of the order of 2 per cent of the house price (almost certainly a minimum), so that a further £400 is lost. The noise sufferer must therefore have £2,400 *in cash* in order to move. We assume he values peace and quiet at more than that, but such sums do not fit neatly into the pattern of everyday purchases analysed in economic textbooks. Quite simply, if the noise sufferer has not saved this sum (plus his removal expenses) he will not be *able* to move. What has happened is that costs and benefits are asymmetric: some have cash flows associated with them, some do not.

Failure to recognise this point leads us to think that the process of 'trading off' costs and benefits occurs regardless of what type of cost and benefit exists – i.e. of whether they have associated cash flows or not. There is every reason to think that the world is imperfect in this sense and that hedonic-style models fail to capture such constraints (Pearce, 1972, 1976).

HYBRID PROPERTY PRICE APPROACHES

We now turn to what we might call 'hybrid' property price approaches, the most famous of which is the study carried out by the Research Team of the Commission on the Third London Airport (hereafter, CTLA) (CTLA, 1970, 1971). It is 'hybrid' in the sense that it does not assume a process of continuous adjustment as in the hedonic attribute models and because, in practice, multiple regression techniques could not be used and resort was had to a different method of estimating price depreciation. Further, whereas the hedonic models nowhere speak of consumers' surplus – the excess of the individual's subjective valuation of a house over and above its market price – the discrete adjustment procedure assumed in the CTLA study requires an estimate of this surplus.

The essential background to the CTLA study was that four sites round London had been shortlisted as sites for London's third airport (the other two being London Heathrow and London Gatwick). Full details are given in CTLA (1971) and an overview is provided in Dasgupta and Pearce (1972). Noise was only one of the many issues analysed in this extensive study and, ultimately, it proved insignificant, at least as far as the CTLA Research Team's study was concerned, when compared to the social losses in terms of lost travelling time. The ultimate recommendation by the Commission of an inland site, Cublington, was rejected by the UK government of the day for reasons that were quite different from those that were given in the press and media. However, our concern is with the methodology and results obtained for the valuation of noise nuisance.

The first requirement was to categorise the types of person affected by the advent of airport noise. These were:

(1) People who are 'natural movers' – i.e. who will be moving anyway for reasons unconnected with noise. If noise increases as these people sell their houses, we can expect house prices to fall and they will bear this loss (D). For these people, consumers' surplus (S) is zero.
(2) People who move *because* of noise. Now, for many of these people, the value they place on their homes exceeds the market valuation by the amount S. Hence, they lose both D and S by moving. In addition, of course, they will incur removal costs (R).

For these people, then, it must be the case that the cost of noise, *N, if they remained,* exceeds $S + D + R$. Consequently $S + D + R$ is a *minimum* estimate of the costs to this category of sufferer.

(3) Those who stay and tolerate noise. They suffer a cost, *N.* Technically, $N < S + D + R$ for these people, and, of course, *N* could be zero.

(4) Those who move into the noisy area to replace natural movers and those who have moved because of noise. *If* these people are fully aware of the new circumstances, it would be reasonable to assume that they are at least compensated by *D,* the depreciation on property they now buy. In fact, of course, *D* could exceed their requirement for compensation, in which case there would be *benefits* (*B*) for this category, such that $B \leqslant D$. The general assumption, however, was to set costs equal to zero for this category.

(5) To these four groups should be added those who lived outside the previously quiet area and who *would have moved in* but for the noise. These people experience a welfare loss, as Pearce (1972) points out. Unfortunately, no evident method exists for evaluating this form of option demand. The category was not considered in the CTLA model.

Apart from estimating the rate of natural movement (which was obtained by looking at rates of movement in the potentially affected areas without airport development) and the numbers of people involved, the model therefore reduced to estimating *D, S, R* and *N.* Removal costs naturally presented little problem, but depreciation, *D,* did. As we have already observed, these could have been obtained by regression technique, but this proved impossible. Instead, estate agents in Gatwick (which was thought similar to the four sites, having no night flights whereas Heathrow does) were asked what impact they thought noise had already had on named properties. In this way it was hoped that the effect of noise alone would be singled out. The actual range of figures derived was very wide indeed, although some confirmation for medium priced houses (£4,000–£8,000) was obtained from a British Airports Authority study and from the Inland Revenue (see Pearce, 1976, p. 19). Table 2.2 assembles the average results for Gatwick and for Heathrow.

Now, placed on a graph the data in Table 2.2 would appear to suggest *linear* relationships between NNI and house price depreciation. Indeed, this apparent linearity is the basis of Walters's claim that noise indices have cardinal properties (Walters, 1975), a claim hotly disputed by Hart (1973) who contests the validity of the construction of the noise and number index in the first place. While such critiques are themselves of immense value, and Hart's paper suggests more than one serious deficiency with NNI (and hence with other indices such as CNR and NEF which tend to be comparatively simple transforms of each other),

Table 2.2   *Percentage Depreciation in House Prices, Heathrow and Gatwick*

| | | Property | | |
		Low price (£4,000)	Medium price (£4,000–8,000)	High price (£8,000)
35–45 NNI	H	0	2·6	3·3
	G	4·5	9·4	16·4
45–55 NNI	H	2·9	6·3	13·3
	G	10·3	16·5	29·0
55 NNI+	H	5·0	10·5	22·5
	G	—	—	—

Note: H = Heathrow
G = Gatwick

we may also note that linearity, if it exists, is an *empirical* characteristic. Yet, for Gatwick we have only *two* observations across wide noise bands, and for Heathrow we have only *three* points. Possibly some comfort is to be derived from the fact that extrapolated backwards the origins of house price/NNI linear functions lie round about the 30 NNI level which corresponds, roughly, to the difference between town and country noise (see Pearce 1976, pp. 20–1). But the truth of the matter is that the CTLA data is altogether too limited, and itself the result of some severe averaging anyway, to be used to support hypotheses of linearity. Yet we saw when reviewing the hedonic price literature that this linearity is often built into the model specifications – that is the 'price' of noise is constant per unit of noise. Further doubt has been cast on this assumption by Waller (1976) who legitimately points out that NNI is logarithmic in scale so that a unit increase in NNI at higher levels of NNI is 'worse' than a unit increase at lower levels. That is, we would expect the price of noise to be higher per unit of noise at the higher levels of noise. If so, the relationship between depreciation (if indeed depreciation is itself a measure of the price of noise) and noise will be curvilinear and not linear. Introducing non-linearity into the models so far discussed could be significant but no work appears to exist containing such a model.

For the CTLA model we are left with trying to find estimates for S and N. The CTLA Research Team considered various ways of estimating S. Strictly, one requires to observe a set of prices freely negotiated between house owner and developer. If these could be observed they might indicate the distribution of house owner's subjective evaluations. These could then be compared to actual market prices, and the difference would be a measure of S, the householder's surplus. However, practical difficulties prevent this approach being used – primarily, no such 'free' negotiations take place in reality – so that a questionnaire approach was adopted. In the CTLA case, six areas in the south of England were chosen for the survey, each of the areas supposedly unaffected by development. Respondents were asked to consider a hypothetical 'large development' and to say 'what price would be just high enough to compensate . . . for leaving this house and moving to another area'. The price quoted was then recorded and the difference was the householder's surplus. In the BAA/METRA survey, respondents were first asked to react to the idea of making a £100 profit by moving: if they responded favourably then their inducement to move must lie below this sum. If they responded unfavourably they were asked, 'What would the difference in price have to be to make you seriously consider moving?', and if they responded that no sum would induce them to move, they were asked, 'You mean that if your house/flat would fetch twice as much as those in other areas, you would still not consider moving?' (BAA/METRA, 1970).

The responses to the CTLA and BAA/METRA surveys are shown in Table 2.3.

Several points may be noted. First, up to the absolute figure of £2,500 the two distributions are broadly in agreement. Secondly, there is complete disparity after this point, most significantly in the number who would not sell at any price. In the BAA/METRA case this is 38 per cent (50 per cent in the separate survey of tenants) and 8 per cent in the CTLA case. There are various explanations. The CTLA argue that the 38 per cent in the BAA/METRA study comprise many people who would have stated very large sums, and that 'the purpose underlying the questions in the Authority's survey seem to have been misunderstood'

Table 2.3 *Householder's Surplus*

Inducement	% Response	
	BAA/METRA	*CTLA*
£150	12	11
£150–450	4	2
£450–950	13	14
£950–1,500	20	19
£1,500–2,500	6	11
£2,500–4,500	⎫	18
£4,500–10,000	⎬ 7	12
£10,000	⎭	5
Would not sell	38	8
	100	100

(CTLA, 1971, p. 275). This explanation is difficult to accept not least because the BAA/METRA survey contained a deliberate question to emphasise to the respondents what sums they were implying when they said this. Hedges (1972) gives various reasons for doubting the results of questionnaire approaches. It is certainly tempting to think that very large offers must have been sufficient to induce their respondents to sell: their failure to state a definite sum has led them to being called 'infinites' because they appear to imply infinite sums for compensation. But this may not be the correct conclusion to draw. It may be that people do not think or behave like the economist's 'rational man' on all occasions: that is, they may not conceptually be able to translate the many intangible items covered by 'householder's surplus' into money terms. If this is true it presents severe methodological problems for cost-benefit studies, but it is at least as consistent a view as supposing that there must be some finite figure for compensation. (See Chapter 7 on Social Severance for a similar view.)

As to those finite values reported by respondents, Mishan (1971) criticises the use of these on the grounds that respondents were given no indication of how far they would have to move to avoid the (hypothetical) development scheme. Whitbread and Bird (1973) adopt a similar stance when they argue that the valuations of *S* are unreliable because respondents were unable to identify from the questionnaire what the alternatives were before them. Indeed, Whitbread and Bird are categorical when they say, 'We know of no way in which surpluses may be reliably observed' (Whitbread and Bird, 1973, p. 199). This verdict underlines general doubts about the validity of the approaches to estimating.

One important deficiency of surveys is that the very *fact* that the survey is taking place makes the respondent believe that there is a connection between disamenity and money values which is capable of being assessed (Hedges, 1972). It also remains true that hypothetical questions are almost certain to induce unreliable responses because the respondent knows he is not being asked to engage in *actual* decisions.

We shall not investigate the methodology used by the CTLA Research Team to calculate *N* since the process was a lengthy one and somewhat tenuous. An excellent description of the procedure is to be found in Paul (1971) and is further dealt with at length in Pearce (1976).

Table 2.1 presented earlier, *if* the price/noise linearity assumption can be justified, suggests noise depreciation indices of 1·0 for Heathrow and 1·3 for Gatwick (standardised for the assumed $25,000 house – see Walters, 1975, p. 104). If any credence can be given to such results, it would mean that London noise sufferers appear to be willing to pay considerably more than their American counterparts for a unit reduction in noise. Indeed, the difference is $250–325 for a unit reduction in NNI in London and only $55–110 in the USA, both relating to periods round about 1970, and for similarly priced houses (we have taken Nelson's lower range of depreciation indices, having argued that Walters's estimates are in need of revision). Since these are willingness to pay measures it is not evident why they should differ so markedly, unless, of course, the methodologies used to derive them are at fault.

Overall it seems impossible to have faith in house price indicators as accurate guides to the social cost of noise. The few studies on traffic noise (Vaughan and Huckins, 1975, Gamble *et al.,* 1974) in the USA do secure negative influences of noise on property prices, but Diffey (1971, 1975) found no such correlation. The range of values derived is too wide to adopt the cautious confidence taken by, say, Walters (1975) when, after reviewing some aircraft noise studies he concludes that 'there is a remarkable consistency in the results'. The very opposite would appear to be the case.

Property price approaches have occupied most of our attention because they have dominated research work in the area. The remainder of the chapter considers some alternative approaches that have been used.

THE EXCLUSION FACILITIES APPROACH

Starkie and Johnson (1975) have proposed a different approach to the valuation of noise costs. They point out that, besides moving to escape noise or staying to suffer it, there is a further option open to householders, namely, to insulate against it. In this way the CTLA model can be modified to allow for this option. Essentially, where the movement decision in the CTLA model depended on:

$$N \lessgtr S + D + R.$$

Starkie and Johnson argue that those who stay to tolerate noise must obey the inequality:

$$S + D + R > N < G + N',$$

where G is the cost of 'exclusion facilities' such as house insulation, fencing (if it is motorway noise), etc., and N' is the valuation of 'residual noise' – i.e. that noise left over even after the introduction of insulation.

Similarly, those who stay but buy exclusion facilities must obey:

$$N > G + N' < S + D + R.$$

The cost of double glazing – which varies with window size – was used as a surrogate for price, thus providing the basis for estimating a demand schedule.

The logic of the above inequalities is simply that households will buy exclusion facilities if the value of noise reduction so secured is more than the expenditure on the facilities, i.e. if:

$$N - N' > G,$$

in which case there will be a surplus gained on G. In this way, expenditure on exclusion facilities represents a minimum valuation of the good peace and quiet. If variations in the price of exclusion facilities can be observed, we can obtain a demand curve the area under which would be a minimum measure of surplus, and hence a value that can be entered into a cost-benefit analysis.

It must be noted that the approach will produce unrepresentative valuations for average households if there is a significant number of movers: the model operates, by definition, only for those who stay. Starkie and Johnson (1975) argue that the bias in this respect is small since they estimate that there are very few households that move because of noise. This is in contrast with Walters's suggestion that movement rates in noisy areas are probably 20–30 per cent above the 'natural' movement rate (Walters, 1975). On the other hand, the Heathrow area which was studied by Starkie and Johnson has a high proportion of tenants who, they argue, are constrained in terms of their ability to move.

Since Starkie and Johnson's population sample was fairly homogeneous, it was assumed that its members had similar incomes. By indirect means this average income was estimated at £1,800, and total willingness to pay for insulation of three bedrooms was £45 and for two living rooms £47, for a given average reduction in noise of 14 dBA. This suggests a willingness to pay of about 5 per cent of income for the total insulation of a house with three bedrooms and two downstairs rooms. Starkie and Johnson further suggest that this is a maximum value since sound insulation has joint-good aspects – it serves also as heat insulation – which means that the expenditures for noise *alone* can be thought of as being less. The figure of 5 per cent of income as the value of 'quiet' compares to Walters's suggestion (1975, p. 76) that the range of maximum values is from 2 per cent (for low income groups) to 7 per cent (for high income groups).

Starkie and Johnson's approach is an interesting one and it is clear that further useful work could be carried out in this general direction. The problems with it are (1) that it cannot be relied upon to provide an average valuation of noise if there is a significant number of people who move because of noise; (2) it provides an average value of $N - N'$ but leaves residual noise unvalued (e.g. outdoor noise), although this may be thought of as possibly cancelling out with the good aspects of insulation; (3) it provides us only with an *average* valuation for a specified range of noise reduction so that we have no *marginal* valuation for a specified range of noise reduction so that we have no *marginal* valuation which can be applied to other ranges; (4) expenditure on double glazing gives us an estimate of what householders are willing to pay for the joint product of noise insulation, thermal insulation *plus* a speculative element in that double glazing tends to raise property prices thus securing the householder a capital gain. Speculative motives are, of course, absent for tenants.

EXPERIMENTAL EVALUATION APPROACHES

The possibility of using a controlled, simulated market experiment to value environmental goods has been investigated by Hoinville and Berthoud (1970a, 1970b), Hoinville (1971), Hoinville and Prescott-Clarke (1972) and Pendse and Wyckoff (1974). The objective is to present controlled subjects with a hypothetical budget which they have then to allocate between a set of 'environmental goods' such as noise reduction, time saving, natural amentiy, and so on. The respondents allocate the budget in such a way as to exhaust the sum they are given and to be indifferent in their final allocation to further trade-offs. The price of each good can be varied to test the reaction of each respondent. The nature of the goods is indicated to the respondent, usually in the form of a picture or, for noise, a tape recording, and, of course, the budget is set so that maximum quantities of all variables cannot be achieved. This forces the respondent to state his trade-off position.

Now in order to find *absolute* values for environmental change it is essential to put at least one absolute value in the experiment. In addition, respondents should be able to choose their own budget size – otherwise there is a risk that this will be arbitrarily selected so that valuations of individual variables will be *relative* valuations only. In Hoinville and Prescott-Clarke (1972) absolute values are secured by introducing values of travelling time taken from United Kingdom Department of the Environment studies, and altering income levels by allowing respondents to pay a 'tax' to secure further improvements. In the Pendse and Wyckoff (1974) study, budget levels were pre-set at 'approximately the annual costs incurred per person for maintenance of the environment under study' but no information is provided as to how this was obtained.

The Hoinville studies have not yet reported absolute values for noise. The Pendse and Wyckoff study does. Some general observations can be made. First, the Hoinville studies suggest that substantial improvements in poor amenity situations are sought by respondents and they are willing to pay for them. In the Pendse and Wyckoff study, however, poor environments did not appear to attract such sensitivity. Hoinville's studies show a marked preference for amenity over accessibility – i.e.

Table 2.4   *Disposition of $18 Budget (Pendse and Wyckoff)*

	Condition of Environment	
	Average	Good
Variable	*$*	*$*
Natural Surroundings	4·5	4·5
Various Noises	1·7	4·5
Recreation Park Facilities	3·9	3·9
Vehicular Traffic	2·0	4·5
Travel Time (Work)	0·9	0·5
Parking Facilities	5·0	7·0

a willingness to give up travel time to secure more amenity – and this is consistent with Pendse and Wyckoff's study.

Table 2.4 above shows Pendse and Wyckoff's results for their $18 budget.

These prices are then taken to be the respondent's valuation of an additional unit of each of the variables. It will be seen that noise valuation increases when the environment is already good.

The difficulties with such experimental approaches are numerous, but it is clear that further work in the area is justified. There is the immediate problem of whether the results obtained from such studies can be extended to real-life situations in which respondents may behave quite differently even though respondents appear both to have understood the 'game' and reacted sensibly. Secondly, there are no real means of validating the results except by comparing any absolute values obtained with other method results. It is not clear if the respondents correctly perceive the alternatives facing them or if they see it as anything other than a 'game'. Thirdly, to date, samples used have been very small.

None the less, the approach is a promising one in many respects.

CONCLUSIONS

Noise nuisance has perhaps attracted more research effort than any other pollutant in terms of attempts to place a monetary valuation on it. Moreover, with air pollution, it has promoted attempts to model its effects on property values in the contexts of spatial general equilibrium models. These attempts are to be applauded, but as we stressed in the introduction to this book little is achieved if the end result is a wide array of estimates when we would expect some similarity in outcome. Of course, there is no particular reason to expect, say, the residents of Washington to value noise in the same way as residents of London. To this end, estimates will differ. At the same time, when wide variations do occur, and this chapter has demonstrated that they exist, contrary to the views taken by other authors, it would seem sensible to have some idea of what explains the variation. Model specifications may be weak and the useful surveys by Walters (1975) and Nelson (1976) help us in this respect. On the other hand, we have also noted that some models actually build in assumptions in such a way that certain results must emerge from the model. Notable here is the requirement that a unit of noise attract the same price regardless of how much is 'consumed' by the individual. This outcome is at odds both with real world economics and with what we know about noise indices. Just what difference relaxing this assumption would make remains to be seen. In the meantime we have a fairly extensive literature which is inconclusive and which certainly has no policy relevance as yet.

NOTES

1 There are numerous measures of noise and noise nuisance. The latter incorporate some index of individuals' subjective assessment of noise, whereas the former will perhaps just measure loudness and frequency of occurrence. Measures of noise annoyance, such as the *noise and number index* (NNI), are logarithmic in scale by virtue of the way they are constructed. As such, an increase from 50 to 51 NNI relates to a more serious increase in noise nuisance than does an increase from 40 to 41 NNI.
2 NEF is frequently used in the United States, whereas NNI tends to be used in the United Kingdom, despite considerable criticism. NEF is defined as:

$$NEF = \overline{EPNL} + 10 \log (N_d + 16 \cdot 7 N_n) - 88,$$

where $\overline{EPNL}$ is the effective perceived noise level, N_d and N_n are the numbers of daytime and nightime flights respectively.
3 1 NEF = 1·5 CNR (Composite Noise Rating) and 1 CNR = 1·5 NNI. Hence, 1 NEF = 2·25 NNI.

REFERENCES

British Airports Authority, *Evidence to Stage V Proceedings of the Commission on the Third London Airport*, Document 5006 and 5006A, 1970.
Colman, A. H., *Aircraft Noise Effects on Property Values*, Environmental Standards Circular, City of Inglewood, California, 1972.
Commission on the Third London Airport, *Papers and Proceedings*, Vol. VIII, chs 18–20 (London: HMSO, 1970).
Commission on the Third London Airport, *Report*, ch. 7, and appendices 22 and 23 (London: HMSO, 1970).
Dasgupta, A. K. and Pearce, D. W., *Cost Benefit Analysis* (London: Macmillan, 1972).
Diffey, J., 'An investigation into the effect of high traffic noise on house prices in a homogeneous sub-market', paper presented to the Centre for Environmental Studies Seminar on House Prices and the Microeconomics of Housing, London. Also M.Sc. thesis, University of Keele, 1975.
Dygert, P. K. and Sanders, D., *On Measuring the Cost of Noise from Subsonic Aircraft* (Berkeley, California: Institute of Transport and Traffic Engineering, 1972).
Dygert, P. K., 'An economic approach to airport noise', *Journal of Air Law and Commerce*, vol. 30, 1964.

Emerson, F. C., 'The determinants of residential value with specified reference to the effects of aircraft nuisance and other environmental features', PhD thesis, University of Minnesota, 1969a.

Emerson, F. C., 'The environmental determinants of residential prices', Western Michigan University, unpublished.

Gamble, H. B., *et al.*, *The Influence of Highway Environmental Effects on Residential Property Values* (Pennsylvania: State University, 1974).

Griliches, Z., *Price Indexes and Quality Change* (Cambridge, Massachusetts: Harvard University Press, 1971).

Hart, P. E., 'Population densities and optimal aircraft flight paths', *Regional Studies*, vol. 7, 1973.

Hedges, B., *Attaching Money Values to Environmental Disturbance* (London: Social Community Planning Research, Paper No. 230, 1972.

Hoinville, G. and Berthoud, R., *Identifying and Evaluating Trade-Off References – An Analysis of Environmental/Accessibility Priorities* London: Social and Community Planning Research, 1970a.

Hoinville, G. and Berthoud, R., *Value of Time: Development Project, Report on Stage 3* Social and Community Planning Research, 1970b.

Hoinville, G., 'Evaluating community preferences', *Environment and Planning*, vol. 3, 1971.

Hoinvill, G. and Prescott-Clarke, P., *Traffic Disturbance and Amenity Values*, Social and Community Planning Research Document 214, London, December 1972.

McClure, P. T., 'Indication of the effect of jet noise on the value of real estate', *American Institute of Aeronautics and Astronautics*, Printed as RAND Paper, p. 4117, 1969.

Mishan, E. J., 'What is wrong with Roskill?', *Journal of Transport Economics and Policy*, vol. 4, no. 2, 1970.

Mieszkowski, P. and Saper, A. M., An Estimate of the Effect of Airport Noise on Property Values', *Journal of Urban Economics*, 1978.

Muth, R., *Cities and Housing* (Chicago: University Press, 1969).

Nelson, J. P., 'An analysis of jet aircraft noise and residential property values', Pennsylvania State University, 1976 (unpublished).

Nelson, J. P., *The Effects of Mobile-Source Air and Noise Pollution on Residential Property Values*, Report DOT-TST-75-76, Department of Transportation, Washington DC, 1975.

Paik, I. K., 'Impact of transportation noise on urban residential property values with special reference to aircraft noise', Consortium of Universities, Washington DC, 1970.

Paul, M. E., 'Can aircraft noise nuisance be measured in money?', *Oxford Economic Papers*, November 1971.

Pearce, D. W., 'The economic evaluation of noise-generating and noise abatement projects', in OECD, *Problems of Environmental Economics* (Paris: OECD, 1972).

Pearce, D. W., *The Social Cost of Noise* (Paris: OECD, 1976).

Pendse, D. and Wyckoff, J., 'Scope for valuation of environmental goods', *Land Economics*, 1974.

Polinsky, A. M. and Shavell, S., 'The air pollution and property value debate', *Review of Economics and Statistics*, vol. 57, February 1975.

Price, I., *The Social Cost of Airport Noise as Measured by Rental Changes: The Case of Logan Airport*, Boston University, Ph.D. thesis, 1974.

Rosen, S., 'Hedonic Prices and Implicit Markets', *Journal of Political Economy*, vol. 82, 1974.

Smith, V. K., 'Residential location and environmental amenities: a review of the evidence', *Journal of Regional Studies*, vol. II, no. 1, 1977.

Starkie, D. and Johnson, D., *The Economic Value of Peace and Quiet* (London: Saxon House, 1975).

Taylor, R., *Noise* (Harmondsworth: Pelican Books, 1970).

Vaughan, R. J. and Huckins, L., *The Economics of Expressway Noise Pollution Abatement* (California: Rand Corporation 1975).

Walters, A., *Aircraft Noise and Prices* (London: OUP, 1975).
Whitbread, M. and Bird, H., 'Rent, surplus and the evaluation of residential environments', *Regional Studies,* June 1973.

Chapter 3

Air Pollution

INTRODUCTION

The previous chapter demonstrated that, while various approaches have been taken with respect to attempts to derive monetary evaluations of noise nuisance, most of them have centred on property price models. In turn, most of these models have used one or other variant of a 'hedonic-price' approach whereby multiple regression equations relating house prices to housing characteristics are analysed for the relevant coefficient relating house price to noise nuisance. It is also true to say that much of the literature on noise nuisance is fairly recent so that, in effect, both theory and practice have been developed simultaneously. Studies of air pollution damage have also concentrated on house price variations, but several differences exist between this work and that for noise. First, the earlier house price studies (e.g. Ridker, 1969) engaged in multiple regression techniques without really investigating the theoretical underpinnings of this approach first. As such, the theory came *after* the empirical attempts to estimate damage. Secondly, whereas noise is a reasonably homogeneous 'bad', air pollution can take on a variety of characteristics, some of which make the pollution invisible to the senses and others of which make it noxious and readily perceived. That is, there are different types of air pollutants and it may matter a great deal which measure is taken. Thirdly, and following from the second point, it seems clear that air pollution *is* linked to ill health, particularly to respiratory illness. Unless individuals perceive this linkage clearly we can have no reason to assume that property price changes, if observed, will 'embody' these health effects. To this extent then, the air pollution cost literature also includes an important element devoted to damage to health. Finally, a number of studies exist which attempt to evaluate air pollution damage to buildings and paintwork through corrosion, damage to livestock and damage to plants, trees and crops. With the possible exception of crop and livestock damage one would expect, in a hedonic-model context, that corrosion damage would be perceived and should therefore be capitalised (negatively) into property prices.

HOUSE PRICE STUDIES: THEORY

As noted above, house price studies relating to air pollution did not initially investigate, in any detail anyway, the methodological basis for using house price changes as indicators of marginal willingness to pay. Chapter 2 demonstrated that severe methodological problems remain. Within the air pollution literature the main methodological arguments have been developed by Anderson and Crocker (1971), Nelson (1975), Polinsky and Shavell (1976), Polinsky and Rubinfeld (1977), Freeman (1974) and Smith (1976, 1977). The dates of these publications may be compared with that of the first major empirical study, that of Ridker (1967).

With noise nuisance we noted that the assumption of mobility in response to the perception of 'bads' was critical to the use of property price changes as measures of damage done by pollution. Where mobility is imperfect, because of constraints or lack of information about pollution or environmental quality in alternative areas, then property price changes will *not* as a rule be measures of damage. The mobility assumption has been critical to the air pollution/property price debate. The problem is best illustrated by the distinction used by Polinsky and Shavell (1976) between small 'open' cities and large cities which may be open or 'closed'. An 'open' city is one where there is free migration in and out in response to city characteristics, including pollution levels. A 'closed' city is one where this kind of mobility does not occur. We may take the extremes of total openness and total closure. Following Strotz (1968), we consider a simple example. Assume total closure and that the city has land which is identical but for the fact that one half is polluted and the other half is not. Polluted land sells at $100 per unit and unpolluted land at $200 per unit. Now assume a programme of environmental improvement such that the polluted land is made unpolluted. No one now has any incentive to move from the polluted to the unpolluted section of the city and land values average out at $150 per unit. What are the gains and losses? Those who rented unpolluted land at $200 now rent it at $150 and therefore gain a surplus of $50 per unit. Those who rented polluted land now find themselves paying $50 more per unit. If they value the improvement positively then their gain must be somewhere between $0 and $50, the upper limit being determined by the fact that they could have paid $200 before to secure unpolluted land. That is, they have paid an extra $50 and hence their surplus could be zero or it could be $50, the difference between what they now pay and what they could previously have paid to secure unpolluted land. If, on the other hand, they value the improvement *negatively* they will have *losses* of between $0 and $50. That is, they pay $150 for unpolluted land, an increase of $50, and if they do not care about the improvement this increase must be a loss. Now, while *total* land values have not changed – the city has the same area now selling at $150 per unit, instead of half at $100 and half at $200 – the price of both polluted and unpolluted land has changed. The benefits appear to be $50 per unit for the unpolluted land, but somewhere between +$50 and −$50 for the polluted land. If preferences were normally distributed in the polluted area, the net gain there would be zero. The benefit to the programme of improvement thus becomes $50 per unit (on the previously unpolluted land), but the *land value* changes are *minus* $50 in the previously unpolluted area and plus $50 in the previously polluted area. *In short, for the closed city, land value changes do not measure programme benefits.*

If the city was open but large we would get similar problems since the prices of its goods compared with other cities would be affected and surpluses *outside* the city would be changed. In the closed city, however, we note that surpluses elsewhere have not been affected. Not surprisingly, therefore, we find that land value changes appear linked to marginal willingness to pay only in *small open* cities. This is the essential conclusion reached by Polinsky and Shavell (1976) and Polinsky and Rubinfeld (1977). What happens when the city is open is that migration occurs inwards if there is environmental improvement, and outwards if there is environmental deterioration. In these circumstances land prices will be bid upwards and the surpluses we noted in the Strotz example would be eliminated or, rather, brought into line with surpluses in other cities. In these circumstances the environmental change does become capitalised in the land value change. The conditions for the use of property prices to measure air pollution damage thus become those of smallness and openness.

Notice that in the above example we were looking at the new set of land values *after* the improvement or deterioration occurred. Since, in general, we are interested in *proposed* programmes of improvement we need some way of predicting these land value changes when we are satisfied that the small, open city conditions are met. It is true, however, that *ex post* studies are valuable in order to see just how much damage has been done. Practitioners now seem agreed that general equilibrium approaches are essential, but practically impossible to manipulate (see Polinsky and Shavell, 1975, and Freeman, 1974) for the large or closed city contexts.

Polinsky and Rubinfeld (1977) provide a valuable assessment of the problems to be encountered by various attempts to model the different locational adjustments that might be made in response to environmental quality changes. Building on the earlier papers by Polinsky and Shavell (1975, 1976), they make one major alteration in assuming that there are different groups within the city. (The Polinsky–Shavell papers assumed a single homogeneous group.) *Within* each group there is homogeneity of tastes, but there are many groups so that they 'compete' with each other. Also, *within* each group there are identical incomes, but per capita incomes vary *between* groups. Given complete mobility adjustments to the existence of amenities, etc., will, according to Polinsky and Rubinfeld, lead to each *group* achieving the same level of utility regardless of where they locate. This result occurs because if one location improves compared to another location, land prices will simply rise in the first location and fall in the second until both locations are equally desirable.

The resulting model is complex and accordingly they seek a simplification by assuming a Cobb–Douglas utility function (see also Walters's model for noise in Chapter 2) for residents. Using this model they conclude that:

(1) Even for small, open cities with one homogeneous group – the one class that emerged apparently safe from the Strotz analysis described earlier – changes in amenities will affect wage rates and transport costs, perhaps attracting more residents into the city and lowering the wage rate, or causing congestion and raising transport costs, and so on. *If* these effects did *not* occur, property value changes corresponding to amenity level changes could be predicted (this says nothing about what the property value changes would *mean* – see below). But if they do occur, then prediction of property price changes would require prediction of the effects on transport costs and wage rates – i.e. we are back to estimating a complex general equilibrium model.

(2) For the small, open city with *heterogeneous* groups we shall have the same problem as in (1) above, but even if general equilibrium effects are ignored then a property price equation needs to be specified for *each group*. But this can only be done if we know where each group will locate itself when all the adjustment procedures have taken place and a new equilibrium occurs. Thus, even apart from the possible effects on wage rates and transport costs 'this seems a rather hopeless task empirically'. (Polinsky and Rubinfeld, 1977.)

(3) For the closed model with a homogeneous group of individuals, all the foregoing problems apply with an extra one for good measure. For now any change in amenity affects the utility level of *all* individuals (see the discussion of the Strotz example above). We are back to solving complex general equilibrium models.

(4) Finally, the closed model with several groups leads to the problem of predicting the change in utility by group, since it can rise for some and fall for others. To assume that utility does not change in either case (3) above or this one will lead to errors in predicting property price changes.

Polinsky and Rubinfeld (1977) then ask whether the property value changes, *even if they could be predicted*, would mean anything – that is, would they be measures of marginal willingness to pay? Again classifying by open and closed areas, they argue that consumers' utility levels are not changed in the open context so that their willingness to pay is zero. Landowners (including residential landowners) will experience positive willingness to pay and hence total willingness to pay *is* measured by changes in land values. (Note that consumers are here regarded as a different group to residential landowners.) But two factors are noteworthy. First, it is *land* values, not property values, that are relevant, and *all* land, residential and business, must be included. In the closed context, consumers may be better off or worse off, so that their utility levels must be allowed for. Overall, changes in *land* values are good estimators for the small, open city. Changes in *property* values will understate willingness to pay (the change in land values will exceed the change in property values).

The real issue, then, appears to lie in whether or not land value changes can be forecast and the Polinsky–Rubinfeld arguments are discouraging in this respect.

Polinsky and Rubinfeld (1977) suggest the rudiments of a better approach in which property prices are expressed as functions of the level of utility in equilibrium, expenditure on goods other than transport, and levels of amenity. But the equation's use is to find the utility function of the consumer so that, once specified, the utility function is used to identify that wage rate which satisfies an indirect utility function equation relating utility to property prices, wage rates and amenity levels and in which an assumed change in amenity is provided. The wage rate satisfying this equation is then used to estimate the difference between it and the actual wage rate, the difference being the marginal willingness to pay for the amenity in question. These sums are then summed over all individuals. While the procedure appears complex, and it certainly has difficult features, the essential idea is to use property price measures in a different way, namely, to go back to the underlying utility function (the specific form of which has to be assumed, of course) and then to estimate the change in wage rates which will correspond to some given change in amenity.

In their empirical application of the approach, Polinsky and Rubinfeld (1977) secure estimates for willingness to pay which systematically *exceed* estimates of property price changes. Their estimates have income taken out as a determining factor in order to compare their results with earlier work such as that of Anderson and Crocker in which income is also absent as a determinant of property price change. Whether income should be included or not has itself been debated. If the model is thought to be analogous to an hedonic approach, it is generally thought that income should be excluded. If it is not analogous, Smith (1976, 1977) argues that income should be included. Polinsky and Rubinfeld are well aware of the bias imparted by excluding income and they suggest that it exaggerates their measure. However, they would not have secured comparison with other models had they included it. Thus, the Polinsky–Rubinfeld work suggests that changes in property values *understate* willingness to pay.

HOUSE PRICE STUDIES: PRACTICE

If the Polinsky–Rubinfeld conclusions are correct, approaches which seek to find the effect of air pollution on property values will tend to understate the benefits of pollution improvement programmes or, conversely, will understate the costs of pollution damage. How far their conclusion is correct depends in part on whether income is to be included as a determinant of property values in models of the Polinsky–Rubinfeld type. This was discussed above. We may now turn to those models which have adopted property value approaches in a more direct fashion.

Ridker and Henning (1967) and Ridker (1967) regressed property values on an index of sulphur pollution across census tracts in St Louis and found a statistically significant negative effect. Other characteristics such as access to roads and public transport were also significant, as was income. We have already noted the debate about including income as an explanatory variable since it will clearly be highly correlated with other variables. However, Ridker (1967) concludes that a fall in sulphur pollution levels by 0.25 mg of $SO_3/100cm^2/day$ would cause an increase in property values of between \$83 and \$245, with the latter figure being more likely. Zerbe (1969) used a model similar to Ridker and secured statistically significant effects for Toronto and Hamilton in Canada. Wieand (1973) repeated the Ridker–Henning study but changed the dependent variable. Whereas Ridker and Henning used a median property value by census tract, Wieand argues that the median property value used in the Ridker–Henning study is in fact a measure of *expenditure* on housing. This is a matter of the statistical source used. Wieand points out that if the property price statistic is in fact housing expenditure, then the relationship between this expenditure and the property *price* will depend on the price elasticity of demand. On the basis of other studies, he suggests this elasticity is about -1 so that expenditure cannot be used as a surrogate for property price. We noted earlier that it is the land price that is needed: property prices will include the value of improvements.

Weiand uses a constructed index of monthly housing expenditure and divides this by residential land area to get a measure of land use intensity. It is this that he regresses on pollution levels, finding *no* statistical relationship. That is, with the correct independent variable, the Ridker–Henning findings are negated. Mullet (1974) criticises

Weiand's statistical approach but not the principle of changing the dependent variable, while Weiand (1974) offers a successful rebuttal of Mullet's criticisms. As such, one must conclude that Weiand has produced a further telling criticism of the use of changes in property values as indicators of marginal willingness to pay for depollution as long as the property values are expenditure estimates and not proper prices. This is particularly applicable to the USA studies which tend to have used the same statistical sources for property value data.

The work of Anderson and Crocker (1971, 1972) found statistically significant relationships between property prices (using median property value, median gross rent and median contract rent in different versions of the regressions) and at least one measure of air pollution. In defending their work against criticism Anderson and Crocker likened their approach to the hedonic price approach discussed in Chapter 2, although unlike other practitioners of this approach they do have income as an independent variable. Freeman (1971) pointed out that their regressions do not isolate demand and supply factors – i.e. the coefficients measure the effects of air pollution on property prices in equilibrium and do not indicate anything about marginal willingness to pay schedules. However, all parties seem agreed that, while such approaches as that adopted by Anderson and Crocker cannot say anything about the effects of large changes in environmental quality (this would require knowledge of the schedule), it is useful for *marginal* changes. We noted this point in the noise debate in Chapter 2. Small (1975) provides a formal proof of the use of the regression coefficient for this purpose and notes that neither income nor utility need be assumed the same for all consumers in order to use such coefficients. See also Freeman (1974).

The work of Deyak and Smith (1974) used a cross-section study based not on tracts within a given city, but across cities. They conclude that air pollution is marginally significant, but they reverse their conclusion in Smith and Deyak (1975) – see also Smith (1976, 1977). As such, their work suggests no significant relationship, although their use of city centre pollution readings for the air pollution measure is likely to impart extensive bias given the variability of pollution levels within cities. Indeed, it is largely this factor that has legitimately inhibited others from engaging in cross-city rather than intra-city analyses.

Nelson (1975) looks at air pollution by city tract for Washington. The hedonic model employed is the same as that for noise described in Chapter 2. The results suggest a statistically significant relationship between property values and air pollution and Nelson argues strongly for the hedonic price interpretation of the coefficients – i.e. he argues that they are measures of willingness to pay for air quality.

Overall, then, the studies of the relationship between air pollution and property values are inconclusive. Certainly, Smith's 1977 judgement that 'policymakers should not be so willing to accept the estimated parameters for air pollution variables for use in benefit-cost analyses of pollution abatement programmes' (Smith, 1977, p. 44) is fully justified. The only proviso must be that work along the lines developed by Nelson (1975, 1976) which has suggested statistically significant relationships is in need of further replication for other areas. Only then might one wish to reverse this overall judgement.

AIR POLLUTION AND HEALTH

The extreme uncertainty surrounding the physical interactions between pollution and health makes it difficult to attach very much credibility to the 'global' estimates of health damage that have been made (Ridker, 1967; PAU, 1972). However, the line of research pursued by Lave and Seskin (1970, 1971, 1972) appears to yield promising results. Their approach has been to correlate *mortality* rates in various regions with air pollution levels in those regions, together with other factors which are thought to explain mortality. The emphasis on mortality rather than the more desirable explained variable, morbidity, arises solely because of statistical data difficulties with the latter. In essence, then, the Lave–Seskin procedure estimates the dose–response relationship. For their UK study (Lave and Seskin, 1970) they used air pollution indices measured by smoke concentrations or SO_2 concentrations. Their only other explanatory variable was a 'socioeconomic index' which was generally a measure of population density, but occasionally a measure of 'social class'. They then regressed mortality rates on the index of pollution and the index of population density, using a linear form. The regressions are broken down into deaths according to bronchitis, lung cancer, other cancers and pneumonia. Interestingly, the correlation coefficients for bronchitis and lung cancer are, in general, higher than for other cancers and pneumonia. This perhaps lends some support to the view that bronchitis is the disease most probably linked with air pollution. The similarity of the coefficients for bronchitis and lung cancer is not in accordance with the medical distinction made between the two by a report of the Royal College of Physicians in 1970 which found little evidence of a lung cancer/air pollution relationship. Overall, however, the Lave–Seskin correlations were poor except for 'males in 26 areas' ($R^2 = 0.766$ to 0.805 depending on the type of socioeconomic variable used). The socioeconomic variable was generally found to have no bearing on mortality rates.

In a similar study of the USA, which updates the 1970 study, Lave (1972) secured far better results with an R^2 of 0.80 to 0.86 depending on the form of equation fitted. In this case, however, total mortality rates were used and these were not classified by cause. The equations used in this study are a little more sophisticated and allow for variations in the age structure and income levels. Additionally, variations in the level of pollution are accounted for by running the regressions with minimum and maximum levels of pollution. The interesting result is that the minimum levels are more significant – perhaps because people adjust to the more conspicuous maximum levels (e.g. persons prone to respiratory illness might stay indoors or take avertive action). Lave (1972) is of the view that the linkage between air pollution and death is 'beyond reasonable doubt'. He argues that the existence of a third factor – e.g. 'urban living' with its alleged stresses and strains – is not consistent with the significant results he obtains when comparing urban areas. Equally, air pollution may be correlated with low income since, intuitively, we might expect low income groups to belong to occupations involving more exposure to air pollution. Lave again argues that the presence of income variables in his equations do not bear this possible relationship out.

The evidence of the Lave and Seskin studies for the USA must certainly be considered impressive. Their earlier results for England suggest a much less stable relationship. The Lave–Seskin approach has been used in the Netherlands (Jansen *et al.*, 1971), but studies there have produced a dose–response relationship far less sensitive to the level of pollution, but none the less significant (e.g. Lave and Seskin's maximum 50 per cent reduction in mortality from bronchitis due to a 50 per cent reduction in air pollution becomes a 6·2 per cent reduction in mortality in the Dutch study). Additionally, the Dutch study extends to morbidity as well as mortality but the methodology and data sources are very unclear. The PAU study (PAU, 1972) also adopts the Lave and Seskin approach and finds independent support for the view that bronchitis deaths could be reduced by 25–75 per cent by bringing pollution down to levels prevailing in clean areas.

Several other studies have taken place on the air pollution–health linkage but they are not numerous, a surprising fact in view of the fact that such studies can short-circuit the otherwise highly complex linkages between physical dose and physical response that would emerge from medical studies. Koshal and Koshal (1973) lend support to the general Lave–Seskin conclusion finding suspended particulates statistically significant in explaining total mortality in forty cities in the USA. They also tested for a lag structure – i.e. for the possibility that mortality in year t is related to air pollution in year $t-n$, but found no significant relationship. Smith (1976, 1977) has also reworked United States air pollution data for fifty metropolitan areas in 1968 and 1969. Testing numerous models he concludes that the results are not statistically robust enough to support an air pollution–health relationship. Rightly, he concludes with a call for further research in this area.

An excellent review of other health and pollution literature is provided in Westman and Conn (1976). Sulphur dioxide and particulates are cited in a number of studies as being significant in their relationship to mortality, heart disease and respiratory disease. Not many studies find linkages to cancer. Clearly, given such suggestive evidence there is a need for a closer and much more extensive look at air pollution and health relationships.

DAMAGE TO MATERIALS, LAND AND AGRICULTURE

Few detailed studies of the monetary cost of physical damage on building, paintwork, laundry, etc. exist. This is perhaps surprising in view of the fact that, on the face of it, such damage represents a 'tangible' effect of pollution. The main studies are those of PAU (1972) for the United Kingdom, Zerbe (1969) for Ontario, Ridker (1967) for the USA and Jansen (1971) for the Netherland. All the studies use similar methodology with varying degrees of success.

The types of damage involved are;

(1) corrosion to buildings and exposed structures which includes damage to ancient monuments, buildings of cultural and historical interest, and so on;
(2) damage to paintwork, necessitating more frequent repainting;
(3) soiling of laundry or fabrics requiring dry-cleaning;
(4) soiling of windows and interiors.

Taking each type of damage in turn, corrosion of buildings has normally been valued by looking at the expenditures necessary to maintain the buildings. This in turn requires knowledge of the rate of corrosion or decay of materials that would have taken place without pollution. In some cases experimental studies have been carried out to test the effects of pollutants on materials. In most economic studies, however, the usual procedure has been to estimate the proportion of exposed surfaces in broadly classified 'polluted' and 'unpolluted' areas, to apply known rates of corrosion due to air pollution, and to then estimate the cost of repainting or replacement of the material. This was the technique used in the PAU study of the UK and followed in other studies.

It is difficult to assess the worth of the results of such studies. Data are clearly very limited and methodology has more than often been confusing. Wyzga (1976) produces the correct formula for estimating the cost of replacement. Thus, if a material subject to no pollution (or some rate which could be achieved by pollution control) is estimated to last ten years but because of pollution is held to last only two years, the loss from having to replace the material earlier than would otherwise have been the case is

$$C^* = \frac{C}{(1+r)^2} - \frac{C}{(1+r)^{10}},$$

where C is the cost of replacement and r is the discount rate. Since, in all likelihood, the cost of the replacement material will differ to that of the original material, and may be more or less depending on the nature of the substitution, the formula requires adjustment to

$$C^* = \frac{C-X}{(1+r)^2} - \frac{C}{(1+r)^{10}},$$

where X is the extra or reduced cost of the new material.

To such losses must be added any extra costs of maintenance incurred over and above replacement and which may take place during the life of the material. Wyzga (1976) also notes that calculations based on type of material rather than by use are misleading in that the way a material is used affects its exposure. In other words, it is better to look at, say, the costs of maintaining and replacing street lamps than at the costs of exposed concrete and metal. The 'component' approach as he calls it was used in the study by Fink (1971) and by ENI (1972).

Damage to paintwork has generally been treated in the same way – by looking at expenditures in polluted as compared to unpolluted areas. PAU used this methodology in their empirical workings and claimed to find little evidence of a higher frequency of painting in polluted as compared to unpolluted areas. For business premises we may note that cleaning tends to be a scheduled feature so that studies of frequency of cleaning are unlikely to reveal a difference. This was noted in Ridker's study (Ridker, 1976) which in fact failed to secure *any* meaningful results from cross-section studies of the type described here. Zerbe (1969) and Michelson (1966) do report results. Ridker also notes that interviews with housewives tended to reveal more about the housewives' desire to impress than about their actual behaviour.

Laundry costs should also be higher if there are significant effects from pollution. Ridker (1967) failed to secure any estimates, mainly due to difficulties in securing data. PAU (1972) report negative correlations between purchases of cleaning materials and air pollution levels, and Ridker failed to secure sufficient co-operation from supermarkets for his proposed study to achieve the required results. The PAU study secured some positive correlation when a specific region was excluded. It is far from evident that the studies allowed for a sufficient number of explanatory factors in attempting to secure a positive correlation.

Window cleaning again presents the problem that, for many buildings, it is a scheduled activity. One might expect the schedules to have shorter intervals in polluted areas, but there is little evidence that this is so (Ridker, 1967; PAU, 1972). The general view appears to be that, as with other cleaning expenditures, variations in taste are the main determinant of frequency and such variations cannot readily be incorporated into multiple regression models.

In all the preceding cases the use of comparative expenditures will *understate* the cost of pollution. This is because any costs borne by individuals will represent the minimum price they have to pay – they might indeed be willing to pay more than this for clean windows, laundry, etc. In other terms, the use of expenditure items fails to reflect the consumers' surplus from cleaner items.

It should be noted that property price studies will, in all likelihood, already embrace some of the materials damage costs since these tend to be perceivable.

While the *nature* of the damage that pollutants can do to crop and livestock is known, precious little quantified evidence is available on the 'dose–response' relationship. As such, we again have the problem that the valuation of such costs is predicted on a highly uncertain physical magnitude. The nature of such damage is described in PAU (1972, p. 140). Yields of commercial crops may be reduced or postponed due to delayed growth. Crops may have quality differences if affected by pollution. Livestock may be similarly affected – fluorosis in cattle is the obvious example cited by PAU. The PAU approach is again to estimate the differences in productivity between clean and polluted areas. This they place as lying between 1·01 and 1·20, but even this wide range is based on admittedly scanty evidence. It should perhaps be remembered that the PAU's task was to find a *national* estimate of damage from air pollution. While such estimates are interesting, they are not likely to be of major significance in policy problems. As such, the very considerable error involved in extrapolating from very limited and localised studies of such things as crop damage to national estimates would be avoided by concentrating on localised studies which have a localised purpose. While it would be useful to think that such studies would give orders of magnitude that could be applied to other study areas, there seems little alternative to accepting that each individual abatement programme would have to be evaluated separately in terms of these kinds of damage. The heterogenous nature of different areas, types of crop, and so on would seem to demand this.

REFERENCES

Anderson, R. and Crocker, T., 'Air pollution and residential property values', *Urban Studies*, vol. 8, no. 3, October 1971.
Anderson, R. and Crocker, T. 'The economics of air pollution' in P. B. Downing, (ed.), *Air Pollution and the Social Sciences* (New York: Praeger, 1971).
Anderson, R. and Crocker, T., 'Air pollution and property values: a reply', *Review of Economics and Statistics*, vol. 54, no. 4, 1972.
Anderson, R. and Crocker, T., Property market equilibria and the environment, Working Paper No. 20, Program in Environmental Economics, University of California at Riverside, 1973.

Barratt, R. and Waddell, T., *The Cost of Air Pollution Damages – A Status Report* (US: EPA, 1971).

Deyak, T. A. and Smith, V. K., 'Residential property values and air pollution: some new evidence', *Quarterly Review of Economics and Business*, Winter 1974.

Fink, F. W., *et al.*, *Technical, Economic Evaluation of Air Pollution Corrosion Costs on Metals in the US* (Columbus, Ohio: Battelle Institute, 1971).

Freeman, A. M., 'On estimating air pollution control benefits from land value studies', *Journal of Environmental Economics and Management*, vol. 1, 1974.

Freeman, A. M., 'Air pollution and property values: a further comment', *Review of Economics and Statistics*, vol. 56, October 1974.

Freeman, A. M., 'Spatial equilibrium, the theory of rents, and the measurement of benefits from public programs', *Quarterly Journal of Economics*, vol. 89, August 1975.

Freeman, A. M., 'Air pollution and property values: a methodological comment', *Review of Economics and Statistics*, vol. 53, no. 4, November 1971.

Jansen, H., *et al.*, *An Estimate of Damage Caused by Air Pollution in the Netherlands in 1970* (Free University of Amsterdam: Institute for Environmental Problems, 1971).

Koshal, R. K. and Koshal, M., 'Environments and urban mortality: an econometric approach', *Environmental Pollution*, vol. 4, June 1973.

Lave, L., 'Air pollution damage: some difficulties in estimating the value of abatement', in A. Kneese and B. Bower, (eds), *Environmental Analysis* (Resources for the Future, Baltimore: Johns Hopkins Press, 1972).

Lave, L., 'Urban externalities', in *Centre for Environmental Studies, Papers from the Urban Economics Conference*, vol. 1 (London: CES, Paper CES CP9, 1973).

Lave, L. and Seskin, E., 'Air pollution and human health', *Science*, vol. 21, August 1970.

Lave, L. and Seskin, E., 'Health and air pollution', *Swedish Journal of Economics*, March 1971.

Lind, R. C., 'Spatial equilibrium, the theory of rents and the measurement of benefits from public programs', *Quarterly Journal of Economics*, vol. 87, no. 2, May 1973.

Mäler, K-G., 'Damage functions and their estimation: a theoretical survey', in OECD, *Environmental Damage Costs* (Paris: OECD, 1974).

Mäler, K-G., *Environmental Economics: A Theoretical Enquiry* (Resources for the Future, Baltimore: Johns Hopkins Press, 1974).

Michelson, I. and Tourin, B., 'Comparative methods for studying the costs of controlling air pollution', *Public Health Reports*, no. 81, 1966.

Mullet, G., 'A comment on air pollution and property values: a study of the St. Louis area', *Journal of Regional Science*, vol. 14, no. 1, April 1974.

Nelson, J. P., *The Effects of Mobile-Source Air and Noise Pollution on Residential Property Values* (Washington DC: US Department of Transportation, 1975).

Nelson, J. P., 'Residential choice, hedonic prices and the demand for urban air quality' (unpublished, 1975).

Nobbs, C. and Pearce, D. W., 'The economics of stock pollutants: the example of cadmium', *International Journal of Environmental Studies*, January 1976.

OECD, *Cadmium and the Environment; Toxicity, Economy, Control*, ENV (73) 45 (Paris: OECD, 1974).

Opschoor, H., 'Damage functions: some theoretical and practical problems', in OECD, *Environmental Damage Costs* (Paris: OECD, 1974).

PAU (Programmes Analysis Unit), *An Economic and Technical Appraisal of Air Pollution in the United Kingdom* (London: HMSO, 1972).

Polinsky, A. M. and Shavell, S., 'The air pollution and property value debate', *Review of Economics and Statistics*, vol. 57, no. 1, February 1975.

Polinsky, A. M. and Shavell, S., Amenities and property values in a general model of an urban area', *Journal of Public Economics*, vol. 5, January–February 1976.

Polinsky, A. M. and Rubinfeld, D., 'Property values and the benefits of environmental improvements theory and measurement', in L. Wingo and A. Evans (eds), *Public Policy and the Quality of Life in Urban Areas* (Baltimore: Johns Hopkins Press, 1977).

Ridker, R. G., *Economic Costs of Air Pollution* (New York: Praeger, 1967).

Ridker, R. G. and Henning, J., 'The determinants of residential property values with special reference to air pollution', *Review of Economics and Statistics*, vol. 49, no. 2, May 1967.

Ridker, R. G., 'Strategies for measuring the cost of air pollution', in H. Wolozin (ed.), *The Economics of Air Pollution* (New York: Norton, 1969).

Royal College of Physicians, *Air Pollution and Health* (London: RCP, 1970).

Small, K. A., 'Air pollution and property values: further comment', *Review of Economics and Statistics*, vol. 57, no. 1, February 1975.

Smith, V. K., 'Mortality – air pollution relationships: a comment', *Journal of the American Statistical Association*, vol. 70, June 1975.

Smith, V. K., 'The measurement of mortality and air pollution relationships', *Environment and Planning*, vol. 8, 1976.

Smith, V. K., *The Economic Consequences of Air Pollution* (Cambridge, Massachusetts: Ballinger, 1976).

Smith, V. K. and Deyak, T. A., 'Measuring the impact of air pollution on property values', *Journal of Regional Science*, vol. 15, December 1975.

Strotz, R., 'The use of land rent changes to measure the welfare benefits of land improvements', in J. E. Haring (ed.), *The New Economics of Regulated Industries: Rate Making in a Dynamic Economy* (Los Angeles: Occidental College, 1968).

Westman, W. E. and Conn, D., *Quantifying Benefits of Pollution Control*, (Energy Resources Conservation and Development Commission, State of California, 1976).

Wieand, K. F., 'Air pollution and property values: a study of the St. Louis area', *Journal of Regional Science*, vol. 13, April 1973.

Wieand, K. F., 'More on air pollution: a reply to Mullet', *Journal of Regional Science*, vol. 14, April 1974.

Wyzga, R., 'A survey of environmental damage functions', in OECD, *Environmental Damage Costs* (OECD: Paris, 1974).

Wyzga, R., *A Handbook of Environmental Damage Functions* (Paris: OECD, 1976).

Yocum, J., 'Effects of air pollution on materials', in A. Stern (ed.), *Air Pollution* (New York: Academic Press, 1962).

Zerbe, R., *The Economics of Air Pollution – A Cost-Benefit Approach* (Toronto: Ontario Department of Public Health, 1969).

Chapter 4

Recreational Land Use

INTRODUCTION

The necessity of evaluating the social costs and benefits of recreational land use can arise in response to a variety of problems. One set of problems can be classified as those involving questions of scale, such as preservation and capital investment (or disinvestment). Examples would be such specific questions as (a) should the recreational capacity of a wilderness area be protected from damage via inroads by mining and lumbering interests? (b) should the level of open space within a certain city be preserved or should it be reallocated to other uses, such as housing or industrial development? and (c) how many indoor sports centres should be built over the next ten years, how large should they be, and where should they be located?

Another set of problems can be classified as those involving questions of management, such as choice of techniques of production, institutional organisation and pricing policy. Examples would be such questions as (a) should we encourage or rely upon private provision and management of golf courses? and (b) should public swimming baths attempt to cover running costs?

Our concern in this chapter will not be to attempt direct answers to these questions but to assess the extent to which research was helped to supply information relevant to an assessment of the social costs and benefits involved, where the information considered to be relevant is a monetary measurement of these social costs and benefits. In short we wish to know if there has been success in estimating the true demand functions.

The discussion in this chapter will be organised as follows. First, we have an introductory section on the nature of the social costs and benefits of recreational land use. Secondly, we discuss the problems involved in the estimation of monetary measures of the social costs and benefits of recreation. Here we will concentrate on the method which has dominated recent research, which is the travel cost approach based on the original work of Clawson (1959). Thirdly, we contrast this approach with an approach to the provision of recreational facilities based on planning standards. Here we will examine some features of the planning standards approach but we will particularly pursue the question of the contribution which could be made by use of the travel cost approach mentioned above. Finally, an attempt at assessment will be made on the progress of past research on the estimation of monetary measures of recreation costs and benefits and on priority areas for future research.

THE NATURE OF SOCIAL COSTS AND BENEFITS OF RECREATIONAL LAND USE

A number of authors have made a distinction between primary and secondary benefits arising from recreation projects. Primary benefits are those which accrue directly to users of (or suppliers of factors of production to) the recreation facility in question. Secondary benefits can be regarded either as those which follow on the impact of the primary benefits or alternatively as all those benefits for which there exists a willingness to pay, which arise due to the recreation facility, and which are excluded by the definition of primary benefits. It may, of course, be difficult to allocate some secondary benefits and even some primary benefits to one particular recreation facility.

1 *Primary Benefits*
The reason why it has been suggested above that it may be difficult to allocate primary benefits to a particular recreation site is because to some extent the experience which gives satisfaction to the recreationist may not be dependent on visiting a particular site. The simplest case to imagine is where a drive without any stops is the experience desired.

Clawson and Knetsch (1966) present a framework which is far more dependent upon visiting a particular site. They categorise the recreation experience as consisting of five major phases: anticipation and planning, travel to the recreation facility, use of the facility, the return journey and recollection of the experience. However, they do acknowledge that there can be great variation in the time and effort expended, as well as the pleasure received during each phase. Also that there may be several sites visited during a particular trip.

Some of these problems mentioned above have particular implications for the technique of estimating monetary measures, and these will be considered later.

2 *Secondary benefits*
A number of types of secondary benefits have been identified.

Income-generating effects Associated with the provision of recreation facilities in an area there will be expenditure by recreationists on goods and services provided, rather *en route* or locally, with consequent increases in local incomes and employment. Thus recreation facilities will influence the regional distribution of income and employment. Work on estimating these effects via regional multipliers has reached a refined stage. Employment multipliers are of most interest here because they may most visibly reflect an increased use of resources which would otherwise be under-utilised. Archer (1974) reported a study which found that £10,000 of tourist expenditure in 1970 in Anglesey created seasonal employment of 4·3 primary jobs and 0·49 indirect jobs. Henderson and Cousins (1975) derived three employment multipliers for seasonal jobs: 0·398 for local areas, 0·412 over the whole of Tayside and a further 0·060 for the rest of Scotland. Archer (1976) seems to give full support to the Henderson and Cousins finding that there is little difference between the employment multipliers resulting from tourist expenditure and other expenditure. This latter fact is the type of information required to decide on the effectiveness of recreation-linked development.

Increase in land values   Knetsch (1964) and David (1968) have demonstrated that proximity to recreation areas or facilities increases the value of land and property in the vicinity. These increases may represent genuine additions to add to primary benefits where they reflect a willingness to pay for general amenity. However, there is a danger of double counting. This will be so when the increase in value represents a capitalisation of primary benefits, where property has been purchased to reduce the travel costs to a particular facility. There will presumably be great variations in the proportion of capitalised primary benefits to true secondary benefits in different areas and in connection with different types of recreation facilities, but no empirical evidence seems to be available on this subject.

One important area which needs further research is the magnitude of secondary benefits, which show up in increases in property values, due to proximity to urban open space and parks. It is here that one suspects that non-user benefits are most significant. What work there is suggests that proximity to open space and parks seems to be relatively unimportant compared to other variables which influence house prices (Ball, 1973).

Option demand   A distinct category of non-user benefits called either the 'option demand' or the 'option value' was postulated by Weisbrod (1964). This is the amount which people would be willing to pay for retention of a recreation area or facility which is not captured by user charges or taxation or even estimable as user's current consumer's surplus. Indeed, the major portion of the option demand is taken to be that of individuals who do not at present use the facility in question and may never, in fact, use it. In short, some individuals might purchase insurance policies to preserve a facility if it were not for the usual difficulties associated with public goods. Within this subject debate has tended to concentrate on whether the option value will tend to be greater than, less than, or equal to, the present value of expected consumer's surplus derived from future use (Krutilla, Cicchetti, Freeman III and Russell, 1972).

However, possibly more important than this additional insurance element may be the existence of a willingness to pay by some individuals in order that others may be able to use recreation facilities. Unfortunately, whatever its quantitative importance, techniques are not yet available which have been exploited for the monetary measurement of the option value. One possible approach may be through studies of individual responses to charitable appeals associated with particular recreations or recreation facilities and attempting to relate these responses to past, present and likely future use. Until satisfactory progress is made in this area we may be guilty of overlooking substantial non-user benefits.

External benefits Under this category we include benefits accruing to individuals which they may not themselves perceive, such as improvements in their physical and mental health. Again the extent of these unperceived benefits seems difficult to measure and no relevant study appears to exist. Also some authors cast the net of external benefits rather wider and include reductions in the costs of crime induced by recreation participation. Seckler (1966, p. 489) says: 'Externalities flowing from outdoor recreation, it seems . . . are quite high . . . \$300–\$400 million dollar annual expenditure . . . could quite easily be paid for in the diminution of crime and mental disorders alone.' Unfortunately this statement is unsupported by any evidence.

Social costs The social costs of recreational land use embraces a wide range of possibilities. Indeed all the resources used in recreational provision will usually carry an opportunity cost, with rare exceptions being the use of land too remote and rugged for other uses and also the use of labour which is unemployed and immobile. However, even where there is no alternative present-day use, recreation use of land may carry congestion costs or ecological costs, with the latter affecting possible use by future generations (Fisher and Krutilla, 1972). Fisher and Krutilla report some progress with regard to measurement of congestion costs, although measurement of ecological costs represents an extremely difficult task.

The opportunity cost of land will tend to be variable within rural areas depending on the presence of mineral deposits or useful aggregates. However, it is within urban areas that variations in opportunity cost will be largest. Although some authors (Evans, 1974) have studied the logic of advocated standards of provision of open space in urban areas (Ministry of Housing and Local Government, 1956) there has been little empirical work on the costs of such provision. However, land value data to fill this gap can be obtained and the greater problem is, as mentioned earlier, the estimation of external and other secondary benefits.

There are also important costs associated with the physical presence of recreationists. In the commercial sector of provision there are often external diseconomies of noise associated with the use of cinemas, discotheques and night clubs, as well as the wide range of damage possible by supporters of professional Association Football Clubs. The literature on recreation has, however, generally been more concerned with congestion, physical damage, and other external diseconomies imposed on residents of the countryside and coastal resorts by day visitors and holiday makers (Patmore, 1972; Countryside Commission, 1969). Nevertheless, no British study appears to have reached the quantification stage in the analysis of external costs. In general, compared to the monetary measurement of the social benefits of recreation there has been a lack of emphasis on the monetary measurement of costs. There is obviously much room for improvement and, in this author's opinion, the cost element probably contains much variability. However, in the rest of the chapter we will reflect the literature and concern ourselves with the monetary measurement of recreation benefits.

METHODS OF ESTIMATING MONETARY MEASURES OF THE BENEFITS OF RECREATION

The search for methods which would help to give monetary measures of recreation benefits began in the United States in the 1940s in connection with the recreational use of National Parks and multiple use water resource projects. Some early methods used, which are not worth discussing here, were most unsound (Outdoor Recreation Resources Review Commission, 1962).

The need for monetary estimation has been justified on a number of grounds. Most common is the reason that recreation is often available at zero or nominal entrance charges. Another reason may be the idea that even where charges are more substantial there may still be a large untapped consumer's surplus in the use of facilities. In fact the methods we discuss below are aimed at estimating the demand curve, and there are many possible interpretations of potential benefits given knowledge of the demand curve (R. J. Smith, 1975).

However, the tasks facing different empirical studies will vary. Where the main concern is to evaluate whether one facility is worth preserving or whether past provision of the facility has proved worthwhile, knowledge of the demand curve for that facility will be adequate. Where the concern is to evaluate whether to introduce one or more facilities, then estimation of a number of demand curves will be necessary and this must include estimation of their inter-relationships as substitutes (Gibson, 1974). We discuss later the extent to which estimation models in the first type of study can be less sophisticated than in the second type.

For any facility it is possible to attempt collection of information on one point on the demand curve: that is observed consumption at the current entrance price. Economists are familiar with the identification problem which implies that demand curves cannot be estimated unless one has observations which includes the supply curve at different levels. However, provided certain assumptions hold, Hotelling (in Prewitt Report, 1949) and Clawson (1959) suggested a method to identify the demand curve using only cross-section data.

The essence of Hotelling's suggestion, which was not commented upon in the Prewitt Report, is contained in the following extract:

> Let concentric zones be defined around each park so that the cost of travel to the park from all points in one of these zones is approximately constant. The persons entering the park in a year, or a suitably chosen sample of them, are to be listed according to the zone from which they come. The fact that they come means that the service of the park is at least worth the cost and this cost can presumably be estimated with fair accuracy. If we assume that the benefits are the same no matter the distance, we have, for all these living near the park, a consumer's surplus consisting of the differences in transportation costs. (Prewitt Report, 1949: letter from H. Hotelling)

This was the first attempt to link the fact that people pay different prices for recreation, due to different travel costs, with consumer's surplus.

Many criticisms have been made of the above technique but all except one can likewise be made against the Clawson method given below. The unique weakness of the Hotelling travel cost technique is that it involves the assumption that all visits are valued equally and therefore that all observed visits would still be undertaken as long as total costs remain below that cost faced by the most distant visitor. This is inconsistent with the notion of downward sloping demand curves. Indeed, when Trice and Wood (1958) attempted to use Hotelling's suggestion their data showed that visits per head of population varied inversely with distance to the recreation sites considered.

Clawson (1959) suggested a technique very close to that mentioned by Hotelling. The same type of data are used, with the addition of zonal population figures so that a relationship can be found between visit rates per head of population and distance or travel costs for any given site. This relationship, the demand curve for the whole recreation experience as defined by Clawson and Knetsch earlier, is shown as Zz for hypothetical data in Figure 4.1(a). If we suppose for the present that a satisfactory measure of travel costs can be made, then Figure 4.1(a) shows three (say, Zone 1, Zone 2 and Zone 3) observations: visits per head of population per annum to the site of Oa, Ob and Oc, at travel costs of OA, OB and OC respectively. This relationship is inverse and it is presumed that visit rates become zero when a travel

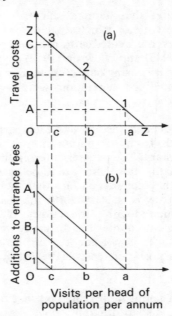

Figure 4.1   (a) *The demand curve for the whole recreation experience: hypothetical data.*
(b) *The response of visit rates to entrance fees for individual zones.*

cost of OZ is reached. Clawson then assumed that visitors will react in a similar manner to variations in travel costs as they do to variations in entrance fees. If this is so then the relationship of visits per head from each zone and total visit costs will be identical (provided there are no differences in tastes and expenditure patterns between zones) and the response curve to additions to entrance fees for the individual zones will be as shown in Figure 4.1(b) with curves aA_1, bB_1, cC_1 being parallel to the demand curve for the whole recreation experience. Also notice that consumer surplus per head of population can be regarded as either areas OaA_1, ObB_1, OcC_1 in Figure 4.1(b) or areas A1Z, B2z, C3z in Figure 4.1(a). The estimate of demand simply involves the usual summation of quantities at given additions to entrance fees across individual zones where in Figure 4.1(b) the quantities at given additions to entrance fees are multiplied by the relevant zonal populations.

We can also summarise this procedure by some elementary algebraic manipulation. Suppose that we have the same data as above for three zones and that for this site j the following function has been fitted for the demand curve for the whole recreation experience:

$$\frac{V_{ij}}{P_i} = w - kC_{ij} \quad \text{and} \quad w - kC_{ij} = 0 \quad \text{when} \quad C_{ij} \geqslant OZ$$

where V_{ij} is visits from zone i to site j (C_{ij} is travel cost from zone i to site j) and P_i is the zonal population. Then the consumer's surplus per head of population to residents of any zone will be the visit rate multiplied by half the distance between the zonal travel costs and those travel costs at which visit rates become zero: this represents, for the linear relationship, the area of the relevant triangle. So, for any given zone

$$\frac{V_{ij}}{P_i}(OZ - C_{ij})\tfrac{1}{2}$$

is consumer's surplus per capita for zone i, and

$$P_i\left[\frac{V_{ij}}{P_i}(OZ - C_{ij})\tfrac{1}{2}\right]$$

is consumer's surplus for zone i.

Summing consumer's surplus for the three zones we get

$$P_1\left[\frac{V_{ij}}{P_1}(OZ - C_{1j})\tfrac{1}{2}\right] + P_2\left[\frac{V_{2j}}{P_2}(OZ - C_{2j})\tfrac{1}{2}\right] + P_3\left[\frac{V_{3j}}{P_3}(OZ - C_{3j})\tfrac{1}{2}\right]$$
$$= \tfrac{1}{2}[V_{1j}(OZ - C_{1j})] + \tfrac{1}{2}[V_{2j}(OZ - C_{2j})] + \tfrac{1}{2}[V_{3j}(OZ - C_{3j})]$$
$$= \tfrac{1}{2}[OZ(V_{1j} + V_{2j} + V_{3j}) - C_{1j}V_{1j} - C_{2j}V_{2j} - C_{3j}V_{3j}]$$

and this final expression shows that consumer's surplus will vary directly with the size of OZ, inversely with the C_{ij}s, and, because OZ is greater than any C_{ij}, directly with the V_{ij}s. Furthermore, as $OZ = w/k$ the consumer's surplus varies directly with the quantity intercept w, and given that k is positive, it also varies inversely with k: that is, given the intercept, the quicker the decay of visits with distance the smaller is the consumer's surplus.

Alternatively we can regard the Clawson method as simply estimating the site demand curve. Using the same demand curve for the whole recreation experience and assuming observations for three zones at zero entrance price, visits at this zero price will be

$$\sum_{i=1}^{3} \frac{V_{ij}^0}{P_i} \cdot P_i = V_j^0 = P_1(w - kC_{1j}) + P_2(w - kC_{2j}) + P_3(w - kC_{3j})$$

and at an addition to entrance fees of Δc_1 visits will be

$$\sum_{i=1}^{3} \frac{V_{ij}^{\Delta c_1}}{P_i} \cdot P_i = V_j^{\Delta c_1} = P_1(w - k(C_{1j} + \Delta c_1)) + P_2(w - k(C_{2j} + \Delta c_1))$$
$$+ P_3(w - k(C_{3j} + \Delta c_1))$$

and

$$V_{ij}^{\Delta c_i} = 0 \quad \text{when } k(C_{ij} + \Delta c_i) \geqslant w.$$

The above simulation can continue until V_j is equal to 0 and a demand curve is estimated over the entire range of possible prices.

So, in summary, Clawson used data on visit rates to sites to estimate a trip generation equation (the demand curve for the whole recreation experience) for that site. The initial specification included only the costs of travelling to the site as an independent variable in the trip generation equation. The marginal decrease of visits with increases in travel costs provides the estimate of the response to increases in entrance fees.

The Clawson method of interpreting the trip generation equation has dominated work on the economics of recreation over the last fifteen years. There has been the occasional advocacy or testing of other methods (Knetsch and Davis, 1966). Also there have been advocates of other interpretations of trip-making behaviour for purposes of estimation of monetary benefits, such as Wood (1971), Pearse (1968) and Norton (1970). These latter efforts are all unsound. Norton and Wood confused travel expenditure with benefits, rather than treating them as costs, and Pearse transferred the Hotelling assumption of equally valued visits to all visitors within each income classification.

Empirical studies using the Clawson approach have been carried out by Merewitz (1966), Stevens (1966), Smith and Kavanagh (1969), Mansfield (1971), Ullman and Volk (1972) and Grubb and Goodwin (1968). Some of these studies were concerned to make refinements or widen the application of the Clawson approach. More recently there has been a number of articles criticising either the earlier empirical studies (Common, 1973; Flegg, 1976) and/or making advances in the application of the basic Clawson interpretation to more complex situations (Gibson and Anderson, 1975; Cheshire and Stabler, 1976). To this can be added a number of earlier American criticisms of the Clawson approach (Seckler, 1966; Carey, 1965).

We can consider post-Clawson research and under two main headings. First, there is research aimed at improving the effectiveness of monetary estimates of a particular site. Secondly, there has been work in respect of the valuation of sites when an increase or decrease in the total supply of facilities is contemplated.

Single-site Estimation

A basic assumption of the Clawson method is that visitors will react in the same way to increases in cost whatever their source. That is, they will be indifferent between increases whether they are caused by a rise in entrance fees or a rise in travel costs. This has been regarded by some writers as a strong assumption (Common, 1973) but no rival suggestions have been made.

However, one difficulty has been taken up by a number of writers, namely, that allowance must be made for the costs of travel time as well as the direct monetary costs of travel. Where this has not been included in the estimate of travel costs there will be an overestimate of zonal responses to increases in total costs. For example, in Figure 4.1 an addition to entrance fees of AB will leave residents of Zone 1 in a different position to that formerly faced by residents of Zone 2. Although they now face total costs (excluding time) of OB, their journey times are lower. This will not hold for all such comparisons. Thus visit rates will not fall to the extent shown in Figure 4.1 and there will be an underestimate of the number of visits at additions to entrance fees and consequently an underestimate of the benefits at the site.

Cesario and Knetsch (1970) suggest explicit inclusion of time as a separate variable in the trip generation function. However they presume that direct estimation of the separate effects of money and time is defeated by the high collinearity between those variables in most sets of travel data. They suggest instead using assumed trade-off functions between time and money which in their later research (Cesario and Knetsch, 1976) takes the form of two methods used;

$$\text{Method I} \quad C_{ij} = (\$0 \cdot 06 D_{ij})(t_i T_{ij})$$
$$\text{Method II} \quad C_{ij} = \$0 \cdot 06 D_{ij} + t_i T_{ij}$$

where C_{ij} is generalised cost of travelling from a county i to a park j, where D_{ij} is distance, t_i is the value of travel time and T_{ij} time. The overall model for which this equation is used we will consider later. Here we must note that the parameter estimates for generalised cost differs greatly between the two methods and that the product form of the trade-off results in higher visitor estimates. In effect Cesario and Knetsch (1970) make the inclusion of time into the Clawson framework a two-stage problem. Not only do we have to assume or estimate the value of time but we have the possibility of trade-off functions between time and money which are non-linear.

The problem has seemed to be less complex to some writers who have simply added estimated time costs, using independently derived values for leisure time. Smith (1970) adds time costs in this way and does a sensitivity analysis of the relationship between benefit estimates and the values assumed for leisure time. Common (1973) used a different approach. This was to test the effectiveness of different data sets for total travel costs with respect to the minimising of squared absolute errors between observed and predicted visits from the trip generation equation. The preferred set suggested the interesting speculation to Common that time costs were negative.

This leads us into the complex question of the effects of utility derived from travel. Various studies have pointed to the fact that utility may not only be dependent on a particular site visit but also on the journey itself (Colenutt, 1969; Elson, 1973; Burton, 1966). This manifested itself not only in the fact that many journeys did not take the shortest routes, but also that many visitors had not planned to visit a specific site. Cheshire and Stabler (1976) have done a relevant case study of visitors to Uffington White Horse in Berkshire. They define visitors as in one of three categories (a) 'pure' visitors who are site-oriented and whose journey is pure cost, (b) 'meanderers' who derive utility from the journey and (c) 'transit visitors' whose journey is made for another purpose but who call in at the site, at presumably lower incremental time and money costs than implied by consideration of their origins. Cheshire and Stabler apply a conventional Clawson analysis to their entire visitor data and then, as a second exercise, apply it only to visit data for the 'pure' visitors. Forty-five per cent of their sample are classified as pure visitors, but the surplus estimates are only 27 per cent of that estimated for all visitors, using a log-linear trip generation function. However, they do not attempt to suggest a procedure for analysing 'meanderers' surplus, and, indeed, suggest that the Clawson approach may have to be abandoned in favour of a general modelling approach such as proposed by Vickerman (1974) or the use of direct questionnaire methods (Bohm, 1972) in order to estimate measures of willingness to pay.

Cheshire and Stabler's particular concern is just one aspect of a large class of behaviour which most threatens the basic foundations of the Clawson method. However, no author has comprehensively dealt with the full range of possible cases.

First, if potential visitors change their residence in order to be near a recreation site the assumption that all zones have the same distribution of tastes collapses. This will lead to underestimation of benefits because there will be less response to additions to entrance fees by residents of inner zones than is implied by the Clawson interpretation. However, this point has been considered of small importance because it is not thought that many recreation sites significantly influence residential choice for many people.

Secondly, visitors may visit a site as only one of a number visited on one trip. They may be staying nearby on holiday or they may be visiting friends. This is distinct from the notion of receiving utility from the journey. Here it is uncertain whether the existence of this phenomenon will lead to over- or underestimation of benefits. For example, someone staying with relatives nearby may have responses to additions to entrance fees similar to an inner zone resident and may gain a surplus greater than, equal to or less than the surplus implied by consideration of his former position (visit rate and travel costs) on the trip generation equation. On balance, it seems likely that this particular class of 'transit' visitor may enjoy a higher consumer's surplus than is implied using the Clawson method. Offsetting this will be a tendency to simulate too great a cost inelasticity in the response curves of inner zones. Thus, the reader can see how complex is the operation of some of these factors within the context of the Clawson framework.

Thirdly, I return to consider the visitor who derives utility from the journey to a recreation site. This is the 'meanderer' studied by Cheshire and Stabler. Unfortunately, there is more complexity to the concept of a 'meanderer' than they seem to realise, with consequent difficulties regarding whether the Clawson method over- or underestimates benefits. For example, utility derived from the journey may be dependent on visiting a particular site: that is, more utility is derived from the journey when it is known that at the end of the trip there will be available a place to stop. Of course, more generally it may not be linked to a specific site but to the expected availability of one of a number of possible sites. If this journey utility reduces cost there is again a two-stage effect within the Clawson framework. The response to entrance fees may be more or less inelastic than is implied by the usual interpretation of the trip generation function. Also for residents of inner zones not enjoying journey utility, benefits will be overestimated. The net result of the two effects is uncertain.

Finally it is also worth remembering that there is the possibility that the journey itself gives disutility over and above the reduction in utility due to money and time costs. Theoretically, this is more straightforward. It will simply result in the Clawson method underestimating benefits.

How widespread are the above phenomena? Journey-derived utility is probably important for informal countryside recreation. Journey-derived disutility is probably relatively most important for sport and recreation in urban areas, especially winter pursuits. Holiday-based visits are obviously relatively greater at sites in the main holiday areas. Residential relocation is probably never of much significance. Overall, the above features will need a large investment of research effort if they are to be successfully incorporated into the distance decay framework for estimating monetary benefits.

There has been much discussion with regard to the specification of the trip generation function. This includes both the choice of functional form and the inclusion of independent variables.

The most common functional forms for the trip generation equations seems to be shared by the logarithmically linear form

$$\ln \left(\frac{V}{P} \right) = a - b \ln C$$

$$\ln V = a - b \ln C + c \ln P$$

and the exponential form

$$\ln\left(\frac{V}{P}\right) = a - bC$$

or

$$\ln V = a - bC + cP,$$

where V is visits, C is costs, P is population and a, b and c are parameters.

Taylor (1971) has shown that many of the Pareto-type double logarithmic transformations used in applied geographic research show evidence of mis-specification when one considers the pattern of the residuals. The pattern of residuals is typically not shown in published work, but in this author's experience of recreation travel data the pattern is distinctly non-random from this transformation. Cheshire and Stabler (1976) however show a typical example with negative residuals (overprediction of visits) at extreme distances and positive residuals (underprediction of visits) at middle distances. They present an *a priori* argument in favour of rejecting the simple logarithmic linear form and achieve a much better fit to the data by use of an asymptotic logarithmic form which simply involves the estimation of an extra parameter which is a constant added to distance before the logarithmic transformation is performed. Their view is that the double-logarithmic transformation is illogical because it fails to account for two important limits: there will be an upper limit to distance travelled and there will be an upper limit to visit rates even at near-zero costs.

There has not been much discussion in published empirical studies of the criteria used for choice of functional form. It is, of course, possible for equations with logarithms as dependent variables to have higher coefficients of determination than equations with the dependent variable in absolute units but to fare relatively badly when compared for the sum of squared absolute errors. However, Common (1973) does not find this to apply to Smith and Kavanagh's (1971) study of Grafham Water.

Indeed these latter authors were conscious of the sensitivity of benefit estimates to the specification of the functional form. Smith (1970) showed that there was a very great difference in the site demand curves estimated by use of the logarithmically linear and exponential forms of the trip generation equation when the level of aggregation allowed only eight zonal observations, and this despite the fact that both forms had an r^2 greater than 0·9. However, Smith showed that this problem disappeared with his data when there was less aggregation. When twenty-seven observations were used the logarithmic linear and exponential forms estimated surplus for Grafham Water at £6,995 and £6,857 respectively.

There has been much criticism of the constraint placed on many trip generation functions that the elasticity of visits with respect to population is unity, by the use of the dependent variable log (V/P). This is an assumption which Common (1973) thinks needs to be tested. His work seems inconclusive regarding this point, but Flegg (1976) shows evidence that in the logarithmic linear model the elasticity is less than unity for visitors to Llandegfedd Reservoir, and Grubb and Goodwin (1968) have a similar result for visitors to Texas reservoirs.

This author can find no convincing argument for this phenomenon. However, there are sound arguments for having a relevant explanatory variable included as an independent variable, not least the fact that its absence may lead to biases in the estimates of the coefficients of the remaining variables (Johnston, 1972, pp. 168–9). This is especially so with aggregated data when there tends to be some collinearity between travel costs and population.

Weber and Hawkins (1971) have shown by a simulation study that the achievement of r^2 greater than 0·9 using the logarithmic linear transformation is not difficult with non-linear data even when it is not, in fact, appropriate for this functional form. However, it seems that careless specification has been fairly common in other areas of applied econometric studies. Research in recreation benefit estimation now seems to be reaching a higher level of sophistication, as evidenced by the techniques applied by V. K. Smith (1975) regarding choice of functional form.

Recently, there has been strong advocacy for using data which are not highly aggregated. Brown and Nawas (1973) demonstrate that using individual data reduces the collinearity, and increases the efficiency of parameter estimates twelvefold in their study, between two independent variables: transfer costs and distance. This disaggregation, they argue, makes it possible to measure individual effects of several variables and avoids the need to assume a trade-off function between money and time (Cesario and Knetsch, 1970). Flegg (1976, p. 358), in his reservoir study, also rejects aggregation into 9 distance zones, preferring to use data based on 121 local authority areas. He has a similar result to Smith (1970), namely, that surplus estimates are not very sensitive to the choice of functional form between the logarithmic linear and the exponential when the data are not highly aggregated. He also points out that aggregation, when the variable is transformed into logarithms, should be geometric not arithmetic.

We must also ask whether we need to include further independent variables other than cost if we have the limited aim of valuing an existing facility. We have already discussed the population variable and concluded that it is best used as an independent variable, both because the elasticity of visits with respect to population may not be unity and because its absence may bias estimates of the cost elasticity.

Ignoring problems of the validity of the Clawson assumptions and specification of functional form, errors in estimation of monetary benefits for single-site studies are going to arise from two main sources: (1) the absence of significant further independent variables which shift the demand curve for the whole recreation experience for individual zones, and (2) bias in estimates of the parameter of costs caused when significant independent variables are excluded which are themselves intercorrelated with travel cost (Johnson, 1972, pp. 168–9).

Two variables which we would expect to have important effects *a priori* are income and some measure of competing recreation opportunities. However, single-site studies seem to have had much difficulty in successfully including such variables. Merewitz (1966) did not find mean income of zones consistently 'useful' in explaining visit rates at Lake of the Ozarks in Missouri. Smith (1970) found insignificant results for his measure of competing recreation opportunities. Also in most of the cases reported by Flegg (1976) mean income of households in zones was not significant, and in all cases mean income of the visitor was not significant. Mansfield (1971) gives a rare exception when he finds a car-ownership variable significant for visit rates to the Lake District.

The author's own conclusions regarding this problem are that in most empirical studies the dangers from excluding variables for income and competing opportunities are minimal providing the data are not highly aggregated. This is because there will in most cases be little collinearity between travel costs and excluded variables using disaggregated data. Of course, if the reaction to travel cost itself is effected by socioeconomic factors, a specification based on uniform $\delta V/\delta Cs$, or on uniform $\delta \ln V/\delta \ln Cs$, across zones will probably lead to inaccurate forecasts.

The Clawson method has been regarded as difficult to apply to facilities which do not attract visitors from a wide catchment area. This, of course, applies to many facilities within urban areas. Here, measurement errors may be very severe with regard to travel costs with consequent effects on the estimates of the trip generation function. There is also the point that single-site studies when the site is only a minor attraction become relatively expensive when using the Clawson method. However, Moncur (1975) reports encouraging results for a study of a site where most visitors came from within a small area.

A number of further points have been made by some authors which should help to improve monetary estimation procedures. Gibson and Anderson (1975) demonstrate the need to derive separate estimates for season ticket holders and day visitors when facilities offer optional tariffs. McConnell and Duff (1976) show that the Clawson method underestimates potential benefits when there is congestion at recreation sites.

Most of the studies we have mentioned in this section have been single-site studies or research on the Clawson method aimed at improving its effectiveness in such studies. The needs for such studies are, we have implied, less than the needs of multi-site studies. However, it is in multi-site studies that the research will, perhaps, be a more useful aid to decision makers and it is to this topic we now turn.

Demand-supply Interaction
A number of authors have realised that a dramatic improvement in forecasting ability could be achieved by further sophistication of the basic trip generation equation.

If travel cost and population of origin zones are the only independent variables in the trip generation equation, then except for population scale effects there is retained the strong assumption that the demand schedule is the same for all distance groups. As mentioned earlier this may not cause serious bias but it does mean a limitation of the Clawson method simply to valuation of the particular recreation resource or facility in question. This is not only because we have not included any characteristics which shift demand curves, such as incomes, car-ownership and the availability and price of substitute recreation facilities, but also excluded are characteristics which represent variations in supply, such as the area of the resource.

Knetsch (1963) suggested the addition of further independent variables, and proposed the following expression

$$V = F(C, Y, S, G)$$

where V is visits per unit of population, C is travel cost, Y is income of population groups, S is the substitute areas that might be relevant for any group, and G is some measure of congestion. Knetsch saw the following gains from such an addition:

Such expressions may have useful predictive value. It is useful to be able to describe the structure of demand for a given area or group of areas but it becomes of increased significance to be able to infer values from such areas to a completely different area or, as may often be the case, an area which has only been proposed. This would seem to be an extremely useful extension of the method for planning purposes, where possibly several different recreation areas are under consideration or where alternative management or development schemes are being considered. Estimates might then be made which would on the basis of the different characteristics and locations of the areas, show the relative demand and value expectations for each . . . (Knetsch, 1963, pp. 391–2)

Forecasting ability is closely linked to the issue of supply–demand interaction. The question uppermost with those decision makers who are concerned with 'value-for-money' in provision (or preservation) of recreational facilities is of the type, 'What effect does the addition (loss) of a new (or an existing) park have on participation in the catchment areas?'. The answer to this question provides knowledge of how many trips have been generated (lost) by the addition (removal) of the park. This is one major source of benefit (loss). The other major source is the benefits (losses) accruing to those who divert trips from (to) other sites. Understanding both features means, in effect, one has knowledge of the demand curve for the new (existing) facility, and the inter-relationship with the demand curves for other facilities.

Can we apply any *a priori* notions to the nature of supply–demand interaction? The simplest case is where the recreation facilities supplying a particular recreation are all considered to be of the same quality by actual and potential participants. In this case more facilities will only generate demand if they are cheaper than existing facilities which, in this context, probably means nearer. However, demand can be generated if more distant facilities receive trips deterred by congestion at nearer facilities.

It is common, however, for certain recreations to be available at facilities which are not homogeneous with respect to quality or supply characteristics. In this case, participants will not necessarily visit the nearest facility. In general, a facility will lead to greater generation effects the more attractive its supply characteristics and the nearer it is to the population concerned. There will be some sort of trade-off in operation; for instance, a large facility at a long distance will have an equivalent effect to some smaller size facility at a shorter distance (Beckmann, 1971). Also, the size of diversion effects should have a direct relationship to the size of the generation effects. This is because

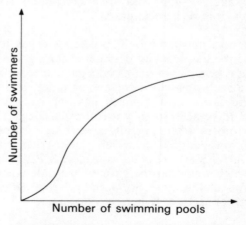

Figure 4.2   *A suggested relationship between number of swimmers and number of swimming pools (Veal, 1970).*

they are sensitive to the same factors: the larger and/or more attractive and the nearer a new facility, the more likely it is that trips will be diverted from other destinations.

This author would also hypothesise that there should be diminishing marginal generation effects due to increasing supplies of facilities. Veal (1970) suggested the relationship shown in Figure 4.2. This is in contrast to a distinct theme apparent in much British discussion of recreation that marginal generation effects are constant.

The satisfactory prediction of supply–demand interaction has been most difficult to achieve. In this respect recreation research has not been unique (Gibson, 1975). Cesario (1969) gives ample demonstration of this difficulty, when he advocates the following model (certain features of which are suppressed in the formulation below):

$$V_{ij} = N_i \frac{\left(\dfrac{A_j}{C_{ij}^{\alpha}}\right)}{\displaystyle\sum_{m=1}^{M} \left(\dfrac{A_m}{C_{im}^{\alpha}}\right)}$$

where V_{ij} is the number of visits from population centre i to site j; C_{ij} is the total money cost of each visit from population centre i to site j; and there are m sites in the system. N_i is the total number of visits from population centre i to the sites in the system, and it is assumed that $N_i = kP_i$ where k is a constant. In essence, the above equation contains a trip distribution function within the brackets and also a trip generation element, N_i. Unfortunately, the trip generation element is not sensitive to increases in available supplies of recreation facilities. In terms of Figure 4.2 it amounts to use of a horizontal generation function at the vertical height kP_i. If an attempt is made to estimate the benefits of or demand for a new recreation facility using the above equation, then, provided the trip distribution function is valid, benefits/demand will be underestimated. The only visits which will be predicted will be those diverted from other sites, caused by their diminished market shares, when the denominator is summed over $m+1$ rather than m sites. The quantitative significance of this omission will vary greatly. Cesario was very conscious of this and stated that the equation above did not achieve the need for equations relating participation in outdoor recreation to what might be termed 'opportunity to participate' (Cesario, 1969, pp. 49–50).

An early attempt to cope with the addition of new facilities in a recreation system was made by Mansfield (1971). The objective of that study was to estimate the benefits derived by visitors to the recreational facilities of the proposed Morcambe Bay barrage at its earliest operating date, 1981. Benefits were interpreted as consumer's surplus accruing to visitors. The first stage in the study was the estimation of trip-making functions to the Lake District. These were derived for three types of trip: day trips, half-day trips, and holiday trips. The functions obtained were:

(1) Day trips

$$T_{iL} = -0.346 + 0.0064W_i + 1229.68C_i^{-2}$$

(2) Half-day trips

$$T_{iL} = -0.158 + 0.0017W_i + 621.95C_i^{-2}$$

(3) Holiday trips

$$\log^e(T_{iL} + 1) = 1.4648 - 0.2581 \log_e C_{iL}$$

$$r^2 = 0.90,$$

where T_{iL} is trips per 1,000 population over the observation period, W_i is cars per 100 households in each zone, and C is the number of distance units between the origin zone and the nearest point of entry to the Lake District. All the coefficients shown above were significant at the 5 per cent level, and those for distance were significant at the 1 per cent level. However the level of aggregation varied from thirty-two origin zones for day and half-day trips to nine broad bands for holiday trips. The specification of the day and half-day trip making function is unusual, but nevertheless this was the first British study to emerge with a significant socioeconomic variable in a recreation trip-making function.

The novel feature of the study though involves the attempt at the second stage to derive estimates of benefits for generated as well as diverted trips from an increased supply of recreation opportunities. The assumption was that Morecambe Bay recreation facilities could be regarded as a perfect substitute to the Lake District. Thus using the trip-making functions estimated for 1981, which were as above but using the relevant projections for car-ownership and travel costs, total trips to the joint Lake District/Morecambe Bay complex were assumed to be a function of the minimum costs of visiting either of the two substitutes. Figure 4.3 below shows the trip-making function for 1981, $T_{iL}T_{iL}$ and the case of an origin zone for which travel costs are lower to Morecambe Bay (C_M) than to the Lake District (C_L). Generated trips are shown as ($OT_M - OT_{LB}$) and diverted trips as ($OT_{LB} - OT_{LA}$). The new total of trips is predicted by the substitution of C_M for C_L in the trip-making function. The number of diverted trips is predicted by multiplication of T_{LB} by the formula (for origin zone i):

$$\frac{C_{iL} - C_{iM}}{\frac{1}{2}(C_{iL} + C_{iM})}$$

and the consumer's surplus gained is:

$$\tfrac{1}{2}(\mathrm{O}T_M - \mathrm{O}T_{LB})(C_L - C_M) \text{ for generated visits,}$$

and

$$(\mathrm{O}T_{LB} - \mathrm{O}T_{LA})(C_L - C_M) \text{ for diverted visits.}$$

No incremental gains accrue to zones for which C_L is less than C_M and the estimated gains from the introduction of the Morecambe Bay facilities are relatively low: whereas the 1981 estimated surplus for the Lake District alone is £227,520 per average week, the estimated surplus for the Morcambe Bay area is only £22,880 per average week. Mansfield's work represents an attempt to include generated growth into the distance–decay method, but even ignoring the issue of the level of aggregation used for the holiday data, there are inconsistencies between the supply–demand interaction assumed and the evaluation of consumer's surplus gains. The inconsistencies are: first, if homogeneity is assumed why is there only partial diversion of trips from origin zones where travel costs are lower to Morecambe Bay than to the Lake District? Secondly, if the number of diverted trips is sensitive to variations in the difference in travel costs, $(C_L - C_M)$, as the formula used for estimating diverted trips assumes, why are all diverted trips evaluated as deriving a consumer's surplus gain equal to the full travel cost difference $(C_L - C_M)$?

Nevertheless, one could say that a great deal was achieved with limited data. The most important limitation was, of course, the absence of any data on how variations in supply variables affects trip

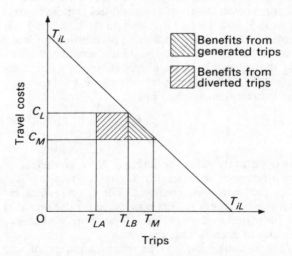

Figure 4.3   *Benefits from provision of Morecambe Bay barrage to recreation trip makers*

generation behaviour and hence the benefits from increased recreational provision.

The most convincing model of supply–demand interaction in the 1960s emerged from a study designed to estimate the potential recreation benefits from reservoirs proposed in the preliminary Texas Water Plan (Grubb and Goodwin, 1968). For this study data on visits to eight reservoirs in Texas during the summer of 1965 were pooled and resulted in the following visitation equation:

$$\log_e (Y + 0.8) = -8.603 + 0.573 \log_e x_1 - 1.186 \log_e x_2 + 0.752 \log_e x_3$$
$$\qquad\quad (2.080)\ (0.044) \qquad\quad (0.075) \qquad\qquad (0.267)$$
$$\qquad\qquad - 0.326 \log_e x_4 + 0.209 \log_e x_5 \quad (r^2 = 0.41)$$
$$\qquad\qquad\quad (0.048) \qquad\quad (0.063)$$

where Y is the number of visitor days from a particular county of origin, x_1 is population of the county of origin of visitors, x_2 is round trip cost of travel from the county of origin of visitors, x_3 is per capita income in the count of origin of visitors, x_4 is a 'gravity' variable, which will be described below and x_5 is size in surface acres of the conservation pool of the reservoir visited.

The figures in brackets in the visitation equation are the standard errors of the regression coefficients and an encouraging feature of the visitation equation is the large number of significant variables it contains, all with the expected signs. However, with the relatively low level of aggregation used the coefficient of determination is low.

The gravity variable x_4 is pertinent to our discussion in this section. The basic aim was to construct a variable reflecting the competitive effect of other reservoirs available to potential visitors to any particular reservoir. Grubb and Goodwin state that they tried to give this variable features compatible with two assumptions. First, the larger the number of reservoirs near any particular county, the less likely are residents of that county to visit a particular reservoir. Secondly, the larger is a reservoir's surface area the more effective it will be in competition for reservoir visits. Thus

$$X_{4j} = \sum_{i=1}^{n} \frac{\log_{10} S_i}{d_i}$$

where X_{4j} is the gravity value for county j, S_i is the surface acre size of the conservation pool in reservoir i, and d_i is the distance from reservoir i to the centre of county i. The n reservoirs included all within 100 miles of county j. This was based on the fact that the 1965 survey used indicated that more than 90 per cent of visitors originated within 100 miles of each sample reservoir.

A complete examination of the characteristics of the Grubb–Goodwin visitation equation would be too lengthy for our purposes here. However, it is sufficient to state that the equation contains the following properties. First, it is possible for recreation visits to respond in either direction, that is, increasing or decreasing, in response to an increased supply of facilities. Secondly, the precise effect depends upon the relative size of the regression coefficients of the gravity variable and the surface acreage variable, but there is a strong tendency for increased supply to have a positive effect on visits. Finally, using the Grubb–Goodwin parameter estimates there is a strong positive effect.

The authors never explicitly state these characteristics of their model, and one does not know how intentional the above effects are. However, they are a source of confidence in the model.

Finally, within this section some recent work by Cesario and Knetsch (1976) shows some measure of progress. They hypothesise the following visitation equation:

$$V_{ij} = g X_i K_i^{(a+1)} \frac{Y_j \exp(dc_{ij})}{K_i}$$

where

$$K_i = \sum_{k=1}^{m} Y_k \exp(dc_{ik})$$

and V_{ij} is the number of visits per unit time made to site j from population centre i; X_i is a measure of the combined effects on recreation trip making of characteristics of population centre i, such as population size and medium income; Y_j is a measure of the combined effects on recreation trip making of characteristics of recreation site j, such as land and water acreage and car-parking spaces; and c_{ij} is the generalised cost of travel from i to j; g, a and d are parameters. Cesario and Knetsch describe K_i as a 'competing opportunities' or 'accessibility' term.

In the visitation equation above there are two distinct components. The first term in square brackets represents a trip generation component with the number of recreation trips as a function of origin characteristics and accessibility. Examination of the K_i term shows that it is assumed that an increase in available sites will have a positive generation effect provided a is greater than -1. No restraint is placed on the parameter value a, but the range $-1 < a < o$ will also give the effect of a diminishing marginal effect of accessibility on recreation trip making and is expected *a priori* by Cesario and Knetsch. The second term in square brackets represents a trip distribution component and is the probability that a trip from centre i will go to site j, and this is given by the ratio of accessibility of j to the total accessibility of all sites.

Not only does this equation have a positive generation effect, but it also has the desirable feature that recreation sites are imperfect substitutes with negative cross-price elasticities, and thus, can cope sensibly with the introduction of new sites. A new site, n, increases accessibility by $Y_n \exp (dc_{in})$ and the increase in the size of the first term will show new visits to the recreation site (generated visits), and the decrease in shares at existing sites caused by the increase in K_i in the distribution component will represent diverted trips.

The above ideas were applied to visit data collected by on-site surveys at eighty-four state parks in Pennsylvania, parts of New York and New Jersey, and amounted to a test area of twenty-three contiguous counties and thirty-eight recreation sites. The precise model specification tested was:

$$V_{ij} = b_0 P_k^{b_1} A_j^{b_2} \exp (b_3 c_{ij}) \sum_{k=1}^{m} A_k^{b_2} \exp (b_3 c_{ik})^{b_4} + E_{ij},$$

where V_{ij} and c_{ij} are as before, P_i is the variable representing X_i and is population of county i, A_j is the variable representing Y_j and is here an index of site j's appeal using weights derived from recreationists and also weights subjectively given by researchers. b_0 to b_4 are parameters, with b_3 corresponding to d, and b_4 to a.

The parameters were estimated using the Marquadt 'compromise' procedure which searches for the minimum using a least-squares criterion. This was necessary because there was no simple transformation of the above model because it was non-linear in parameters. The signs and magnitudes of all the parameters were plausible, and for a multiplicative model of the travel cost variable gave $b_3 = -0.944$ and $b_4 = -0.575$. Especially encouraging was the fact that this model succeeded in explaining 87 per cent of the variance in visits, which was impressive at this level of aggregation.

We will postpone a summary on progress in estimation of monetary measures in order to consider a different type of approach to recreational provision below. This is based on planning standards and aims to provide facilities to meet these standards.

THE PROVISION OF RECREATIONAL FACILITIES BY THE USE OF PLANNING STANDARDS

Impetus to a major investment programme in sports facilities in England and Wales was provided by the Sports Council's advocacy in *Provision for Sport* (Sports Council, 1972) of standards implying the need for construction of 447 swimming pools, 815 indoor sports centres and 970 nine-hole golf courses. The capital cost of this programme, excluding professional fees and land costs, was (at 1972 prices) £71·9 million for swimming pools, £148·4 million for indoor sports centres and £43·6 million for golf courses. The percentage increase in supply embodied in these proposals was dramatic being near 50 per cent for golf courses, 80 per cent for swimming pools and much more for indoor sports centres, as only twenty-seven of the latter were open or given loan sanction by the end of 1969.

Let us study the method of appraising swimming pools requirements and then compare it with the methods based on travel cost/visit relationships which form the base of estimation techniques for monetary measurement.

The Sports Council aimed at a standard of provision of a certain area of pool water per 1,000 population which they called the 'Water Area Requirement' (WAR). This WAR was set at a level of 30 square feet of water area to each person in the water pool during the average weekly peak hour over the months May to September, excluding August. The WAR can be expressed as one equation:

$$WAR = (AF)(P)(G)(Prop.)(N)(W)(WAP),$$

where   AF = Attendance factor: visits per head of catchment area population, assumed to be 2·5 in urban areas, and 3·0 in rural areas.

       P = Registrar General's 1968-based 1981 population projections.

       G = Growth factor: index of change in Attendance Factor, assumed to be 1·25.

  Prop. = Proportion of annual attendance during May to September, excluding August, assumed to be 0·4675.

      N = Number of weeks during May to September, excluding August: seventeen.

      K = Proportion of weekly average demand attending during the peak hour, assumed to be 0·0375.

      W = Proportion of peak hour attendance in the water, assumed to be 0·6.

  WAP = Water area required per person in the water, assumed to be 30 square feet.

The above formula involves many assumptions. One could profitably test the sensitivity of the 'required' building programme to all of these assumptions. However, distance-decay type methods relating visit rates to distance have usefulness in relation to one specific assumption above, and that is the attendance factor. The attendance factor is a constant in the formula and yet it is apparent that if there is distance-decay, the attendance factor (which is a measure of V/P) is a variable.

The Sports Council itself quotes evidence of distance-decay. In order for the above WAR equation to be usable it must represent a situation where after the increase in swimming pools has occurred there is an equilibrium with the attendance factor equal to 2·5 and 3·0 in urban and rural areas respectively. If we assume homogeneity and therefore that extra swimming pools simply contract catchment areas we can by consideration of distance-decay behaviour test the likely effect of increasing supplies on (a) the number of swimming pool visits per head of population and (b) the number of visits to each swimming pool.

Remember that an 80 per cent increase in swimming pools is recommended. In Figure 4.4 population is distributed equally along the line YY (our argument is not affected by considering a two-dimensional distribution of population), with a swimming pool located at X. ZZ measures the distance for which the swimming pool X is nearest before the increase in supply, and Z_1Z_1 measures the above distance after the 80 per cent increase in supply, with $ZZ/Z_1Z_1 = 1·8$. In Figure 4.4 three alternative distance-decay curves are shown relating visits to distance: CEDEC, BFDFB and ADA. Now if the data show that ADA is the typical behaviour a contraction of market areas from ZZ to Z_1Z_1 will have no affect on the attendance factor at each pool, but there are effects for curve BFDFB, and more marked effects for CEDEC. Visits per pool will fall from BDB to Z_1FDFZ_1 for curve BFDFB, and will fall from ZCEDECZ to Z_1EDEZ_1 for curve CEDEC.

Thus visits per pool vary both with the relationship of visit decay to distance and with the market areas given to each pool. The Sports Council do not provide direct evidence on how great a proportion of visitors to existing pools will be diverted to new pools, and one can only say that the realism of their assumed attendance factor in the situation

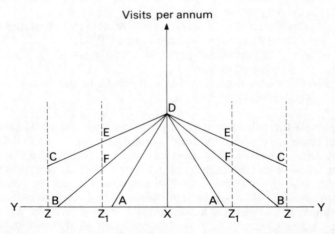

Visits per annum

Figure 4.4   *Alternative distance-decay behaviour for a swimming pool located at X*

of increased supply still needs to be tested *and* that it probably can be tested by using existing data.

This is as far as one can go without moving into territory not explored by the Sports Council. However, distance-decay curves are only part of the technique of estimating monetary measures. The Clawson method could be used to give measures of (a) the sensitivity of demand, especially peak hour demand, to variations in charges, and (b) the incremental benefits from building extra swimming pools. I will leave this subject here, but must mention that in my opinion a Clawson-type analysis would be most worthwhile.

CONCLUSIONS

With regard to the estimation of the primary benefits of recreation there has been a great deal of progress. The number of multi-site studies which successfully include a number of significant independent variables is limited. However, remember that ten years ago none existed. One thing which may inhibit progress and application is the large data requirement for achieving supply–demand interaction in recreation trip-making models.

The Clawson method for converting recreation trip-making equations into monetary estimates involves a number of problems. Some are common to much applied econometric work, such as specification of functional form, and progress here should be little different from that for other parts of the subject. However, there are also the problems listed earlier, such as utility derived from travel, where it has yet to be shown (a) the range of situations where they will be important, and (b) whether the Clawson method can be modified to apply to more difficult situations or whether it has to be abandoned.

However, less progress has been made with regard to the estimation of the secondary benefits of recreation, and the obstacles to progress here seem very severe. For the option value no direct consumption data can possibly be obtained. For reductions in crime and medical expenditure due to recreation, the factors to be quantified probably interact in a complex manner and it is unlikely that recreation is one of the major determinants so that its effects will be difficult to isolate. This is likely to have most effect in the evaluation of projects in urban areas. Not only are secondary benefits relatively more important but also opportunity costs are usually highest in urban areas. We may add to this the greater difficulty of applying the Clawson method accurately for urban project evaluation due to the greater susceptibility to measurement errors in the data. Urban project valuation is the more urgent and more difficult, but is less well researched than rural project evaluation. We must hope the next ten years will see the emergence of urban studies which are as convincing as some of the rural supply–demand interaction studies discussed earlier.

REFERENCES

Archer, B., 'The impact of recreation on local economies', *Planning Outlook*, special issue, *Planning for Recreation*, 1974, pp. 16–27.

Archer, B., 'The anatomy of a multiplier', *Regional Studies*, vol. 10, 1976, pp. 71–7.

Ball, M. J., 'Recent empirical work on the determinants of relative house prices', *Urban Studies*, vol. 10, 1973, pp. 213–33.

Beckmann, M. J., 'Market share, distance, and potential', *Regional and Urban Economics*, vol. 1, 1971, pp. 3–18.

Bohm, P., 'Estimating demand for public goods: an experiment', *European Economic Review*, vol. 3, 1972, pp. 111–30.

Brown, W. G., and Nawas, F., 'Impact of aggregation on the estimation of outdoor recreation demand functions', *American Journal of Agricultural Economics*, vol. 55, 1973, pp. 246–9.

Burton, T. L., *Windsor Great Park: a recreation study* (Wye College Studies in Rural Land Use, No. 8, 1967).

Carey, O. L., 'The economics of recreation: progress and problems', *Western Economic Journal*, vol. 3, 1965, pp. 172–81.

Cesario, F. J., 'Operations research in outdoor recreation', *Journal of Leisure Research*, vol. 1, 1969, pp. 33–51.

Cesario, F. J., and Knetsch, J. L., 'Time bias in recreation benefit estimates', *Water Resources Research*, vol. 6, 1970, pp. 700–4.

Cesario, F. J., and Knetsch, J. L., 'A recreation site demand and benefit estimation model', *Regional Studies*, vol. 10, 1976, pp. 97–104.

Cheshire, P. C., and Stabler, M. J., 'Joint consumption benefits in recreational site surplus; an empirical estimate', *Regional Studies*, vol. 10, 1976, pp. 343–51.

Clawson, M., *Methods of measuring demand for and value of outdoor recreation* (RFF Reprint No. 10, Washington DC: Resources for the Future Inc., 1959).

Clawson, M., and Knetsch, J. L., *Economics of Outdoor Recreation* (Baltimore: Johns Hopkins Press, 1966).

Colenutt, R. J., 'Modelling travel patterns of day visitors to the countryside', *Area*, vol. 1, 1969, pp. 43–7.

Common, M. S., 'A note on the use of the Clawson method for the evaluation of recreation site benefits', *Regional Studies*, vol. 7, 1973, pp. 401–7.

Countryside Commission/Sports Council, *Coastal Recreation and Holidays* (London: HMSO, 1969).

David, E. L., 'Lakeshore property values: a guide to public investment in recreation', *Water Resources Research*, vol. 4, 1968, pp. 697–707.

Elson, M. J., 'Some factors affecting the incidence and distribution of week-end recreation motoring trips', *Oxford Agrarian Studies*, vol. 2, 1973, pp. 161–79.

Evans, A. W., 'The economics of the urban recreational system', in *Studies in Social Science and Planning*, ed. J. Forbes (Edinburgh: Scottish Academic Press, 1974, pp. 249–66.

Fisher, A. C., and Krutilla, J. V., 'Determination of optimal capacity of resource-based recreation facilities', *Natural Resources Journal*, vol. 12, 1972, pp. 417–44.

Flegg, A. T., 'Methodological problems in estimating recreational demand functions and evaluating recreational benefits', *Regional Studies*, vol. 10, 1976, pp. 352–62.

Flowerdew, A. D. J., 'Economic aspects of urban models', Urban Economics Conference Paper (London: Centre for Environmental Studies, 1971).

Gibson, J. G., 'Recreation cost–benefit analysis: a review of English case studies', *Planning Outlook*, special issue, *Planning for Recreation*, 1974, pp. 28–46.

Gibson, J. G., 'The intervening-opportunities model of migration: a critique', *Socio-Economic Planning Sciences*, vol. 9, 1975, pp. 205–8.

Gibson, J. G., and Anderson, R. W., 'The estimation of consumers' surplus from a recreational facility with optional tariffs', *Journal of Applied Economics*, vol. 7, 1975, pp. 73–9.

Grubb, H. W., and Goodwin, J. T., *Economic evaluation of water oriented recreation in the preliminary Texas Water Plan* (Report 84, Austin: Texas Water Development Board, 1968).

Henderson, D. M., and Cousins, R. L., *The economic impact of tourism: a case study in Greater Tayside* (Edinburgh: Scottish Tourist Board, 1975).

Johnston, J., *Econometric Methods*, 2nd edn (New York: McGraw-Hill, 1972).

Knetsch, J. L., 'Outdoor recreation demands and benefits', *Land Economics*, vol. 39, 1963, pp. 387–96.

Knetsch, J. L., 'The influence of reservoir projects on land values', *Journal of Farm Economics*, vol. 46, 1964, pp. 231–43.

Knetsch, J. L., and Davis, R. K., 'Comparisons of methods for recreation evaluation', in *Water Research*, ed. A. V. Kneese and S. C. Smith (Washington DC: Johns Hopkins Press, 1966), pp. 121–42.

Krutilla, J. V., Cicchetti, C. J., Freeman III, A. M., and Russell, C. S., 'Observations on the economics of irreplaceable assets', in *Environmental Quality Analysis*, ed. A. V. Kneese and B. T. Bower (Baltimore: Johns Hopkins Press 1972), pp. 69–112.

McConnell, K. E., and Duff, V. A., 'Estimating net benefits of recreation under conditions of excess demand', *Journal of Environmental Economics and Management*, vol. 2, 1975, pp. 224–30.

Mansfield, N. W., 'The estimation of benefits from recreation sites and the provision of a new recreation facility', *Regional Studies*, vol. 5, 1971, pp. 55–69.

Merewitz, L., 'Recreational benefits of water resource developments', *Water Resources Research*, vol. 2, 1966, pp. 626–40.

Ministry of Housing and Local Government, *Open Spaces* (Technical Memorandum No. 6, London: 1956).

Moncur, J. T., 'Estimating the value of alternative outdoor recreation facilities within a small area', *Journal of Leisure Research*, vol. 7, 1975, pp. 301–11.

Norton, G. A., 'Public outdoor recreation and resource allocation: a welfare approach', *Land Economics*, vol. 46, 1970, pp. 414–22.

Outdoor Recreation Resources Review Commission, *Economic Studies of Outdoor Recreation* (Study Report No. 24, Washington DC: US Government Printing Office, 1962).

Patmore, J. A., *Land and Leisure* (London: Penguin Books, 1972)

Pearse, P. H., 'A new approach to the evaluation of non-priced recreational resources', *Land Economics*, vol. 44, 1968, pp. 87–97.

Prewitt, R. A., *The Economics of Public Recreation – an Economic Study of the Monetary Evaluation of Recreation in the National Parks* (Washington DC: National Park Service, 1949).

Seckler, D. W., 'On the uses and abuses of economic science in evaluating public outdoor recreation', *Land Economics*, vol. 42, 1966, pp. 485–94.

Smith, R. J., *The Evaluation of Recreation Benefits: Some Problems of the Clawson Method* (Discussion Paper No. 318, Birmingham: Faculty of Commerce and Social Science, 1970).

Smith, R. J., 'Problems of interpreting recreation benefits from a recreation demand curve', in *Recreational Economics and Analysis*, ed. G. A. C. Searle (Harlow: Longman, 1975), pp. 62–74.

Smith, R. J., and Kavanagh, N. J., 'The measurement of benefits of trout fishing: preliminary results of a study at Grafham Water, Great Ouse Water Authority, Huntingdonshire', *Journal of Leisure Research*, vol. 1, 1969, pp. 316–32.

Smith, V. K., 'Travel cost demand models for wilderness recreation: a problem of non-tested hypotheses', *Land Economics*, vol. 5, 1975, pp. 103–11.

Sports Council, *Provision for Sport* (London: HMSO, 1972).

Stevens, J. B., 'Recreation benefits from water pollution control', *Water Resources Research*, vol. 2, 1966, pp. 167–82.

Taylor, P. J., 'Distance transformations and distance decay functions', *Geographical Analysis*, vol. 3, 1971, pp. 221–38.

Trice, A. H., and Wood, S. E., 'Measurement of recreation benefits', *Land Economics*, vol. 34, 1958, pp. 195–207.

Ullman, E. L., and Volk, D. J., 'An operational model for predicting reservoir attendance and benefits: implications of a location approach to water recreation', *Papers of the Michigan Academy of Science, Arts, and Letters*, vol. 67, 1962, pp. 473–84.

Veal, A. J., 'The theory', in T. L. Burton, *Experiments in Recreation Research* (London: Allen & Unwin, 1971), pp. 307–44.

Vickerman, R. W., 'The evaluation of benefits from recreational projects', *Urban Studies*, vol. 11, 1974, pp. 277–88.

Weber, J. E., and Hawkins, C. A., 'The estimation of constant elasticities', *Southern Economic Journal*, vol. 38, 1971, pp. 185–92.

Weisbrod, B., 'Collective consumption services of individual consumption goods', *Quarterly Journal of Economics*, vol. 78, 1964, pp. 471–7.

Wood, D. F., 'The distance travelled approach for measuring value of recreation areas: an application', *Land Economics*, vol. 37, 1961, pp. 363–9.

Chapter 5

Water Pollution

Water pollution can be defined as the introduction of waste or other substances into the environmental media (water resources) on a scale that causes damage to living systems, hazards to human health, reductions in fishery productivity, impairment of quality for various other water uses, or reduction of amenity (Kinnersley, 1973). In short, water pollution is present when a quality in the water inflicts either an economic burden or aesthetic distress on the users (Dinius, 1972). Water resources are used for a variety of purposes and their required quality will vary with the use in question. Each beneficial use, while depending upon the maintenance of a particular water-quality level, also involves possible damages leading to a deterioration in the quality of water when it is re-used. Man's utilisation of water resources can be broadly divided into two categories: withdrawal uses, which include municipal and industrial water supply and agricultural irrigation; and in-stream uses, such as a variety of water-based recreational activities, aesthetic enjoyment, commercial fishing and the use of a watercourse for effluent removal. High water-quality standards are required for drinking purposes and some industrial processes; while recreation is made more enjoyable and irrigation more productive the higher the water-quality level. On the other hand, the quality may not be of great importance in industrial cooling processes or if the watercourse is being used as an effluent dump.

Most water pollution problems are generated by municipal and industrial waste emissions or agricultural land drainage and usually result from a mixture of more than one type. The various pollutants introduced into the water combine to produce a wide range of possible pollution damages. For a short non-technical survey of the possible pollution impacts and their ecological consequences see Armstrong (1973) and Dodson (1973). There are physical effects produced such as oil filming, detergent foaming, gross turbidity, discoloration, or unnaturally high water temperatures. Any biodegradable organic matter emitted into a water body will serve to reduce oxygen levels, while toxic pollutants such as cyanides, heavy metals, etc., can produce fish and aquatic fauna kills. The combined (synergistic) toxic effects of a number of these toxic pollutants are, however, not known with any certainty. Excessive additions of chloride and sulphate result in mineralising effects which can cause economic damages to households in the form of corrosion, encrustation and despoilation of pipes, plumbing fixtures, water heaters and other appliances. Nitrates and phosphates derived from domestic sewage and agricultural land drainage can, in the presence of sunlight, lead to the eutrophication of water bodies. The process of eutrophication results in an over-enrichment of the water by the nutrients. The consequent increased production of algae and other aquatic plants leads to deoxygenation, deterioration of fisheries and can reduce the recreational and aesthetic enjoyment of the water body. Excessive growths of micro-organisms can cause taints in water and make filtration and purification difficult. Henderson (1972) warns, however, that it is necessary to bear in mind that from an ecological point of view water bodies serve as the natural recipients of nutrients and other constituents derived from plant, soil, animal and other sources most of which are vital or beneficial to aquatic life or to the land-making process. These natural constituents are sometimes in undersupply while at other times they will be oversupplied and may thus pollute. The net detrimental effect of pollution can be caused by these natural contributions and/or man-made or man-induced conditions. Separating man-made from natural pollution impacts is in many instances a formidable scientific task. This makes accurate economic evaluation of a number of possible water pollution damages currently unfeasible.

Kneese and Bower (1968) stress that the achievement of an economically optimal level of water quality requires the delineation of the damage-cost function, which relates the amount of waste discharged to the damages inflicted. This pollution quantification exercise is made extremely complex, however, because of the multi-dimensional nature of water usages, qualities and receptors. The different water uses and benefit or cost recipients may compete with or complement one another. Moreover, each recipient may be uniquely sensitive to different components of water quality. Freeman (1975) states that 'water quality cannot be represented by a single number on some scale but rather is an n-dimensional vector of the relevant parameters. Further, water quality varies across space and time, making the task of measurement and description even more complicated.' The National Commission on Water Quality (1975) in the USA used five variables: dissolved oxygen (DO) and DO depletion, nutrients (nitrate and phosphorus), turbidity and suspended solids, total dissolved solids and coliform bacteria, in its assessment of the nation's water quality problems and conditions. The above list is not fully comprehensive and probably reflects the availability or rather lack of availability of hard scientific data derived from continual monitoring. An increase in the magnitude of one quality component may affect one use favourably while simultaneously affecting an alternative use negatively. Very cold water is best for industrial cooling, for example, whereas warm water is best for irrigation. Not all wastes have a detrimental effect on water quality. Claims have been made, for instance that a waste product (ferrous sulphate solution) derived from the use of sulphuric acid as a steel rod descaling agent in industry can actually improve water quality in certain circumstances. When added to sewage effluent the ferrous sulphate solution can solidify any phosphorus present, thus enabling it to be removed before the effluent enters a watercourse. The removal of the phosphorus would reduce any eutrophication conditions present in the receiving water body.

Dinius (1972) has constructed a rudimentary social accounting system for evaluating water resources. His system requires the actual physical measurement of important polluting substances in the water and then the conversion of the individual substance quantities into a single broad quality unit. A standardised rating scale was constructed to express the relationship between the existence of various pollutants in the water and the degree of damage or distress that each separate pollutant inflicted on the various classes of water users. This system has its limitations, however, due to the fact that as yet science has not provided us with a complete understanding of the links between many water-quality parameters and pollution discharge rates. Much evidence is also still required before we can know with any certainty what indices of water quality are relevant to the different water uses. Thus the Dinius rating scale contains a number of subjective judgements as opposed to hard evidence. In a survey of empirical water-quality benefit-cost studies Tihansky (1975) concludes that while studies dealing with industrial, agricultural and municipal water supplies are generally based on a sound conceptual base the same cannot be said of recreational usage studies (see also Whiteley and Dendy, 1968). He also stresses that there is an overall dearth of empirically derived damage functions. Nearly all recreation damage curves are hypothetical and in the limited number of studies presenting actual damage curves these are often based on very small samples of observation points.

WATER USES AND RELATED POLLUTION DAMAGE COSTS

A number of writers (Bower and Kneese, 1968; Haveman, 1974; Wyzga, 1974) have concluded that, based on the limited empirical evidence available, the primary damage costs of water pollution are those imposed on the recreational services yielded by the environment. This conclusion is reinforced by the results of the Delaware Estuary Study (FWPCA, 1966). A number of attempts that have been made to estimate industrial damage from polluted water have shown them to be minimal. For many industrial processes (e.g. cooling) water of almost any quality is acceptable, and for other uses (e.g. food processing) the required quality standard is so high that practically all water needs to be treated. Further, the treatment costs are relatively insensitive to the quality of intake water. Thus the Delaware study concludes that the benefits of raw water quality improvement which could be identified as accruing to municipal and industrial water users were very small compared with the costs of improvement. In fact, improvements in water quality with respect to some parameters could increase industrial damages, e.g. higher DO levels tend to increase corrosion in cooling equipment. Tihansky (1975) agrees that recreation activities along water bodies generally sustain the largest damages when water-quality levels fall, but that other economic damages could not be dismissed as insignificant. He demonstrates (Tihansky, 1974), for example, that the economic damages from domestic water-supply use are substantial and that such damages could be considered in defining water-quality standards. Household appliances and personal items in contact with mains water are subject to physical damages from chemical and other constituents of the water. Many so-called comprehensive water-quality damage studies unfortunately include an incomplete list of water-use categories. Some water uses are deliberately omitted because of the complex difficulties stressed by Henderson (1972) involved in segregating man-made from natural water-quality problems. The quantity of total dissolved solids in domestic water supplies, for instance, is a function of both natural processes of soil erosion and groundwater conditions and also certain agricultural practices which stimulate increased soil erosion rates and groundwater infiltration.

DOMESTIC WATER-SUPPLY DAMAGES

Poor water quality will increase the treatment costs for domestic water supplies and may also introduce toxic substances which affect the safety and palatability of the drinking water if normal treatment processes are unable to remove them. Conventional treatment techniques remove or reduce organic matter, suspended matter, hardness and iron and manganese from the water. Nevertheless, there are substances, such as nitrate which are not removed by normal treatment. For a discussion of the special methods available for nitrogen and phosphorus removal and their costs see Bayley (1970) and Brown (1975). The existence of impurities in domestic water supplies can lead to a product that is not aesthetically pleasing due to an unpleasant taste and/or odour. Human health can be affected in a variety of ways ranging from short-term outbreaks of bacteria-related diseases to chronic long-term health effects due to the accumulation of impurities such as mercury or nitrate-related compounds in the human body. Lyon (1970) and Freeman

(1975) note that very little information exists on the possible long-term adverse health effects of continual ingestion of heavy metals, inorganic salts or persistent hydrocarbons. The dose-response relationship between pollution and ill health is still an extremely uncertain one. Waste oil can contaminate drinking water and has been cited by one authority as the main source of carcinogene hydrocarbons in purified drinking water, but the evidence is inconclusive. The general effects of waste oil on ecosystem functioning are simply not known. Schroeder (1960) has shown that there is a highly significant inverse correlation between the hardness of drinking water (particularly calcium content) and deaths from cardiovascular disease. The exact mode of action of cardiovascular pathogenesis related to the mineral content of drinking water has, however, not been made clear. There is a lack of detailed epidemological and other health data on which to establish a firm dose-response relationship. Moreover, water-borne pollutants are transmitted through a complex mechanism of inter-related uses: drinking and culinary uses, water-based recreation, agricultural intake water and aquatic food uses. To trace the full extent of these complex effects is currently unfeasible.

The complexity of the problem is well illustrated by the Wabigoon river case in Canada. The Wabigoon and English river system in Canada has become seriously polluted by waste emissions from industrial plants including a pulp and paper plant. In particular, toxic mercury pollution appears to have been building up over a period of years. A wide range of damages have occurred but their full extent is difficult to measure accurately. The known adverse economic effects have been the closure of a valuable commercial fishery and two of the largest tourist lodges in the region. This has resulted in a significant loss of jobs and income among the local Indian population dependent on the fishing and tourist industries. The social damages inflicted on the local community are harder to quantify but, perhaps the most disturbing damages are the possible long-term health effects. Some Indians have shown symptoms of a form of mercury poisoning (minimata disease) but as yet no unequivocal proof of mercury poisoning has been established.

Growing concern has been expressed in the UK in recent years regarding the concentration of nitrate in certain river and well waters. At high concentrations nitrate in the water supply may cause methaemoglobinaemia (blue baby disease) in infants. Nitrates are derived from various sources; surface waters may contain nitrate from sewage effluents, from agricultural land run-off and also from the atmosphere through rainfall. Agriculture appears to be an important pollution source because of the nitrate-nitrogen lost in drainage from farmland which often enters sources of drinking water (see Haith, 1976). In some UK water supplies concentrations have from time to time exceeded the 11·3 mg/l of NO_3-N which the World Health

Organisation gives as the upper limit of their 'recommended' category (Cooke, 1975; Goodman, 1975). Davey (1970) investigated nitrate concentrations in drinking water from aquifers beneath chalk formations in north Lincolnshire; later Sumner (1973) found that the average concentration of 10·7 mg/l of NO_3–N in 1970 had risen to 13·7 mg/l by 1972 in the village of Barrow-on-Humber. The incidence of infantile methaemoglobinaemia is small and the number of cases confirmed in the UK has been less than ten in twenty years. Nevertheless, some investigators have suggested that in some individuals the nitrates formed in the body from nitrates may be transformed into nitroso compounds some of which are thought to be carcinogenic. High nitrate concentrations in drinking water must therefore be judged potentially dangerous until further research has been carried out. It may also prove rather difficult to diminish nitrate concentrations in water percolating down from areas used for intensive arable agriculture.

Any evaluation of these possible but as yet not fully understood health damages will have to include estimates of:

(1) resource costs in the form of medical expenses associated with pollution-induced health damages. Various attempts have been made to measure hospital costs on a per patient basis allowing for 'case mix' and, as a preliminary approach, these data could be used in a damage cost study (see, for example, Beresford, 1972; Lavers, 1972);
(2) the value of a lost life. Mooney (1977) has surveyed the 'health economics' literature which deals with this question (see Chapter 6);
(3) the value of impairment due to disease.

Tihansky (1975) has summarised attempts that have been made in the USA to estimate national health costs of polluted water such as those by Liu (1972) and Lackner and Sokoloski (1973). The latter investigators estimated the national benefits that would result if water-borne communicable diseases such as infectious hepatitis and typhoid fever were reduced. Outbreaks of the disease were costed on the basis of ten days' lost income and the resource costs of a five-day stay in hospital. Outbreaks of gastro-enteritis were also evaluated. It was estimated that the unit social cost per case was $100 and that there were approximately 1 million cases of gastro-enteritis per annum in the USA. The final cost figures were increased by a factor of five (the contagion multiplier) to allow for the highly infectious nature of hepatitis and typhoid fever, and were then doubled to take account of the national economic impacts of personal expenses. Liu (1972) estimates that 2 million working days are lost in the USA due to acute gastro-enteritis and diarrhoea at an average lost wage of $30 a day. He also estimates that the value of the 1,000 deaths due to infectious hepatitis per year is around $100,000 per life. Tihansky (1975) concludes, however, that much of the data used in these studies are subjective and that these damage estimates are at best 'guesstimates'.

Mains water constituents are also capable of causing other types of welfare costs to households. Patterson and Banker (1968) pointed out that household appliances and plumbing which come into frequent contact with mains water are subject to abrasive, corrosive and other damaging effects of certain mineral constituents in water. There are both short- and long-term household economic damage costs. Daily expenditures for soap and detergents, as well as operating costs of appliances usage, can increase. In the longer term, the service life of household items suffers from contact with poor water quality. The Delaware Estuary Study (FWPCA, 1966) neglected these impacts, the rationale being that existing treatment plants remove all objectionable water pollutants prior to household distribution. Tihansky (1974) argues that this is a misconception and that total dissolved solids and hardness are among those elements not treated fully enough to eliminate the possibility of substantial household damage costs. Tihansky's own study (Tihansky, 1974) of the economic damages from residential use of mineralised water supply estimates total annual damages to US residents in 1970 to be in the range $0·65–$3·45 billion, the mean being $1·75 billion. This mean translates to $8·6 per person annually. Hardness was found to be the most damaging water constituent, costing $1·14 billion annually compared to $0·61 billion for total dissolved solids. It is necessary to bear in mind, however, that both the constituents examined by Tihansky are partly natural in origin and therefore their impacts are difficult to interpret in evaluating man-induced pollution abatement programmes. Lawrence (1975) has constructed a simple composite graphical estimation of indirect costs of urban water use for the Los Angeles river Planning Area (containing some 7 million people) based on previous cost studies undertaken in the USA. The study examines only the relationship between total dissolved solids and total hardness in the water and the consequent damage costs. He cited research studies (for example, Leeds *et al.*, 1963, 1970; Patterson and Banker, 1968) which estimate that the approximate life of domestic water heaters (ten to thirteen years at a water-quality level of 200 mg/l TDS) declined by one year for every 200 mg/l additional TDS. A generalised curve developed from these reported data indicated that for an installed heater cost of $100 and interest at 6 per cent, the domestic water heater cost rose from $17 per acre-ft (nearly 1·4 cents per m³) at 200 mg/l TDS to $21 per acre-ft (1·7 cents per m³) at 800 mg/l TDS. These results were expressed on an overall municipal water system basis where the per capita water consumption averaged 0·2 acre-ft (247 m³) annually. Lawrence (1975) also constructed a cost curve indicating damage to domestic plumbing as a function of TDS. The curve itself was based on data from a number of states in the Western USA. A nearly linear curve appeared to rise from $95 per acre-ft (7·7 cents per m³) at 200 mg/l TDS to $106 per acre-ft (nearly 8·6 cents per m³) at 800 mg/l TDS.

IRRIGATION WATER DAMAGES

The chemical and bacteriological quality of water may affect its suitability for irrigation. Polluted water can have adverse effects on crop yields and on irrigation equipment. River water containing detergents has been known to wash out the lubricants from irrigation oscillators and pumps. Very soft waters tend to be acid in character and therefore corrosive; and an excessive amount of suspended solids in the water will necessitate frequent cleaning of the filters and nozzles. Nevertheless, the most serious impacts are likely to occur if the irrigation water is too saline. Salts affect plant growth adversely in a number of ways; they can physically prevent water uptake by plants (osmotic effects); they are able to affect the metabolic reactions of plant (toxic effects); and indirectly they induce changes in soil structure, permeability and aeration. Pinock (1969) has developed an economic analysis of the effects of different levels of water quality on output and income for irrigated agriculture. The author himself warns, however, that physical data relating crop yields to irrigation water quality under field operating conditions are sparse. Thus empirical situations that would permit the establishment of damages and their monetary equivalents relating to different levels of water quality were not used. Instead the study focused on available laboratory experimental work. Crop yields and budgeted income effects were studied for three electrical conductivities of irrigation water; EC = 1·25 (1960), 1·44 (1980) and 1·93 (2010). Two point estimates of salinity damage were reported; in 1980 damages were $1,350, a negligible percentage of the projected total value of output for agriculture in the study district; by the year 2010 damages were expected to increase to $854,679 or a 1·8 per cent reduction in the total value of output in 2010.

An Australian study (Callinan and Webster, 1971) has attempted to estimate farm crop losses and some of the social costs of farm failures due to excessive salinity water conditions. Unfortunately the evaluation procedure used is rather subjective. The authors merely assume that farmer re-establishment costs are fixed amounts per capita and that the corresponding social cost is 25 per cent of the economic cost. Vincent and Russell (1971) present a more comprehensive analysis of saline water damages in the Colorado river basin. This study examines losses to municipal, industrial and agricultural water as well as the indirect economic losses to the regional economy. The upper end of their estimated damage curve terminates at the projected salinity concentration level for 1980 if no salinity control measures are implemented. On this basis damage costs of around $26–7 million are indicated for 1980. Once again due to data deficiencies concerning the full effects of saline water damages the investigators derived their estimates by applying Bayesian probability theory. Thus the cost figures must be considered as only rough orders of magnitude. Moore *et al.* (1974) confirm that the total concentration of dissolved salts expressed in parts per million or electroconductivity has been found to be the most important single criterion of irrigation water quality. The adverse effects of a saline irrigation water can be offset by application of additional amounts of irrigation water. The use of extra water leaches accumulated soils through the root zone but this process requires excellent naturally draining soil or an investment in artificial drainage. Alternatively, by holding the amount of irrigation water applied to a constant level, the growers can either accept a lower yield from a salt-sensitive crop or shift to a lower valued but more salt-tolerant crop. Moore *et al.* (1974) have developed a production function of the following form:

$$y = f(W_q, W_i/K, L, R, \ldots),$$

where W_q = supply of water, W_i = irrigation water quality in terms of EC, K = capital, L = labour, R = rainfall.

The function relates irrigated crop yield to the quality and supply of irrigation water. The study results indicate that a deterioration of the water supply in the Colorado river at Imperial Dam from the current (1974) level of EC = 1·5 to the projected level for the year 2000 of EC = 2·0 would cause a decline in the return to land and water of about 14 per cent for Imperial Valley farmers. Further deterioration of water quality in the lower Colorado river to EC = 3·0 would cause a decline of about 26 per cent in net returns. Since most of the additional salt load in the lower Colorado river is projected to come from additional upstream irrigation development it is possible to value the downstream impact of this external diseconomy. The estimated annual cost to downstream growers in the year 2000 when the projected water quality is likely to be EC = 2·0 would be approximately $7·6 billion. Kneese and Bower (1968) warn, however, that although water-quality deterioration is reflected in crop yields, the extent to which crop yields are reduced overall is a function of a complexity of inter-related factors including climate, soil types and farm management.

INDUSTRIAL INTAKE WATER DAMAGES

It seems generally agreed in the literature (Keese and Bower, 1968; Haveman, 1974; Freeman, 1975) on the basis of limited empirical evidence that the industrial damages from polluted water are not economically significant. Studies made of the petroleum refining, fruit and vegetable canning, thermal power and beet sugar industries confirm that industrial costs are relatively insensitive to intake water quality within comparatively wide ranges. The standard of water quality required depends in part on whether the water is to be used for processing, as boiler feedwater, for cooling or for sanitary purposes. Feedwater for high pressure, high temperature boilers requires a very high quality standard; concentrations of total dissolved solids for such use are stringently controlled. On the other hand it has been argued that cooling water can be of almost any quality level with respect to total dissolved solids and even biological oxygen demand. The Appalachian Regional Commission (1969) in the USA sponsored a study of the economic damages due to excess acidity in the intake water. Damage impacts such as excess treatment costs and boiler replacement costs were quantified. The study used linear damage curves to relate acidity levels of intake water to costs of lime neutralisation. The linearity assumption in the damage estimates, however, was not apparently tested by empirical observations.

Lawrence (1975) has constructed a generalised graphical relationship between total dissolved solids levels in intake water and industrial damage costs. The principal effects, he argues, of high TDS *per se* are increased potentials for corrosion, dezinclification, and some increased costs for cooling water systems and industrial processing. Thus boiler feed, cooling tower make-up and industrial process water usually require specific treatment, e.g. softening, de-alkalising, demineralisation or ameliorative additives, or any combination of the four. A linear relationship was assumed between industrial water treatment costs and TDS, corresponding to about $11 per acre-ft (0·9 cents per m^3) at 200 mg/l TDS and $44 per acre-ft (3·6 cents per m^3) at 800 mg/l TDS. Lawrence (1975) also presented a total impact cost curve for urban consumers, including both industrial and non-industrial users. The curve was developed for a range of TDS between 200 mg/l and 800 mg/l and a range of total hardness (TH) between 100 mg/l and 400 mg/l. In 1974 conditions total costs in the Los Angeles River Planning Study Area were estimated to range between about $25 per acre-ft (2·0 cents per m^3) per 100 mg/l TDS at the low TDS range and about $35 per acre-ft (2·8 cents per m^3) per 100 mg/l TDS at the high TDS range. Since the Lawrence study used data gathered from a range of previous damage studies, its accuracy is dependent on the degree of subjectivity used in the original studies. Thus, as Lawrence himself points out, the cost curves should only be considered as approximations to the real indirect quality related costs to urban consumers resulting from water use.

COMMERCIAL FISHING DAMAGE COSTS

Water pollution can adversely affect commercial fisheries production in a number of ways: the spawning runs of fish like salmon and herring can be reduced or even destroyed; toxic pollutants can damage estuarine areas which may be the basis of the food chain for fish; finally while the fish may survive the pollution they are often so contaminated as to be unfit for human consumption. Kneese and Bower (1968) note that the impacts of various pollutants on selected species of fish have been the subject of many investigations which unfortunately have yielded a wide variety of results. The impact of the pollutants on fish populations varies with the physical and chemical composition of the water. Synergistic effects can result in large fish kills but can also produce converse results in certain circumstances. Kneese and Bower (1968) conclude that the most important factor in determining aquatic life tolerance to pollutants is the time-concentration relationship.

Tihansky (1975) has surveyed a number of estimates that have been made in the USA of total national fish losses (dockside revenue) from DDT, mercury and pathogenic organism pollution. The damage estimates currently available must, he argues, be judged highly conjectural as fish kills have not been carefully monitored. Holden and Caines (1974) while examining the nutrient status of Loch Leven, a shallow lake in east Scotland, reported that due to the eutrophic state of the water, annual fish catches (trout) have declined from a maximum of almost 90,000 in 1960 to less than 20,000 in 1970. This decline has been paralleled by the increased eutrophication of the loch waters.

AESTHETIC AND RECREATIONAL DAMAGE COSTS

While it is generally agreed in the literature on water pollution that some of the significant losses associated with this pollution are those related to aesthetics and recreation, it is, nevertheless, recognised that water quality is only one of a range of variables that influence water-based recreational demand. Knetsch (1974), for example, argues that the availability of alternative recreational facilities is probably the most important determinant of recreational response to a particular site and not small changes in water quality. The majority of the early attempts to measure recreational losses or benefits were all derived from the distance-based demand curve model exemplified by the work of Clawson and Knetsch (1971) and Merewitz (1966). All these early studies, however, fail to include any kind of water-quality parameter (the exception being the Stevens, 1966, 1967 model). They therefore provide no evidence on the differential willingness of participants to pay for generalised recreation under differing water-quality conditions.

In general, while a fairly extensive literature exists, precise quantitative evidence on the water-quality dose-response relationship remains limited. Ideally in order to construct recreational demand curves as functions of water quality one needs to correlate variables such as visit rate data or recreational sports club membership with cross-sectional and time series differences in water quality. While it is true that water quality in general has been and is monitored to some extent, visit rates have not been. One of the earliest attempts to quantify the recreational benefits of hypothesised improvement in water quality appears in the Delaware Estuary Comprehensive Study (FWPCA, 1966). This study suggests that more than 95 per cent of the clean-up benefits were due to the Delaware river's recreational potential. In a study of the Lake d'Annecy site in France, Deportes (1972) claims to have established, on the basis of time series data, a negative relationship between a decline in water quality and adjusted tourist visitation data. In fact, the study does not contain hard data on the volume of tourists over a period of years. Instead the author relies on proxy variables such as variations in the volume of road traffic around the lake. The reliability of these proxy variables, however, is not sufficient to establish any firm negative relationship between declining water quality and reduced tourist volume. Further, rough evidence is presented in an Italian study (Muraro, 1974) which examined five major lakes in northern Italy. The difference between tourist activity rates (number of tourist days) in polluted and non-polluted areas was established and then evaluated at some subjective price per activity-day. Insufficient detail was presented to assess adequately the methodology used but one could question how exactly a 'suitable value' was arrived at to price each activity-day; and how far the approach adjusted for the many other factors likely to affect tourist demand.

The US National Commission on Water Quality (1975) argued that participants in water-based recreation would be major beneficiaries of the improved water quality implicit in the 1972 US Federal Water Pollution Control Act Amendments. The Commission undertook a series of national surveys to determine the full benefits different groups would receive from the improved water quality. Nationally, it was estimated that if all the beaches currently closed to swimming (lake, river and ocean swimming) as a result of water pollution were to be opened this could provide up to 121 million additional swimming days during the summer season. Both freshwater fishing and boating were also predicted to increase substantially as a result of the 1972 Act.

The Clawson–Knetsch (1971) model can, in principle, provide a measurement of the recreational benefits or losses due to water quality changes but only in an *ex-post* sense. One would need to know the visit rate before and after a change in water quality at a particular site. The *post* water-quality change demand curve should be above (below) and to the right (left) of the *pre* water quality change demand curve depending on whether water pollution improves or deteriorates.

Following the method of Mäler (1971), the recreational benefits or losses would be equal to the area between the two demand curves (ABDC) in Figure 5.1.

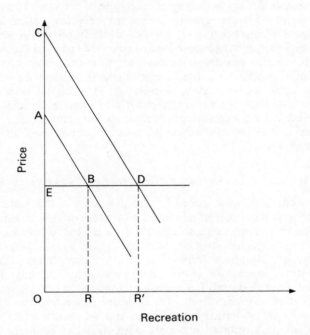

Figure 5.1 *Recreational benefits from water quality improvement*

Mäler argues that where a public good (water quality, in terms of its impact on fish stocks) is complementary to a private consumption good (sports fishing) the benefits of increasing water quality can be estimated from information on the private good's demand. In Figure 5.1, assume the income compensated demand curve for fishing shifts from AB to CD due to an improvement in water quality. Thus in theoretical terms the physical recreational response to the given water-quality change is BD and the monetary evaluation (consumer surplus) of this response is ACDB. In the real world concealed in this shift from point B to D are some formidable scientific and pyschological data constraints. Empirically we need to know what the precise effects of a particular pollution emission are on water quality. Further, we would like to know precisely the differential physical response of participants under improving and deteriorating water-quality conditions. Considerable empirical evidence is required (and so far has not been forthcoming) on participant perceptions of and reactions to different types of water pollution – i.e. suspended solids, dissolved oxygen deficiency, etc. Russell (1972) argues that participant response to changes in water quality is probably conditioned by the joint effect of the changing mix of recreation activities enjoyed with changing water-quality conditions and the simultaneously changing quality of each type of activity experience. In general terms, if water-quality levels are very low, often the only activity possible is boating. If quality levels improve, however, the boating experience may become more enjoyable (due to the reduction of river odour, for example). At the same time the water may now be capable of supporting a limited range of coarse fish species which will stimulate some sports angling activity. At even higher water-quality levels the full range of water-contact activities and trout fishing would be stimulated. Thus a continuum of recreational demand curves will be associated with the continuum of possible environmental (water-) quality states.

WATER QUALITY STANDARDS AND QUALITY PERCEPTION

A fundamental question posed by the inclusion of the water-quality variable is just what empirical measure of water quality is appropriate in a given recreation demand model? It is probably true to say that the value of water for any single recreational use will depend on a number of quality characteristics. To further complicate matters, an increase in the magnitude of one quality characteristic may affect one recreational use favourably while simultaneously affecting an alternative recreation use negatively. Thus higher water temperatures may make for better swimming conditions but adversely affect trout or salmon fishing. A reduced industrial acid emission level will improve the fishing potential of a river but may not improve swimming prospects due to possible stimulation of algae growth and consequent 'green slime' water conditions. A minimum water-quality standard for recreation would be water free from floating or suspended solids, objectionable colours and foul odours. At this minimum quality-level boating would be tolerable. For water-contact recreation the water quality would need to be higher and while meeting boating standards should also be relatively free from pathogenic organisms and contain no toxic substances. It is not possible to move very far from the level of generality in this discussion of water-quality measures because of the complexity and data limitation constraints. In an authoritative survey McKee and Wolfe (1963) confirm that there is a distinct lack of firm evidence concerning the relationship between water quality and its effect on swimmers.

Water-quality criteria and standards, while perhaps technically adequate for the recreation user's health and safety, may not necessarily guarantee the qualities that attract or deter potential recreational users.

The National Commission on Water Quality (1975) has attempted to determine a relationship between water quality and human perceptions of water quality. Survey research was apparently used to develop a 'perceived water-quality index'. No detail is given by the commission of the index itself and other similar attempts to construct such an index by different researchers have not been conspicuously successful. A number of writers have made preliminary studies of recreationalists' water-quality perceptions and how their perceptions influence the type and frequency of recreational activity (Barker, 1967; Bishop and Aukerman, 1970; David, 1971; Simpson and Kamitakahara, 1971; Ditton and Goodale, 1973; Dornbusch and Barrager, 1973). The David (1971) study results suggest that the presence of algae is the most important indication of pollution to most people, with dark, cloudy and murky water being ranked second in importance. Dornbusch and Barrager (1973), using an interview survey, claim to have established that the majority of residents living near a water resource are aware of any improvement in water quality that takes place. The two researchers had to abandon the attempt to construct a water-quality index, however, because of the familiar data constraints. Other investigators (Willeke, 1968) recognised that non-users also perceive the environment in certain ways and act on these perceptions. Willeke examined the relationship between the perceived pollution of San Francisco Bay and its use for major recreation activities. He surveyed representative samples rather than just recreation participant samples. Ditton and Goodale (1973) investigated the Green Bay area on Lake Michigan. This bay has been used for commercial fishing, shipping, recreation and as a waste sink. As a result of pollution several water uses in the area – domestic water supply, body-contact water recreation and sport fishing – have been impaired. The Green Bay study attempted to identify how people perceived the bay as a recreation resource, how these perceptions differed between groups, and how these perceptions related to recreation use patterns. The researchers claim that participants and those who use the bay were less apt to cite characteristics such as unpleasant smell and dead fish as major problems and more apt to cite such problems as winds, waves and cloudiness. Perceptions also differed among user groups with swimmers and boaters differing most and fishermen occupying a position between the two groups. Kneese (1968) and Freeman (1975) both conclude that the difficulties in tracing out the scientific effects of a pollution emission on the many parameters of water quality and, in turn, their effects on recreationists' perception of quality and use of water, plus the limited progress achieved to date in this area, substantially constrain the effectiveness of water-quality improvement cost-benefit studies.

In the face of the scientifically and psychologically complex set of problems set by water-quality parameters and human perception of such parameters, many cost-benefit studies have fallen back on the use of DO as their sole index of water pollution. A group of inter-related studies (Davidson, Adams and Seneca, 1966; Tomazinis and Gabbour, 1967) investigating pollution and recreation on the Delaware river are prime examples of DO-based water quality models. Davidson *et al.* (1966) recognised that many conditions affect water quality, but for pragmatic reasons used DO as a first approximation of an index of water quality. They postulate that at least 3 mg/l of oxygen are necessary for sport fishing and 5 mg/l for swimming. Ackerman (1974) points out that the DO parameter does indeed have an impact on several important river uses and, moreover, is measurable, thereby fitting neatly into any modelling process. Nevertheless, Ackerman stresses that it is a recognised fact that DO alone, while being a necessary indicator, is far from a sufficient indicator of water quality. Although a DO level near zero and the resulting odour inhibits any form of recreational activity, a higher DO level does not necessarily indicate that the river is suitable for recreation. A relatively high DO level will not ensure that the water looks clean to the typical swimmer, fisherman or boater. As David (1971) pointed out, murky water is perceived to mean polluted water in many people's minds. Dark murky water is in fact mainly the result of turbidity conditions and not DO levels.

CLAWSON–KNETSCH-TYPE MODELS INCORPORATING THE WATER-QUALITY VARIABLE

Stevens (1966), when analysing a sports fishing resource (Yaquina Bay, Oregon), defined water quality as the number of fish caught per angler-trip, or the success/effort ratio. Stevens first estimated Clawson–Knetsch-type demand equations for three types of fishing activity assuming a given level of water quality. He then regressed a fishing participation rate variable (total angling effort) on an income variable and a per capita daily fishing cost variable. A deterioration in water quality is assumed to inhibit angling success (Stevens subjectively assumes a 50 per cent reduction in angling success in his model). Two types of data were used to construct the *pre* and *post* water-quality change angling demand curves; time series data from other sport-fishing areas along the Oregon coast and cross-sectional data derived from a mail questionnaire. The losses due to the deterioration in water quality can be estimated from the difference between the two demand curves derived from total angling effort before and after the change in quality.

Reiling *et al.* (1973) in similar fashion to Stevens used the consumer surplus method of estimating recreation benefits in a study of Upper Klamath Lake, Oregon. The researchers used subjectively determined 'use-intensity level' variables for swimming, boating, water-skiing and fishing in order to indicate the desirability of the site for that activity.

A participation variable was then regressed on travel cost, on-site cost and use-intensity levels variables. In order to compute the likely benefits from a given improvement in water quality the researchers merely substituted higher values of the use-intensity variables in the equation. Actual water-quality changes were analysed in a two-step procedure. First, the removal of blue-green algae was hypothesised to increase boating and water-skiing activities. Subsequent decreases in water temperature and cleaner beach areas were then expected to increase swimming and fishing participation rates. Oxygen deficiency was not considered on the grounds that participants' perception of it was apparently marginal.

Burt (1969) has argued that Stevens' definition of welfare change in his original study is incorrect and that his methodology is logically invalid. Moreover, neither the Stevens nor the Reiling model contains a satisfactory solution to the water-quality selection and impact problems. Neither model contains a sufficient basis for relating changes in its water-quality measure to varying pollution emissions; or for establishing recreationist perception of and response to changes in quality. Stevens merely assumes that pollution leads to a 50 per cent reduction in angling success. Reiling *et al.* (1973) go directly to use-intensity variables in order to establish a relationship between recreational demand and changes in water quality.

PRIVATE LAND VALUES AND THE WATER-QUALITY VARIABLE

David (1968) has attempted to test the proposition that an individual's willingness to pay for an improved water-quality level will be equal to the marginal differential in waterside property rents, with respect to water quality. David claims that substantial property on the shoreline of the lake study areas was positively correlated with good water-quality conditions and higher property values. The quality variable used by David, however, was based only on cross-section data. A multiple-site property value model has also been constructed for the US Environmental Protection Agency by Dornbusch and Barrager (1973). There are a number of operational drawbacks to the use of this type of model. Where resources are open both to private use, benefits associated with the latter use will not be reflected in waterside property values. The property evaluation process itself and the large number of variables that can be expected to influence land values also present difficulties. David's quality variable was derived from a judgemental measure of pollution of the lakewater provided by officials of state agencies. Leaving on one side the complexities of defining the water-quality variable, it is still an open question as to whether the official criteria for classification coincided with those factors which influence potential property owners' perception of water quality.

PUBLIC RECREATION EXPENDITURE VALUATION AND THE WATER-QUALITY VARIABLE

Russell (1972) sees the collective evaluation of a recreation resource that is available to users at a zero price as the outcome of a kind of balancing process, given that the total participant body is made of separate interest groups, swimmers, fishermen, etc. For this reason Russell utilises data that already reflect some collective political evaluation process – i.e. a municipality parks and recreation expenditure budget. It is possible to interpret these data as a measure of the municipal benefits of water-quality improvements in fact foregone. The budget would represent some upper limit on a municipality's evaluation of the recreation benefits yielded by a water-quality improvement programme. An attempt was made to test this hypothesis empirically using water-quality data for adjacent rivers to explain the residual variation in municipal recreation budgets (allowing for the effects of socioeconomic variables). In the small fifteen-city sample tested, no significant relation was found between residual variation in the per capita recreation budget and DO- and coliform-bacteria-based water-quality variables.

INTERVIEW TECHNIQUES AND THEIR LIMITATIONS

In a number of studies recreation participants are asked how often they would have used a particular water resource if water quality had been high. By comparing the responses to the questionnaire with existing visitation rates (at current, lower levels of water quality) an estimate can be made of the increased rate of participation. The problems with the technique are how to induce respondents to give unbiased answers to questions about their willingness to pay for recreation; and how to structure questions concerning changes in water quality that do not pose over-hypothetical and probably difficult-to-visualise alternatives to the interviewees. Bohm (1971) suggests that the bias problem could be overcome by leaving the individuals questioned uncertain how, if at all, their response might affect their liability to pay. Tideman (1971) believes it may be possible to design suitable questionnaires so that one, known to yield underestimates, could be applied to one random sample of participants at the same time as another, known to yield overestimates, is applied to a second random sample. The two sets of results should then yield an interval which contains the true willingness to pay for recreation (with a certain probability). Both the Bohm and Tideman approaches, however, require fairly sophisticated respondents acting in a totally rational manner.

PARTICIPATION-PROBABILITY MODELS

This approach does not attempt to estimate a fully identified recreation demand curve, but instead relies on reduced form prediction equations. It is assumed that improvements in water quality increase the supply of recreation sites and so-called participation rates. The recreation benefits, however, can only be evaluated by inferring from some exogenous source the value of a recreation day. The Delaware Estuary Study (FWPCA, 1966) utilised participation rate data compiled by a special Outdoor Recreation Resources Review Commission (ORRRC, 1962) in order to aid the estimation of the water-based recreational demand of the population in its study area. The Delaware study produced estimates of the quantifiable recreational benefits yielded by five hypothesised water-quality programmes on the Delaware river.

A second participation rate model for the Delaware constructed by Davidson *et al.* (1966) incorporated its own survey to obtain estimates of participation probability as a function of several socioeconomic and physical variables. The Davidson model predicts a substantial increase in recreational demand (with the exception of swimming) due to improvements in water quality as reflected by increased water-site availability. Russell (1972) criticises the Davidson study on the grounds that only discrete improvements in water quality are allowed for. What the model fails to pick up, Russell argues, is the continuously changing quality of the specific recreation activity itself. Tihansky (1975) comments that the crude assumption, implicit in the Davidson model (and other participation rate models), that recreation demand will increase in proportion to water availability is convenient but remains to be proven. Further, the model's index of the adequacy of recreational facilities is interpreted rather subjectively. Nevertheless, the Davidson model does incorporate to some extent the problem of alternative and competing resources which Knetsch (1974) stresses. The Delaware study absolutely fails systematically to take into account this availability variable.

Improvements in water quality do represent increases in the supply of water-based recreational resources but the crucial factor, however, is the magnitude of the change in quality. Small improvements in existing levels of water quality result in participation cost reductions for already existing recreational experiences. Substantial improvements in water quality may well be perceived to yield recreational opportunities that are significantly different to existing possibilities. Ackerman (1974) argued that the DECS grossly overestimates pollution clean-up benefits because it underestimates the recreational opportunities already open to the population of the study area. Given the full range of recreational opportunities, any newly created estuarine recreation opportunities (due to reduced pollution) merely represent lower cost alternatives to already existing facilities.

In the Cicchetti *et al.* (1969) participation-probability model participation rates are explained by means of a two-step procedure. In the first step an attempt was made to determine the conditional probability for participation in a specific activity. The researchers admit, however, that data constraints made it impossible to determine precisely the specific recreational opportunities open to an individual. As a second-best solution a general inventory of factors such as water acreage and miles to the nearest large body of water by county thoughout the USA was compiled. The second step of the analysis involves the determination of the level of participation for all those individuals previously determined to be participants in a particular activity. A number of significant relations were then established between certain variables and observed variations in participation levels. It appeared that the regions which possessed relatively large quantities of high quality recreation water recorded a greater number of swimming activity-days. The presence of large quantities of water not suitable for swimming but adequate for other water-related recreation resulted in a relative decrease in the number of swimming-days per participant. Both the county and state acres of polluted recreation per water capita variables had a negative effect on fishing activity, Mäler and Wyzga (1976) have constructed a general theoretical model which also attempts to take into account the problem of alternative and competing resources. The informational requirement of this model, however, would appear to be some way in excess of current or even likely medium-term data capacities.

Three basic problems remain to be overcome systematically. We need a more complete understanding of the links between many water-quality parameters and pollution discharge rates. Much evidence is still required before we are able to select the appropriate water-quality variables for use in any benefit-cost model. We still do not know with any certainty what indices of water quality are relevant to the different recreational and other uses of water. Finally, it is not clear how recreation participants in particular will respond to changes in different quality parameters. The US National Commission on Water Quality summarised the state of the art accurately. It concluded that 'fundamental source materials for characterising recreational behaviour, identifying the determinants of such behaviour and documentary linkages between water quality and recreation frequently are incomplete, compiled on an inappropriate basis or out of date. The development of the relevant theoretical considerations and empirical procedures is in its infancy. Should there be continued interest in information relating to the quantification of economic impacts of water quality changes in leisure time activity, a basic and comprehensive data collection and analysis programme needs to be initiated.' While damage studies for other water uses have been based on a sounder conceptual basis, data collection and evaluation procedures remain deficient.

REFERENCES

Ackerman, B., *et al.*, *The Uncertain Search for Environmental Quality: The Costs and Benefits of Controlling Pollution Along the Delaware Estuary* (New York: Free Press, 1974).

Appalachian Regional Commission, *Acid Maine Drainage in Appalachia*, vol. 1 (Washington DC: 1969).

Amstrong, N. E., 'Steps to understanding ecological assessment of pollution', in *Water Quality Management and Pollution Control Problems*, ed. S. H. Jenkins (Oxford: Pergamon Press, 1973).

Barker, M. L., 'The perception of water quality as a factor in consumer attitudes and space preferences in outdoor recreation', MA thesis, Department of Geography, University of Toronto, Toronto.

Bayley, R. W., 'Nitrogen and phosphorus removal: methods and costs', *Water Treatment and Examination*, vol. 19, 1970, pp. 294–319.

Beresford, J. C., 'Use of hospital costs in planning', in *The Economics of Medical Care*, ed. M. Hauser (London: Allen & Unwin, 1972).

Bishop, D. W. and Aukerman, R., 'Water quality criteria for selected recreational uses', Research Report 33 (Urbana: Water Resources Centre, University of Illinois, 1970).

David, E. C., 'Public perceptions of water quality', *Water Resources Research*, vol. 7, no. 3, 1971.

Davidson, P., *et al.*, 'The social value of water recreational facilities resulting from an improvement in water quality: the Delaware estuary', in *Water Research*, ed. A. V. Kneese, and S. C. Smith (Baltimore: Johns Hopkins Press, 1966).

Deportes, J. P., 'Problèmes économiques liés a l'assainissement du lac d'Annécy' (Thonon: Institut National de la Recherche Agronomique, Station d'hydrobiologie lacustre, 1972).

Dinius, H., 'Social accounting systems for evaluating water resources', *Water Resources Research*, vol. 8, no. 5, 1972.

Ditton, R. B. and Goodale, T. L., 'Water quality perception and the recreational uses of Green Bay, Lake Michigan', *Water Resources Research*, vol. 9, no. 3, 1973.

Dodson, W. G., *An Examination of the Economic Impact of Pollution Control upon Georgia's Water Using Industries* (Washington DC: US Office of Water Resources Research, 1973).

Dornsbusch, D. M. and Barrager, S., *Benefits of Water Pollution Control on Property Values* (Washington DC: US Environment Protection Agency, 1973).

Federal Water Pollution Control Administration, *Delaware Estuary Comprehensive Study; Preliminary Report and Findings* (Philadelphia: US Department of the Interior, 1966).

Freeman, A. M., 'A survey of the technique for measuring the benefits of water quality improvement', in *Cost-Benefit Analysis and Water Pollution Policy*, ed. H. M. Peskin and E. P. Seskin (Washington DC: The Urban Institute, 1975).

Goodman, A. H., 'Potable water is not pure but it must be wholesome – how do we make it so?', in *Agriculture and Water Quality*, Ministry of Agriculture, Fisheries and Food Technical Bulletin 32 (London: HMSO, 1975).

Haith, D. A., 'Land use and water quality in New York rivers', *Journal of Environmental Engineering Division, Proceedings of the American Society of Civil Engineers*, 1976.

Haveman, R., 'On estimating environmental damage: a survey of recent research in the US', in *Environmental Damage Costs*, OECD (Paris: OECD, 1974).

Henderson, J. M., 'Water pollution – facts and fantasies', *Journal of Sanitary Engineering Division, Proceedings of the American Society of Civil Engineers*, vol. 98, 1972.

Holden, A. V. and Caines, L.A., 'Nutrient chemistry of Loch Leven, Kinross', in *Proceedings of the Royal Society of Edinburgh* (Edinburgh: 1974).

Kinnersly, D. J., 'Water pollution', in *After Keynes*, ed. J. Robinson (Oxford: Basil Blackwell, 1973).

Kneese, A. V., 'Economics and the quality of the environment: some empirical experiences', in *Social Sciences and the Environment*, ed. M. Garnsey and J. Gibbs (Boulder: University of Colorado Press, 1968).

Kneese, A. V. and Bower, B., *Managing Water Quality: Economics, Technology, Institutions* (Baltimore: Resources for the Future, John Hopkins Press, 1968).

Knetsch, J. L., *Outdoor Recreation and Water Resources Planning* (Washington DC: American Geophysical Union, 1974).

Lackner, J. and Sokoloski, A. A., 'Safe drinking water act of 1973: estimates of benefits and costs' (Washington DC: Environmental Protection Agency, 1973).

Lawrence, C. H., 'Estimating indirect costs of urban water use', *Journal of Environmental Engineering Division, Proceedings of the American Society of Civil Engineers,* 1975.

Leeds, Hill and Jewett, Inc., *Need for Dilution of Colorado River Water,* report to San Diego County Water Authority (San Diego: San Diego County Water Authority, 1963).

Leeds, Hill and Jewett, Inc., 'Consumer Costs as Related to Quality of Water Supply', report to Santa Ana Watershed Planning Agency (Santa Ana: Santa Ana Watershed Planning Agency, 1970).

Liu, O. C., *Proposal on Research of Enteric Virus-Related Diseases'* (Washington DC: Environmental Protection Agency, 1973).

Lyon, W. A., 'Water and health – are we concerned enough?', *Journal of Sanitary Engineering Division, Proceedings of the American Society of Civil Engineers,* 1970.

Mäler, K. G., 'A method of estimating social benefits from pollution control', *Swedish Journal of Economics,* 1971.

Mäler, K. G. and Wyzga, R. E., *Economic Measurement of Environmental Damage* (Paris: OECD, 1976).

McKee, J. E. and Wolf, H. W., *Water Quality Criteria* (Sacramento: State Water Resources Control Board California, 1963).

Moore, C. V., *et. al.,* 'Effects of Colorado river water quality and supply on irrigated agriculture', *Water Resources Research,* vol. 10, no. 2, 1974.

Muraro, G., 'Estimate of the economic damage caused by pollution: the Italian experience', in *Environmental Damage Costs,* OECD (Paris: OECD, 1974).

National Commission on Water Quality, 'Staff draft report' (Washington DC: US Government Printing Office, 1975).

Outdoor Recreation Resources Review Commission, 'Outdoor recreation resources review commission reports', nos 19, 20, 26 (Washington DC: US Government Printing Office, 1962).

Patterson, W. L. and Banker, R. F., 'Effects of highly mineralised water on household plumbing and appliances', *Journal of the American Water Works Association,* vol. 60, no. 9, 1968.

Pinock, M. G., 'Assessing impacts of declining water quality on gross value output of agriculture', *Water Resources Research,* vol. 5, no. 1, 1969.

Reiling, D., *et al.* 'Economic benefits from an improvement in water quality' (Washington DC: Environmental Protection Agency, 1973).

Russell, C. S., 'Municipal evaluation of regional water quality management', in *Models for Managing Regional Water Quality,* ed. H. Jacoby and H. Thomas (Massachusetts: Harvard University Press, 1972).

Schroeder, H. A., 'Relation between mortality from cardiovascular disease and treated water supplies', *Journal of the American Medical Association,* 1960.

Simpson, W. G. and Kamitakahara, G. K., *Opinions on Recreation and Pollution in Lake Ontario* (Toronto: University of Toronto Great Lakes Institute, 1971).

Stevens, J. B., 'Recreation benefits from water pollution control', *Water Resources Research,* vol. 2, no. 2, 1966.

Stevens, J. B. 'Recreation benefits from water pollution control: a further note on benefit evaluation', *Water Resources Research,* vol. 3, no. 1, 1967.

Sumner, M. E., '*Further Investigations into Nitrate Pollution of Chalk Borehole Water Supplies',* (Scunthorpe: North Lindsey Water Board, 1973).

Tideman, T. N., 'The efficient provision of public goods', in *Public Prices for Public Products,* ed. S. J. Mushkin (Washington DC: The Urban Institute, 1972).

Tihansky, D. P., 'Economic damages from residential use of mineralised water supply', *Water Resources Research*, vol. 10, 1974.

Tihansky, D. P., 'A survey of empirical benefit studies', in *Cost-Benefit Analysis and Water Pollution Policy*, ed. H. M. Peskin and E. P. Seskin (Washington DC: The Urban Institute, 1975).

Tomazinis, A. R. and Gabbour, I., *Water-Oriented Recreation Benefits: A Study of the Recreation Benefits Derivable from Various Levels of Water Quality of the Delaware River* (Philadelphia: University of Pennsylvannia Institute for Environmental Studies, 1967).

Vincent, J. R. and Russell, J. D., 'Alternatives for salinity management in the Colorado river basin', *Water Resources Bulletin*, vol. 7, no. 4, 1971.

Whiteley, V. and Dendy, B. B., 'Conceptual problems in water quality economics', *Journal of Sanitary Engineering Division, Proceedings of the American Society of Civil Engineers*, 1968.

Willeke, E., 'Effects of water pollution in San Francisco Bay', Report EEP-29 (Stanford: Stanford University, 1968).

Wzga, R., 'A survey of environmental damage functions', in *Environmental Damage Costs*, OECD (Paris: OECD, 1974).

Chapter 6

Human Life and Suffering

INTRODUCTION

This chapter is concerned with some of the attempts that have been made to place a value on human life and suffering. Most of the research in this field has been concerned with mortality rather than morbidity and it is consequently life and death, rather than injury and non-fatal illness, which is the main issue discussed, although many of the approaches apply whether or not death or risk of death is involved. The interest and the literature in evaluation of life and limb has been growing rapidly in the last decade but since much of it, particularly the older literature, is somewhat repetitive this chapter does not attempt to review it comprehensively. (For more extensive reviews see Jones-Lee, 1976, and Mooney, 1977.)

Most of the more recent research in this field has adopted a consumer sovereignty view of cost-benefit analysis, adopting the dictum that the consumer knows his own best good. While this has an intellectual appeal to it (and the author has to declare his somewhat muted support of it – muted because of the realities of decision making in such policy areas as health care and safety legislation), it is not the sole criterion on which cost-benefit studies and hence valuation procedures can rest (see Nash *et al.* 1975). Consequently the next section attempts to examine the relevance of this particular view of cost-benefit analysis to the areas of policy making most concerned with the saving of life and the reduction of morbidity.

In the section dealing with 'Methods of Valuation', various approaches to valuation of life are examined. The human capital approach to valuation, the one most frequently found in practice, is discussed and some of the problems associated with it are highlighted. The approach, which examines *ex-post* the implicit values in public decision making, is then considered and the virtue of consistency in life valuation is developed. Some of the more recent attempts to switch the emphasis to a probability framework, i.e. risk of death, are examined. After looking briefly at the question of non-fatal illness and injury, some conclusions on the value of the research in the field to date are drawn in the final section.

In examining different approaches to valuation of life and suffering there are a number of issues which are important. First, on what principles does the approach stand? Thirdly, what are the advantages of its use?

In considering these aspects there are a number of objectives to be borne in mind in attempting to value life and suffering. There is of course the primary question of how much as a society we are prepared to spend on various policies for the saving of life or reduction in risk of death and decreases in morbidity and injury. But in addition there is the extra dimension of the non-homogeneity of the outputs involved. 'Lives saved' or increases in life expectancy and the quality of life involved are very different outputs in a project involving renal dialysis from what they are in the Green Cross Code road safety publicity directed at children. Despite this there is a need for consistency in terms of opportunity cost across the whole field of life-saving policies. Like lives saved should be valued alike. Further, the outputs can be defined in different ways. For example, road improvements may result in the saving of life, the reduction of risk of death and/or the reduction in anxiety (or increased peace of mind) associated with driving. Does a publicity campaign which raises the level of perception of risk for elderly pedestrians in crossing the road necessarily result in a positive benefit if it saves lives but at the same time increases the anxiety level of the elderly pedestrian?

These issues all relate to the question of the appropriate social welfare function (SWF). Different SWFs arise as the objectives of policy change. It is possible to argue the merits of different objectives and, having examined various approaches to life valuation, some of the more important aspects of the appropriate SWFs in different circumstances will be discussed.

SOME BASIC QUESTIONS

It is usually assumed in cost-benefit analysis that it is the consumer who is the best judge of the utility which he obtains from a particular good or service. From this notion of consumer sovereignty it is assumed that the relevant questions to be posed are to the consumers themselves. Thus, in attempting to decide whether or not society is likely to be better off if a particular project is undertaken, it is to those affected, in terms of both benefits and costs, that we should turn to determine the values to be placed on the benefits and costs. Thus if an individual is made better off by the undertaking of a particular project, the relevant measure of the value to him is his compensating variation, i.e. the maximum sum he would be prepared to pay rather than forgo the benefits to him of the project being considered.

But such an approach implies many prior judgements. First, it assumes that the consumer *is* the best person to make the necessary value judgements. Secondly, it is assumed that the individual *believes* he is the best person. Thirdly, it is assumed that the individual *can* make the judgements and fourthly, it assumes that the individual *wants* to make the value judgements.

Now in the context of valuation of life some of these assumptions are questionable. Many of the public sector areas which are concerned in some way at least with valuation of life are not subject to the degree of consumer sovereignty which the normal theory of cost-benefit analysis assumes. A listing of some of the areas involved – health care, road safety, fire prevention, crime prevention, siting of nuclear power stations and building regulations – indicates immediately that questions of public goods, merit goods, paternalism and consumer ignorance arise in many of these policy areas.

This means that the application of cost-benefit analysis is not as straightforward in valuing life and suffering as it perhaps is in other cases (although some of the same problems are of a more general nature). Let us examine health care as an example.

Health care in the United Kingdom is provided almost wholly within the national health service. For the individual consumer of health care, the choices he can exercise are limited. He has the choice to consult a doctor or not; he has, within limits, the choice to accept or reject a doctor's advice and treatment; he seldom has any choice regarding the nature of the treatment; and beyond withdrawing from the process he has little choice as to the extent of treatment (and in some instances even withdrawal is difficult).

The output of the health care system is composed of increased life expectancy, decreased morbidity and increased comfort and mobility. In many instances, however, the consumer has little knowledge either of his present state of ill health or his future state of health, with or without treatment. His perception is generally poor and as a result it can be argued that part of the output of the health care system is information. But how can the rational consumer form judgements about the value of health care if part of the output of the health care industry is itself providing information about the rest of the output? For example, a woman who attends a clinic for cervical cancer screening is dependent on medical advice as to the likely effects of screening.

Against such a background to what extent should consumer sovereignty be applied to health care and other areas of life saving? There does not appear to be any definitive view that one can take on this which is devoid of value judgements. While this is unexceptional the nature of the underlying value judgements are of some importance.

Is the individual consumer the best person to make the necessary value judgements? These value judgements relate to two factors – first the nature and quantity of the output and secondly the value of the output. Now in many instances the individual can be provided with information about the nature and quantity of the output by the relevant experts. For example, much of the publicity aimed at the prevention of accidents and illness is not so much directed at raising the level of expected utility associated with particular goods or services but rather providing information about the nature of the outputs involved, e.g. using statistics to indicate the effect on injury probabilities of wearing a seat belt or the increased mortality risk associated with smoking. In addition information can be provided to allow individuals to form better judgements about the value of the outputs. Again, using the same examples, publicity on seat belts has used individuals injured in accidents to make statements such as 'I wish I'd worn my seat belt'. Anti-smoking publicity has indicated the difficulties involved in becoming romantically attached if an individual smells of cigarette smoke.

But individuals may well be myopic and even if they appear to accept the evidence they may choose, perhaps rightly, to ignore it. They may believe that the risks involved are so small or so distant that no change in behaviour is justified. Yet a government which has to face a situation in which about 7,000 people die on the roads each year has greater difficulty in dismissing risks as negligible or distant.

In such circumstances the government may decide that it cannot accept the misperceptions of individuals either as to the nature and level of the outputs involved or as to the value attached to such outputs. For example, in the United Kingdom the government has made it illegal to ride a motorcycle without a crash helmet. (Of course, there are instances where the government legislates because externalities are important, e.g. in public health legislation, but externalities in the case of crash helmets are relatively small.)

The issue of the measurement of risk in life and health threatening situations is an important one. We can draw a distinction between two types of measurement of risk. There is the classical or frequency notion of probability. This type of probability is normally exemplified by dice throwing or coin tossing and assumes that there is a finite number of well-defined possible outcomes, many repeated trials which are independent of one another and resultant frequencies for the known possible outcomes.

But there is also the concept of risk of probability based on individuals' judgements and perceptions, e.g. the probability of rain on a particular day. This requires little or much information on the part of the individual, depending on how important it is to him to make an accurate judgement.

In the context of life saving, while there is no exact parallel with the former type of risk, none the less as an approximation to it there is, for example, the Department of Transport's 'objective' assessment, based on detailed knowledge of past accidents and future trends, of the estimated risk of death or injury in the coming year for the average motorist. At the same time and in direct parallel with the second type of risk outlined above, there is the individual motorist's judgement of risk in the coming year. The former is called the 'objective' risk, the latter the 'subjective' risk. Given that these two estimates may differ, which is the appropriate measure to use in policy making? Even if these two estimates do not differ what is more strictly relevant, and more likely to result in disparities between the two measures, is the differential effect on risk – both objective and subjective – of introducing some new risk-reducing policy.

Mishan (1971) has argued that it is the 'subjective' measure of risk and risk reduction which is relevant. He takes as his starting point a potential Pareto improvement, i.e. 'one in which the net gains can so be distributed that at least one person is made better off with none being made worse off'. He then argues: 'In determining whether a potential Pareto improvement has been met economists are generally agreed – either as a canon of faith, as a political tenet, or as an act of expediency – to accept the dictum that each person knows his own interest best.' Mishan continues: 'If, therefore, the economist is told that a person A is indifferent as between not assuming a particular risk and assuming it along with a sum of money, *V*, then, on the Pareto principle, the sum *V* has to be accepted as the relevant cost of his being exposed to that risk.'

Mishan thus chooses to ignore all the issues in our initial questions and assumes that all the normal cost-benefit concepts and criteria *must* apply. Indeed he advocates the principle so strongly that in a footnote he states: 'Person A, for example, may find himself disabled for life and rue his decision to take the risk. But this example is only a more painful one of the fact that people come to regret a great many of the choices they make, *notwithstanding which they would resent any interference with their future choices*' (our emphasis). The question this begs is whether in all cases they *would* resent any interference and even if they did whether in the long run the 'cost' of the resentment would be greater or less than the benefit of interference.

In public policy making the extent to which governments should attempt to bridge any potential gap between expected utility and realised utility is a difficult issue, but it does not appear desirable simply to ignore it as Mishan attempts to do. While he favours the refining and dissemination of information, it is open for debate whether this is sufficient. Mishan goes too far in assuming that one particular set of value judgements, i.e. those contained within the potential Pareto improvement criteria, is correct for cost-benefit studies and the only one that is correct. Nash *et al.* (1975) accept the possibility of different approaches when they state: 'There are many different ways of performing cost-benefit analysis, each of which is logically consistent within a particular set of moral notions . . . there can be no uniquely 'proper' way to do cost-benefit analysis.' They suggest that 'the choice between methods is in the end an ethical one'.

Does the individual believe he is the best person to make the judgement? This is an important question, because if he does not then it would seem that the concept of consumer sovereignty will tend to break down and will *have* to be replaced. But if we so desire it does seem possible to contain this within a consumer sovereignty framework. If individuals are prepared to argue that they are not in a position to judge on the value of the output involved (either because they do not comprehend fully the output involved and/or they do not know how to value it), then they may be prepared to be told what their compensating variation should be. (Legislation on the compulsory wearing of seat belts may be a case in point.)

Of course, if we resort to the view that the goods and services associated with decreased mortality and suffering are merit goods, then the question of what the consumer believes is in his best interest is no longer relevant. What only remains is the extent to which the consumers' views are reflected in the valuation of merit goods.

Can the individual make the relevant value judgements? This is related to the above two issues but it may be the case that even if the individual consumer is considered to be the best judge of his utility and he himself believes this to be the case, he still may not be able to make the judgements required. This is closely related to the question of information. In some instances it is difficult to provide consumers with the necessary information to make the required judgements. For example, in health care some forms of treatment are so complex (e.g. certain drug therapies with possible adverse effects) and likely impacts themselves so uncertain that the individual may not be able to comprehend all the relevant factors to an extent which would be sufficient to allow him to make judgements about the valuation of the treatment involved. Again it may be that the individual will be happy to allow others to exercise their judgements on his behalf.

Does the individual want to make the appropriate value judgements? In some cases individuals may prefer to have decisions removed from their concern and prefer that experts replace him in the decision process. Again this would imply an acceptance by the consumer of certain goods as merit goods. Yet, somewhat paradoxically, if the individual wishes to exercise this choice in the belief that this is in his own best interest, perhaps this could still be contained within a consumer sovereignty principle.

What we can draw from this discussion is rather murky. It would seem that there is a continuum of possible approaches to valuation of life and suffering stretching from on the one hand a complete consumer sovereignty approach to on the other a set of wholly imposed values associated with merit goods and at some distance from a complete reflection of consumers' preferences.

METHODS OF VALUATION

It is now generally accepted – at least among economists – that there is nothing immoral about attempting to place a value on human life. Doubting Thomases still exist but by and large these are to be found outside the disciples of economics. To those who doubt the *morality* of life valuation it must be said that, whether we like it or not, valuations are placed on life every day. This applies both at the level of the individual and at the level of public policy. For example, like the chicken, one crosses the road to get to the other side; there is frequently in this motorised age a risk of death involved in crossing, but the benefit of doing so must be greater than the 'cost' of the risk, otherwise we would stay put. In public policy making values of life are implied in decisions regarding the level and deployment of resources of such diverse activities as the building of a bypass, the screening of women for breast cancer, investment in dust suppression in coal mines, publicity in fire prevention, violent crime prevention, building regulations, railway signalling systems, swimming instructions for schoolchildren and anti-pollution legislation. Frequently, in fact almost always, the values implied in such decisions do not emerge into the light of day; they remain hidden behind the verbiage of official decision making. In this section some of the methods used and/or proposed for life valuation are outlined and an attempt made to indicate their advantages and disadvantages. Few of these methods are dismissed out of hand on the grounds that while far from perfect many may have a contribution to make to improved decision making.

It is important to stress what this section is not about. It is essentially concerned with the conceptual problems of life valuation. Consequently little is said about the operational issues associated with introducing such values into the decision-making process. Again, while it is true that in many respects saving a life may be considered as an extreme case of preventing injury or illness, this section does not examine the question of valuing non-fatal injury or illness in detail although this is considered briefly, shortly. As a final point before reviewing various approaches to valuation of life, it is important that one criterion used in choosing between approaches is that of the validity of the methods in the eyes of the potential users – the decision makers themselves. Unless they have some confidence in the derivation of the values, the valuation of life will remain a purely academic pastime.

The most frequently found method of valuation – and one which has progressed little since Sir William Petty (1699) propounded it in the seventeenth century – is what might be termed the *accounting approach*. This method, whose twentieth-century followers include Dublin and Lotka (1946), Reynolds (1956), Weisbrod (1961), Klarman (1965), Rice and Cooper (1967), Dawson (1967, 1971) and Hanlon (1969), is largely drawn from the human capital school of thought. The value of life is usually equated with the value of a man's labour (assuming the validity of the marginal productivity of labour theory). The discounted stream of future earnings from the time of death (or more precisely from the time death would have occurred but for some intervention) is equated with the value of life. In some cases, e.g. Dawson (1967, 1971), a somewhat arbitrary sum is added to this figure to allow for 'subjective' costs – pain, suffering and grief. The argument about whether one should reduce this sum by the value of the discounted stream of the individual's future consumption is judged to be a matter to be determined by the use made of the emergent values. If we are concerned with the *ex-ante* valuation of a project which is estimated to save x lives, then the valuation of the x lives should be made gross of consumption. The x individuals concerned will be alive, will be members of society and consequently their future consumption can be taken as a benefit to future society. If on the other hand we are concerned to measure the effect on the surviving population of lives lost as a result of, for example, lung cancer last year then the net of consumption estimate is appropriate, although not a measurement of any great relevance.

This valuation methodology is by and large an 'imposed' valuation system which only pays lip service to the concept of consumers' preferences. It can be argued that the valuation of lost output can be considered as the minimum that society *ought* to be prepared to pay to save a life, and if we wish to adopt a social welfare function with Gross National Product as its base then this would be the type of approach to adopt. There is no reason to believe however that there is any necessary relationship between what society *should* be prepared to pay and what society *would* be prepared to pay. The approach makes no attempt to determine what potential victims' views are on the question of how much *they* would be prepared to pay to reduce the chance of their own mortality. (This is the basic theme of Schelling's article, 1968, emphasised in his title 'The Life You Save May Be Your Own'.) Various attempts have been made, for example, by Dawson (1967), and to a lesser extent by Weisbrod (1961) and Klarman (1965), to take account of 'non-economic' values – pain, suffering, grief, etc. Dawson states: 'there are . . . other costs such as suffering and bereavement, that fall upon individuals. Although these are difficult to express in monetary terms their existence is very real to the persons concerned.' His estimate of £5,000, at the time, for these 'subjective costs was derived from a net of consumption approach as follows. 'The use of subjective value of £5,000 for a death means that when only paid output is valued the total average cost of a death is positive in all age and sex groups. £5,000 is thus a minimum value; for if the community wishes to save the lives of persons although it would gain from their death, then the amount of gain which it forgoes is a minimum estimate of the value that is placed on keeping them alive.'

A partial support of the human capital type of approach has been provided by Culyer and Akehurst (1974). Their approach assumes that the measure to be used for life valuation is not earnings but rather the economic surplus from working.

Various other adjustments have been made to the basic approach by a number of writers. For example, Weisbrod (1961) imputes a value to housewives' services; Rice and Cooper (1967) concentrate on the differential values of life which the method raises; Klarman (1965) uses a money-valued proxy to estimate the 'subjective' costs of syphilis; and Hanlon (1969) places emphasis on the various 'debit' items involved – from the economic incapacity of the mother to be through to the risk of premature death.

Thus, while there may be *some* relationship between what an individual would be prepared to pay to prevent his demise (or reduce the risk of his demise) and his future earnings, it is unlikely that there is a one-to-one relationship. It is perfectly reasonable to see the relationship as a functional one but it must be accepted that the logic of treating it as an accounting one cannot be contained within the concept of consumer sovereignty. The values emerging from this approach can be defended as logical minima within a largely merit goods view of policy making. To introduce the valuation of the 'subjective' costs into this approach, while one can appreciate the importance of doing so, would seem to result in a mix of moral values on which the approach stands.

A second approach suggests that a study of decisions involving life-saving activities in the public sector might provide us with an *implicit value of life* or more realistically a series of implicit values. There is considerable merit in this approach which even although it has certain 'vicious circle' features might at least allow some improvement in the sense of greater consistency to be made in the allocation of resources to life-saving activities throughout the public sector. *A priori,* it could be argued that – at least as a first approximation – the value of life should be consistent in decisions both between and within road safety, health, fire prevention, etc. If we could establish that on the basis of past decisions the implied value of life generally lay within a fairly narrow range normally distributed about some mean value, then this mean might be interpreted as the 'public sector value'. When past decisions revealed implied values well or below this 'public sector value' these could then be subject to further investigation to determine why there appeared to be over- or underinvestment in these areas. For the future, decisions on investment for life saving would be made on the basis of the then explicit 'public sector value'. The necessary conditions for the approach to be valid are indicated by Harrison (1974) and discussed in detail by Mooney (1977).

A limited amount of research has been done in this area. The results are inevitably somewhat tentative and are very much dependent on the assumptions used. However they do suggest an enormously wide range in life values from more than £20 million as a result of certain changes made in building structures and regulations following the Ronan Point disaster (Sinclair *et al.*, 1972), to (it has been claimed) less than £50 in the case of an infrequently used test in pregnant women which might prevent some still-births (Leach, 1972).

One form of the socially implied valuation method lies in court awards. At first sight it might appear that one could assume that judges, however imperfectly, attempt to reflect some societal valuation of life in determining awards for damages in the event of a death. One of the major disadvantages of this approach is that the award is made *ex-post* and no attempt is made to estimate the value to the life killed of his existence had he not been killed. As far as compensation to the deceased's relatives is concerned, damages in the case of a death reflect only the pecuniary loss to the relatives as a result of the death of the person injured. Any suffering by the deceased or any anguish of the relatives from the loss of the deceased cannot be taken into account in the award of damages. It would also be more accurate to say that the courts should look to economists for guidance rather than vice versa. This point is made explicitly by Elliot and Street (1968). Regarding the courts they state: 'They do not listen to expert evidence, whether of actuaries or economists, which might assist them in their calculations.' (The position is different in the case of non-fatal injuries and an approach to valuation of these using court awards is discussed below.)

But it is important to be aware of the limitations associated with this type of approach. The first and major problem is that, while by definition any decision regarding the level of investment in any activity which can affect the risk of death must embody an implied value of life, it may be the case that the decision reached was not a rational decision based on the known expected number of lives saved. Given this, it is hardly surprising that wide variations in values emerge. The second difficulty is that frequently it is not possible to obtain a marginal implied value and we have to make do with averages. Where there are major discontinuities it may only be possible to estimate a minimum value implied by a certain decision. In other cases (e.g. cervical cancer screening) where there is a fairly continuous supply curve of the service involved the actual marginal value may be determined. Again at the opposite end of the spectrum where some policy has *not* been implemented it may be possible to infer a *maximum* valuation of life. A third difficulty is that many decisions concerned with life-saving activities also provide other benefits – reduction in injury, morbidity, property damage, etc. While is such cases it may be possible to allow for certain of these factors to be deducted in monetary terms before estimating the implied value of life or suffering, this may not always be possible. A more practical difficulty facing any researchers in this area is that it may simply not be possible to obtain the data necessary to determine the basis used in reaching a decision.

This difficulty of determining the basis of the decision is particularly acute in the field of health. It is only in fairly recent times that much has been done by way of controlled trials to test the effectiveness of different types of treatment. Most of the medical practices encompassed within the NHS undoubtedly do have an impact for the good. But any precise measurement of the impact is frequently very difficult, if not impossible. While in the past in the field of road safety it has proved possible to mount experiments to determine the effectiveness of various 'treatments' (e.g. the monitoring of accidents on the M1 motorway to provide a comparison of the number and nature of accidents on those sections with central reservation barriers as against those with no barrier) the situation is much more difficult in the health field. Immediately it is apparent that a certain type of treatment provides some positive benefit, no matter how small, it then becomes 'unethical' to mount a controlled trial in which some patients are given treatment and others not (thereby determining the extent of the benefit). While it may be right that this should be deemed 'unethical' it does create sizeable problems in improving the allocation of resources between treatments.

Further difficulties arise in the 'public sector implied value' approach in that the outputs of different life-saving programmes may not be homogeneous lives saved. Some programmes will be concerned with young lives, others with the aged. Some will result in complete recovery or the prospect of a full life; others will leave the saved incapacitated in some way or other, in addition even like lives saved may be valued differently in the sense that if society fears death in one way more than another (e.g. fire and road accidents) then measures to prevent fires may be valued more highly than road accident remedial measures. Again, if death at home is considered more abhorrent than death as a football spectator, this may be reflected in differential standards, and hence differential costs and implied values, in building regulations for houses and football grounds.

One way of determining the extent to which some of these factors might influence the 'public sector value' in particular circumstances has been proposed by Feldstein (1970). He takes the case of an official in a health department who has to decide on the allocation of resources to different sections of the community and specifically what relative values to place on the saving of the life of a child and of a young adult (i.e. the ratio of W_1/W_2). He suggests that the official may say that $W_2 > W_1$ but is unable to decide the ratio. He argues that the ratio can be determined by posing the problem in the following way:

You have indicated that W_2 exceeds W_1. Now consider a situation in which there are two patients, one in each group. Each has a probability of 0·2 of dying unless treated by a particular drug. There is only enough of the drug to treat one of them. If treatment would reduce the probability of death to 0·1 in both cases, your statement that $W_2 > W_1$, implies that you would give the treatment to the older patient. But what if the drug was less effective for the older patient? If $W_1 > 0$, then if the drug is sufficiently less effective in reducing the probability of death for the older patient, you would treat the younger patient. More formally, if treatment lowers the probability of death for the younger patient from $0·2$ to $0·1$, then there is some probability $P > 0·1$ such that if treatment lowered the probability of death for the older patient from $0·2$ to P you would be indifferent between treating the older and the younger patient. What is P? [The implied ratio of W_1 to W_2 is given by $2 - 10P$.]

To what extent it is worthwhile pursuing Feldstein's suggestion is in many ways secondary to the importance of actively pursuing the derivation of the 'public sector value' or a series of implied values. There does appear to be sufficient of value in this approach to justify more research in this area to determine as many of the implied values of life as data will allow. In this way at least an increased degree of consistency in life values might be introduced to policy making in the public sector. It has also the very real merit of being relatively simple to apply.

The lack of consumer orientation in the 'lost output' method of valuation led eventually to the publication of an important paper by Schelling (1968) and later to further developments along similar lines by Jones-Lee (1969, 1971, 1976) and Mishan (1971). The basic point Schelling makes is that if we have a programme to save lives and want to measure the benefits of this programme then what we ought to ask is 'What is it worth to the people who stand to benefit from it?. He emphasises the need to take account of consumer preferences and suggests that rather than attempting to value life *per se* we should concentrate on *valuing changes in small risks of death*. This he claims 'makes the evaluation more casual and takes the pricelessness and the pretentiousness out of a potentially awesome choice'.

Schelling accepts that there may be a problem in evaluating small changes in risk but claims that these can be overcome by a 'scaling of risks'. It may not be possible for an individual to grasp the meaning of a 1 in 1,000 chance although a 1 in 10 chance is probably manageable. He continues:

[The individual] is asked, for example, what reduction in income after taxes he would incur in perpetuity to avoid a 10 per cent chance of death ... Suppose he says that he will give up one-third of his income to avoid an immediate 10 per cent chance of dying. How can it be calculated from this what he might give to avoid 1 chance in 1,000 of dying?

Schelling suggests – and most of us would agree – that dividing both figures by 100 is unrealistic. As an alternative he proposes that the man might be asked 'what fraction of his income would he give up to avoid a one-tenth chance of losing one-third of his income . . . The process could be repeated for a one-hundredth chance of losing a third of his income.' A possible criticism of Schelling's 'scaling of risks' is that only if the sums involved by way of income loss and the effect on safety were small could it be considered that we were getting a true measure of the marginal valuation. The criticism carries little weight, however, in that the changes in risk levels with which we are likely to be involved are almost always very small.

Jones-Lee (1969, 1974, 1976) was the next to follow in Schelling's footsteps. His basic premise is that 'if cost-benefit analysis is to be employed *and* the consumer's surplus approach adopted for those goods for which market information *is* available then consistency would seem to demand the development of procedures for eliciting some indication of the sums people would be prepared to forfeit to effect changes in the level of provision of those goods for which market information is not available'.

Jones-Lee's (1976) theoretical framework is developed on the following lines. He adopts a subjective probability approach and draws on the literature on the theory of choice under uncertainty. (See, for example Hirshleifer, 1965, 1966; Knight, 1921; Shackle, 1949; von Neumann and Morgenstern, 1958.) He starts 'by considering a single-period, discrete-time problem . . . [in which] . . . the individual begins the current period with wealth $\bar{w}$ and associates a subjective probability $\bar{p}$ ($o < \bar{p} < 1$) with the outcome of his own death during this period' first for an uninsured individual. It follows that his initial expected utility is

$$E(U) = (1 - \bar{p})L(\bar{w}) + \bar{p}D(\bar{w})$$

where $E(U)$ is his initial expected utility; $(1-\bar{p})$ is his subjective probability of surviving the period; $L(\bar{w})$ is his utility of wealth function conditional on survival; $\bar{p}$ is his subjective probability of dying during the period; and $D(\bar{w})$ is his utility of wealth function conditional on death during the period.

If the individual is given the chance of reducing his risk of death during the period then he will be prepared to trade wealth for an increased probability of survival. The maximum sum he will be prepared to trade will leave him indifferent between the initial situation and the new, reduced-risk situation. This maximum sum v will therefore satisfy the following condition:

$$(1 - p)L(\bar{w} - v) + pD(\bar{w} - v) = (1 - \bar{p})L(\bar{w}) + \bar{p}D(\bar{w})$$

where the symbols are as before and p is the reduced probability of death. Thus v is the compensating variation for the increase in the individual's probability of surviving the period, i.e. for the decrease in risk of death from $\bar{p}$ to p.

Jones-Lee goes on to establish the general properties of the relationship between v and p as implied by the above relationship before applying the theory to an insured individual for the single-period case, and for individuals both insured and uninsured in the continuous-time case.

Mishan (1971) followed the approach of Schelling and Jones-Lee and spelt out his theoretical framework for the application of cost-benefit analysis in this field of life valuation and at the same time mounted an important critique of some of the other approaches proposed. Mishan suggests that in the valuation of a reduction-in-risk approach we need to consider four types of risk. The first of these is the direct risk which people voluntarily assume. Accepting individuals' perception of risk, Mishan argues that the demand for a particular good or service which involves some element of risk to life will be determined by the benefit obtained net of the perceived risk. He argues that: 'a cost-benefit study of a highway project which is expected to increase the number of casualties need make no allowance for the expected loss of life, provided . . . that this is the only type of risk' (i.e. the voluntarily assumed direct risk). Mishan continues: 'The benefits to be measured are ultimately the maximum sums motorists are willing to pay for the new highway system in full cognisance of the additional risks they assume.' Some of the risk to an individual using the road will be imposed by others. However, in so far as the individual can still avoid these risks (which are external diseconomies internal to the industry) then the demand for the road will be determined by the benefit net of both the types of risk considered above.

Now if we accept Mishan's statement that it is perceived risk which is important then this means that in some sense the use of the road will be less than optimal if individuals' perception of risk is not equal to actual risk. Demand will be less than or greater than optimal depending upon whether perceptions are higher or lower respectively than actual. In so far as perceptions are inaccurate more people will die than would otherwise be the case.

Mishan's other types of risk are:

1 the direct involuntary risk of death, such as that arising from disposal of radioactive waste material;
2 and 3 the two components of risk associated with concern for other people's lives – the two components being financial and psychic.

Thus in any policy field involving life saving, in order to measure the benefits of the scheme we need to value up to four types of risk (although not all will necessarily exist in any specific policy) – voluntarily assumed direct risk, involuntary direct risk, financial risk to others and psychic risk to others.

One other aspect which is discussed by Schelling (1968) and Mooney (1977) of the approach of valuation of reduction in risk of death is worthy of mention. There may well be two component parts to such a reduction. There is the question of reduced risk *per se*, i.e. the increased probability of avoiding death or of extending life. But there is also the question of the reduced anxiety associated with decreased risk of death or, as Schelling calls it, increased peace of mind. The separation of these two component parts may be important particularly with respect to the issue of the linearity or otherwise of the utility of risk function. While we know little about the shape of this function, one reasonable hypothesis would be that if we were to separate the function for these two separate components, then the utility of risk *per se* function might well be linear but the function of the utility of peace of mind related to risk might well be non-linear. It might also be that on the question of whether to use an objective or subjective measure of risk the former might be applicable to risk *per se* because it is the objective measure which indicates for a population how many deaths occur. The subjective measure might be more applicable to anxiety or peace of mind because, while education on risk is possible, it is the individual's subjective assessment of the risk which must ultimately form the basis of his anxiety. This separation of the value of risk *per se* and the value of anxiety associated with risk has a parallel in value in use and value in anticipation in some of the literature on option values (see, for example, Weisbrod, 1964, and Zeckhauser, 1970.

The value of a reduction-in-risk approach has been applied on relatively few occasions. There are two possible ways of tackling the problems – first, to study individual behaviour in risk situations and secondly, to apply interview or questionnaire techniques to elicit information about how individuals might behave in largely hypothetical situations.

Melinek (1974) examines a few instances of individuals' behaviour in risk situations and for example estimates the value of life for driving speed and the use of pedestrian subways, both involving trade-offs between risk and time, as £73,500 and £66,500 respectively. Mooney (1977) has indicated the use of the approach in the context of danger money paid in the construction industry. Ghosh *et al.* (1975), assuming optimal motorway speed equals the average at 58·8 m.p.h., the price of petrol (then) at 35p per gallon, and the value of time at £1·00 per hour, estimate the value of life at £94,000. Needleman (1976), using a similar model to that of Jones-Lee (1976), uses data on kidney donors to obtain some 'coefficients of concern' of various relationships (e.g. spouse's concern for spouse). Jones-Lee (1976) uses a questionnaire technique to elicit from individuals what trade-offs they would make between safety and wealth. The individual is asked to make choices between two airlines which are identical except for their safety record and fares.

It is apparent that the number of situations in which individual behaviour towards risk of death (or injury and illness) can be measured are relatively few and although more areas could be investigated there appear to be limits to how far behaviour in risk situations is an appropriate approach. If individuals' perceptions *and* misperceptions are accepted, as Mishan (1971) would wish, then the behavioural approach could yield further dividends. But if 'objective' measures of risk are appropriate then unless more research is conducted into the relationship between 'objective' and 'subjective' risk, the Jones-Lee type of approach is likely to prove more appropriate.

Most of the emphasis to date on valuation of the cost of disease and injury has been on life and death. To some extent this is odd and yet the main reason for it perhaps lies in the fact that death, despite what has already been said about the differing nature of the various outputs of life saving policies, is relatively speaking much more homogenous than morbidity and non-fatal injury. In addition, the question of accurate perception of risk is likely to be a greater problem in investigations relating to non-fatal disease and injury problems than fatal simply because the outcome for the individual is in most cases less traumatic.

However, the techniques indicated above for valuing life are applicable, with suitable modifications, to non-fatal situations. For example, Dawson (1967, 1971) also estimates the cost of non-fatal injuries; Klarman (1965) uses his money-valued proxies for non-fatal cases of syphilis as well as fatal; the approach of looking at implied values in public decision making can be applied to less serious diseases and injuries and not just policies involving life saving; and Jones-Lee (1976) shows that his approach, with modification, does not only apply to fatalities.

One study by Rosser and Watts (1971) has used court awards for injury damages to place relative values on different non-fatal conditions. The advantage of using this approach in the context of non-fatal conditions is that awards for non-fatal injuries are not restricted to compensation for pecuniary loss to the extent that they are for fatal injuries. While of interest in the total context of valuation of life and suffering, the levels of compensation paid in court awards appear to be determined too much by 'rules of thumb' to be of much value in determining publicly implied values. (See Harrison, 1974, for a discussion of rules of thumb in implied values.)

CONCLUSION

The above discussion of valuation of life and suffering has considered three principal approaches to valuation – the human capital approach;

the social or public decision making implied-values approach; and the reduction-in-risk approach. The choice between these approaches is to a large extent a matter of value or even moral judgements and is determined by the philosophy underlying the different social welfare functions (SWFs).

If the SWF is to be GNP-based, and that solely, then the human capital approach is applicable. The approach has the merit of being relatively easy to apply and is the one most commonly encountered. In most instances it ignores the question of consumer sovereignty and the attempts to add in an element of consumer sovereignty suggest some mix of the values underlying the SWF. None the less, if the appropriate decision makers chose to use the approach to provide minimum values of life and state the ethic on which it rests then the approach is defensible.

In the approach based on public decision making implied values, the underlying value system assumes that the political process is the final arbiter in determining how resources should be allocated to different social objectives. It takes the existing institutional framework as given and assumes that the main problem lies in achieving consistency in ensuring that like outputs are valued alike. In doing so it implicitly assumes that the existing total budget for life saving is already optimal and that the problem of resource allocation can be constrained to maximising the social welfare arising from the efficient deployment of this budget.

As has been indicated, the outputs of life-saving programmes are not homogeneous – all lives saved are not alike. Consequently one of the main problems to be solved within the approach is that of the relative values to be placed on the saving of lives of different ages, in different circumstances, etc. If anxiety associated with risk of death is considered relevant to the SWF then the approach requires a consistent attitude not only to like lives saved but also to like anxiety reduced or avoided.

There is a certain 'vicious circle' ring to the approach but if the underlying value judgement associated with the SWF is primarily related to consistency, then the vicious circle aspect is a necessary ingredient. The approach is relatively simple to apply at a crude level and the existing evidence on the wide range of implied values in some past decisions suggests that social welfare from life-saving policies is not being maximised within the existing budget. The main problem in application is in obtaining sufficient and accurate information on past decisions, and how they were reached, to allow the implied values to be made explicit.

Given the wide range of implied values which appear to exist at present, then a crude application to more areas would be valuable. But the issue of relative values attaching to dissimilar lives saved cannot be wholly ignored and is a problem which no one as yet appears to have tackled. If it is not examined then the merit of the approach, i.e.

increased consistency in decisions in life-saving policy making and thereby increased social welfare in health care, road safety, fire prevention, etc., may be lost as apparent inconsistencies are defended on the basis of dissimilar outputs.

The underlying moral values of the SWF in the approach using reduction in risk for the individual at risk are based in consumer sovereignty and to that extent the approach reflects the basis of most welfare economics. If we assume that the individual at risk is the best judge of his own interest, believes he is the best judge, can make the necessary judgements and wants to make the necessary judgements, then this approach is the one to be adopted. The approach can allow for different attitudes to risk of death and suffering as between different individuals and different circumstances. In doing so it encompasses the question of anxiety associated with risk directly.

What measurement of risk is appropriate is of some importance in the approach. The choice lies between adopting measure of risk and risk reduction or a subjective measure. Adopting the former assumes that the consumer is not given sovereignty over the output measurement but only over the valuation of the output. The latter leaves the consumer to form judgements about both measurement and valuation. Which is to be used is again determined by the values underlying the SWF.

In the application of the approach a number of problems arise. In so far as individual behaviour is studied to derive values, then the number of situations in which data will allow values to emerge is limited. In addition if individuals' perception of risk and risk changes is not accurate and the extent of the misperception is unknown then only if subjective measures of risk are deemed to be appropriate will behavioural studies produce true values. If the objective measurement of risk is to be used then only if the extent of misperception is known can true values emerge.

If the direct questionnaire technique is used to apply the approach then there is the common difficulty with this technique of not being sure that the preferences revealed by individuals are an accurate reflection of what they would do in practice. For example, it is possible that the anxiety part of the utility of risk function may be understated.

The data requirements for the approach to be used are also considerable. It is not enough to indicate output in terms of the number of lives expected to be saved from a particular measure. It requires that these be related to the population at risk. In so far as the approach has the advantage of providing different values for different lives in different circumstances, it also follows that different data sets are required for each situation. However some pattern may emerge which will allow an understanding of why values differ in different situations and thus reduce the need for extensive data.

The approach is still in its infancy and what is now required is much more extensive use of it at an applied level. It would also be desirable to examine the extent to which misperceptions of risk levels exist and their magnitude as this may help to resolve the question of the appropriate measurement of risk (i.e. subjective or objective).

In terms of public policy making which of the above approaches is to be adopted is finally a moral judgement. The policy areas involved – health care, road safety, fire prevention, etc. – are such as to make the choice less clear-cut. If it is accepted that the outputs involved are largely merit goods then there is a case for using the human capital approach and even more so for attempting to introduce increased consistency through examining more of the implied values in public policy making. If increased consumer orientation is seen as desirable then more empirical work is required on the consumer sovereignty approach of valuing reductions in risk for individuals at risk.

As a partial compromise the author would suggest that there will almost certainly always be an element of merit goods associated with health care and other life-saving areas and perhaps this is in any case what most consumers want (which is perhaps rather paradoxical!). If this is correct, then by pursuing the proposal on implied values in past decisions and reducing the amount of inconsistency, this will lead to increased social welfare. At the same time if further advances can be made in determining consumers' values for reductions in risk of death then in time it may be possible to incorporate some of these into the decision process. While the concept of merit goods with a flavour of consumer sovereignty is perhaps a little bewildering, it may well not be very far removed from some of the rather confused moral underlying decision making in the policy areas concerned.

REFERENCES

Culyer, A. J. and Akehurst, R., 'On the economic surplus and the value of life', *Bulletin of Economic Research,* vol. 26, 1974, pp. 63–78.

Dawson, R. F. F., *Cost of Road Accidents in Great Britain* (Crowthorne: Road Research Laboratory, 1967).

Dawson, R. F. F., *Current Costs of Road Accidents in Great Britain* (Crowthorne: Road Research Laboratory, 1971).

Dublin, L. I. and Lotka, A. J., *The Money Value of a Man* (New York: Ronald Press, 1946).

Elliott, D. W. and Street, H., *Road Accidents* (Harmondsworth: Penguin, 1968).

Feldstein, M. S., 'Health sector planning in developing countries', *Economica,* vol. 37, no. 146, 1970, pp. 139–63.

Ghosh, D., Lees, D. and Seal, W., 'Optimal motorway speed and some values of time and life', *The Manchester School of Economic and Social Studies,* vol. XLIII, 1975, pp. 134–43.

Hanlon, J. J., *Principles of Public Health Administration,* 5th edn (St Louis: C.V. Mosby, 1969).

Harrison, A. J., *The Economics of Transport Appraisal* (London: Croom Helm, 1974).

Hirshleifer, J., 'Investment decisions under uncertainty – choice – theoretic approaches', *Quarterly Journal of Economics,* vol. LXXIX, no. 4, 1965, pp. 509–36.

Hirshleifer, J., 'Investment decisions under uncertainty: applications of the state preference approach', *Quarterly Journal of Economics*, vol. LXXX, no. 2, 1966, pp. 272–7.

Jones-Lee, M. W., 'Valuation of reduction in probability of death by road accident', *Journal of Transport Economics and Policy*, vol. 3, no. 1, 1969, pp. 37–47.

Jones-Lee, M. W., 'The value of changes in the probability of death or injury', *Journal of Political Economy*, vol. 82, 1974, pp. 835–50.

Jones-Lee, M. W., *The Value of Life, an Economic Analysis* (London: Martin Robertson, 1976).

Klarman, H. E., 'Syphilis control programs', in *Measuring Benefits of Government Investments*, ed R. Dorfman (Washington DC: The Brookings Institution, 1965).

Knight, F. R., *Risk, Uncertainty and Profit* (Boston and New York: Houghton Mifflin, 1921).

Leach, G., *The Biocrats* (Harmondsworth: Pelican, 1972).

Melinek, S. J., 'A method of evaluating human life for economics purposes', *Accident Analysis and Prevention*, vol. 6, 1974, pp. 103–14.

Mishan, E. J., *Cost-Benefit Analysis* (London: Allen & Unwin, 1971).

Mooney, G. H., *The Valuation of Human Life* (London: Macmillan, 1977).

Nash, C., Pearce, D. W. and Stanley, J., 'An evaluation of cost-benefit criteria', *Scottish Journal of Political Economy*, vol. XXII, no. 2, 1975, pp. 121–33.

Needleman, L., 'Valuing other people's lives', *The Manchester School of Economic and Social Studies*, vol. 4, 1976, pp. 309–42.

von Neumann, J. and Morgenstern, P., *Theory of Games and Economic Behaviour* (Princeton, NJ: Princeton University Press, 1953).

Petty, Sir W., *Political Arithmetic or a Discourse Concerning the Extent and Value of Lands, People, Buildings, etc.* (London: Robert Clavel, 1699).

Reynolds, D. J., 'The cost of road accidents', *Journal of the Royal Statistical Society*, vol. 119, 1956, pp. 393–408.

Rice, D. P. and Cooper, B. S., 'The economic value of human life', *American Journal of Public Health*, vol. 57, 1967, pp. 1954–66.

Rosser, R. and Watts, V., 'The measurement of hospital output', Paper presented to the Operational Research Society Conference, Lancaster, September 1971.

Schelling, T. C., 'The life you save may be your own', in *Problems in Public Expenditure Analysis*, ed. S. B. Chase (Washington DC: The Brookings Institution, 1968).

Schackle, G. L. S., *Expectation in Economics* (Cambridge: CUP, 1949).

Sinclair, T. C., Marstrand, P. and Newick, P., *Human Life and Safety in Relation to Technical Change* (University of Sussex, 1972).

Weisbrod, B. A., *Economics of Public Health* (Philadelphia: University of Pennsylvania Press, 1961).

Weisbrod, B. A., 'Collective-consumption services of individual consumption goods', *Quarterly Journal of Economics*, vol. LXXVIII, no. 3, 1964, pp. 471–7.

Zeckhauser, R., 'Uncertainty and the need for collective action', in *Public Expenditures and Policy Analysis*, ed. R. H. Haveman and J. Margolis (Chicago: Markham Publishing Company, 1970).

Chapter 7

Social Severance*

INTRODUCTION

During the late 1960s and early 1970s, a rapid growth occurred in the application of evaluation tools to major transport projects. In the United Kingdom, largely under the influence of the Department of the Environment, the framework for such growth of evaluation was the formal cost-benefit model. Analysts sought to identify an enlarged range of impacts of transport projects, to measure these impacts in physical terms as far as possible and place monetary values on the impacts. In the event of impacts having no obvious physical measure, attempts were occasionally made to go more directly to monetary valuations. In the United States a similar growth in impact analysis occurred, although the evaluation approach was less concerned with expression of all impacts in monetary terms, increased attention being focused on evaluation in a political framework. 'Social severance' gained widespread recognition during this period as an important possible consequence of public projects. The British Urban Motorways Committee (1972), for example, listed severance as one of the main areas requiring research in the planning of major urban roads.

Work on a number of consequences of changes to the urban environment has reached a reasonable level of understanding in the definition and measurement of problems (e.g. noise, air pollution). The same cannot be said in regard to social severance. Relocation severance has received the most attention, but even in this case only a few works examine the determinants and nature of social severance. Barrier severance has only recently received attention. Harrison has observed that 'the basic concepts needed to define and describe the nature of [barrier severance] . . . are only just being developed' (Harrison, 1974, p. 132), and severance by traffic in residential streets has only recently been a focus for research (Appleyard and Lintell, 1970). The effect of other environmental features on social interaction and social severance is not well understood, though there are signs of increasing interest in this topic.

* In the preparation of this chapter, helpful comments were received from Mandy Sinclair, Paul Hooper and Ross King.

The terms social severance, social disruption and related terms are used in distinct ways. *Social severence* is seen as the rupture or impairment of relationships between people, relationships between people and institutions or relationships between people and places. *Social bonds* are the relationships which people have with other people, institutions and with particular places. *Social disruption* is a more comprehensive term than social severance. It includes social severance and factors other than social severance which dislocate a person's identity, pattern of life or psychological well-being, for example worry caused by high unemployment. That is, social severance is socially disruptive, but factors other than social severance may contribute to social disruption. *Social evaluation* is evaluation according to criteria concerning social well-being. *Social well-being* constitutes a state influenced by, *inter alia*, social bonds.

It is not a simple matter to draw these distinctions. In practice any public project has a large range of effects which may be considered at a number of levels. It is not usually possible, or perhaps even desirable, to disentangle precisely all the effects at all levels of analysis. For example, it is usually not clear whether social disruption has been caused by social severance or other factors. Consequently, there is no attempt to push the operative definitions to their limit in this chapter. It is argued, however, that it is necessary to understand the nature of social bonds before social severance can be understood or evaluated.

The following section briefly examines the cost-benefit framework for the valuation of severance. By documenting the cost-benefit approach to a specific problem, highway or urban renewal projects involving housing resumption, some of the limitations of this approach are manifested. The criticisms of the cost-benefit approach to social severance suggest the need for an alternative approach. A perspective on the social assessment of severance is developed in the third section. Key types of social severance effects, and key types of determinants of social severance are noted. Philosophical and conceptual alternatives in the analysis of social bonds are discussed.

Significant work contributing to an understanding of social severance is then considered. Discussion is provided under headings corresponding to the research method employed: participant observation, group techniques and survey methods. Key factors influencing the nature and intensity of social severance are presented. Using the discussion of social severance as a guide, the final section examines some tentative ideas on how social evaluation may be related to economic evaluation, and how in the future social evaluation may be employed.

THE COST-BENEFIT APPROACH

The traditional approach to cost-benefit analysis seeks to identify who gains and loses as a consequence of public projects and to measure the gain and loss in money terms. The criterion for quantifying benefits and costs at the individual level is generally Hicks's measure of compensating variation (Hicks, 1956). Attempts have been made to apply this notion to the monetary valuation of social severance.

Downs (1970) categorised the costs to residential households associated with urban renewal or highway construction in built-up urban areas under the following headings:

(1) losses imposed on residential households by displacement itself;
(2) losses imposed upon residential households by uncertainties and delays;
(3) losses imposed upon residential households not directly displaced but located in surrounding areas.

The first and third categories are of most relevance to social severance, though uncertainties and delays may induce severance effects. Attempts to measure losses (1) and (3) above in monetary terms are discussed to illustrate the application of the cost-benefit approach.

Compulsory *acquisition* of owner-occupied residences for a public use, as described in (1) above, may impose the following costs (or occasionally benefits) on affected households (based on Downs, 1970):

(a) loss of property;
(b) removal costs;
(c) costs of seeking alternative housing;
(d) higher housing costs imposed by the non-availability of equivalent housing at the same price as that acquired;
(e) disruption costs (particularly severance of established personal and environmental relationships);
(f) changed operating costs.

Costs (b) to (f) will also be relevant to relocating tenants.

It should be noted that households who relocate will normally trade between the cost categories (b) to (f) above. It could be argued that each of the costs (b) to (d) and (f) has a severance component. For example, households may incur increased operating costs in order to lower severance costs. Notionally then 'severance cost' could be defined as the sum of the severance components of costs (b) to (f). Category (e) costs are the most contentious in evaluation, and these costs are the focus for the following discussion.

The householders' surplus approach provides a possible avenue to monetary valuation of severance costs. The householder's surplus, for an owner occupying his residence, is defined as the monetary value of the property to him over and above its market price (assessed in the absence of blight). A similar concept also applies to tenants. If the householder's surplus could be taken as a valid measure of the sum of costs (b) to (f) above, then disruption costs (category (e)) could be measured in money terms by deduction, since costs (b), (c), (d) and (f) are reasonably amenable to monetary quantification (see, for example, Holdsworth, 1973). However, if the householder's surplus is a completely valid measure of the sum of costs (b) to (e), there would seldom be any need to compute separately disruption costs for the purposes of evaluation. The key issue is whether the householders' surplus approach does adequately incorporate disruption costs.

The Roskill Commission research team, investigating the possible siting of the Third London Airport, attempted to ascertain the mean size of householders' surplus in monetary terms by use of a questionnaire survey amongst owners not affected by any proposed development (see for example, Flowerdew, 1972). Respondents were asked to consider a hypothetical 'large development' and to say 'what price would be just high enough to compensate ... for leaving this house and moving to another area' (Commission on the Third London Airport, CTLA, 1970). The householders' surplus was calculated by subtracting the market price of their house from the price cited in response to the previous question.

Mishan (1970) has criticised the approach of the Roskill Commission research team on the grounds that respondents were given no indication of how far they would have to move to avoid the hypothetical development. Neither severance costs, nor any change in operating, housing or other costs to offset severance costs, could be realistically assessed by the respondent. Mishan's criticism, however, accepts that in principle such cost can be quantified in monetary terms.

The Urban Motorways Project Team (UMPT, 1973) also used a hypothetical question approach to investigate householders' surplus, seeking to avoid the difficulty pointed out by Mishan in regard to the earlier Roskill work. This study found that 12 per cent of respondents claimed that no amount would induce them to move and a further 17 per cent were unable to state an amount within an interview situation. The Roskill team had found that 8 per cent of respondents would not sell (CTLA, 1970). Mishan (1970) argued that those respondents in the Roskill study who would not sell should have been treated as having an infinite householders' surplus.

The losses imposed on those *adjacent* to urban renewal or a highway were also considered by Downs (1970). The costs relevant to severance include:

(1) disruption of local communications through blocking of streets;
(2) reduction in quantity and quality of commercial and other services available in the area because they have left or been displaced;
(3) reduction in employment opportunities and increased costs of

travelling to work because firms have been compelled to move elsewhere or have gone out of business.

In general these are costs of maintaining a particular activity pattern in the presence of a public project, or costs of replacing that activity pattern with an alternative pattern preferred in the presence of the project, or costs attributable to lost opportunities.

The Urban Motorways Project Team (UMPT, 1973) carried out investigations into problems perceived by households located within 180 metres of major roads. This work provides one basis for the analysis of costs imposed on those adjacent to a major road. The most important problems identified were those related to severance, including difficulties in crossing the relevant road on foot and access to shops. More respondents considered they were annoyed by such problems than were annoyed by noise, fumes, dirt, vibration and loss of privacy. The study sought to establish what level of monetary compensation would be acceptable for those who experienced environmental disadvantages deriving from the presence of the road.

Table 7.1   *Choice between compensation and removal of* all *environmental problems*

	Distance band		
	0–60 m	61–120 m	121–180 m
Category of informant	%	%	%
Compensation acceptable:			
£20–£50	11	20	18
£60–£100	4	3	0
£101–£1,000	6	4	3
£1,001–£3,000	4	1	0
£3,001–£7,000	7	2	0
Don't know amount	14	10	15
No compensation acceptable: removal of all problems preferred	55	60	64
Totals	101	100	100
Base for percentages =	(85)	(101)	(39)*

* The figures in this column are based on a small number of interviews and should be treated with caution.
Source: Urban Motorways Project Team (UMPT, 1973, p. 206).

Table 7.1 indicates that well over half the respondents would prefer the removal of all environmental problems, monetary compensation being unacceptable. A further 10 to 15 per cent did not know what sum (if any) would be appropriate. For those who did state an acceptable amount of compensation, there was no indication of the social severance component.

The monetary valuation of social severance as a component of householders' surplus assumes that social and economic welfare are uni-dimensional, and measurable in money terms. Rebuttal of this line of reasoning is not considered in depth (see, for example, Cropsey, 1955). However, it is argued that people have transactions with their environment at a wide range of levels, for example, social, political, physical and economic. Their transactions in one sphere may be related to their transactions in another. Their welfare in one sphere may be related to their welfare in another, but it is inadequate to assume that all forms of welfare are measurable in monetary terms.

In the studies described in the previous section, a significantly large proportion of people either preferred not to be relocated, or preferred removal of environmental problems to monetary compensation, or were unable to state a suitable amount of compensation. People adjacent to a major road perceived severance as the most important problem stemming from the road, and for the majority of them, monetary compensation was not acceptable. Monetary valuation of social welfare was apparently inapplicable, at least for some people.

There is considerable confirming evidence to suggest that the experience of severance for many people is in no way reducible to money terms. For example, Fied (1967) in his study of relocation in the West End of Boston termed experience as one of 'grief' manifested in the 'feelings of painful loss, the continued longing, the general depressive tone, frequent symptoms of psychological or social or somatic distress, the active work required in adapting to the altered situation, the sense of helplessness, the occasional expressions of both direct and displaced anger, and tendencies to idealize the lost place' (Fried, 1967, pp. 359–60).

The more severe cases of grief in Fried's study included responses like the following: ' "I felt as though I had lost everything" . . . "I felt like taking the gaspipe", "I lost all the friends I knew" ' (Fried, 1967, p. 360). Of course the intensity of grief varied greatly and some of those relocated experienced no apparent loss. However, for some households a relocation experience may constitute something that is qualitatively quite different to the kind of allocation activity that is involved in buying (say) bread, milk and consumer durables. Application of the cost-benefit calculus in such circumstances is quite misplaced.

There is also reason to doubt that those who do state an amount of compensation which would be sufficient for them are actually trading dimensions of their life in the manner required by cost-benefit theory. There is considerable work which suggests the situational nature of human behaviour (e.g. Goffman, 1959; Garfinkel, 1972; Glaser and Strauss, 1972). The interview situation itself may have influenced the amount of householders' surplus stated (cf. Becker and Greer, 1972). There is pressure on respondents to state a compensation amount. This pressure is not balanced by pressure that such an amount is not applicable to them. Without probing there is no certainty that people are indeed placing a monetary value on their proximity to, for example, friends, kin, familiar places or potential psychological disruption. Their knowledge on which to base such a judgement is probably severely limited and their resultant personal assessment of compensation open to doubt. There is also reason to expect that some respondents suspected the motives of the questionnaire and, in responding, reacted to the motives they perceived behind it.

A hypothetical 'large project' is unlikely to have equal 'impact' to an actual project. An actual project is not merely a physical facility. It is introduced by specific organisations or political institutions. It is often seen as serving the interests of specific groups in society. It may be opposed or supported by other groups with which the residents may or may not identify (e.g. local businessmen, resident groups or unions). These components are part of the relevant environment within which people assess the impact of a project on their lives and predict the extent of social disruption, including social severance. The use of a hypothetical project to assess social disruption ignores the political, social and other relevant attributes which inevitably accompany any actual project, and which may influence the degree of severance experienced or predicted by respondents.

While it is acknowledged that the practical and administrative problems of compensation do not affect the principle of determining monetary values using the householders' surplus technique, they do affect the evaluation of projects. The fact that compensation may be rarely paid, and for administrative reasons, if paid, will rarely correspond to actual losses, has an effect on the evaluation of projects. The economic disruption caused by shortfall in compensation may cause social disruption. This point is only tangentially addressed but is a potentially important factor in evaluation.

The traditional application of cost-benefit analysis has subsumed social factors within the cost-benefit framework. At a minimum, the problems associated with the application of cost-benefit analysis to social factors imply the need for a form of social impact analysis. The shortcomings of defining social impact analysis as relevant to a residue of factors not considered by the cost-benefit framework have been dealt with by Healey (1974). By contrast, social analysis and social evaluation should be seen as offering a distinct perspective on human experience, in many respects complementing an economic perspective.

A PERSPECTIVE ON THE SOCIAL ASSESSMENT OF SEVERANCE

Significant limitations have been found in the application of the cost-benefit approach. This serves as a salutary reminder of the complexity of human experience. As Gans remarks, '. . . when I studied people and communities, it turned out that their notion of the good life . . . [was concerned with] work, income, health, family, neighbours, friends, church, and, if they were home owners, space, comfort, status, and property values' (Gans, 1968, p. 1). It has been argued that social bonds, unlike consumer goods, are not generally perceivable as suitable for notional or actual trading in the market place (although monetary costs of maintaining given bonds may be measurable). Well-being depends on monetary matters but also *inter alia* on social factors, like proximity to friends, familiar neighbours and kin.

The social assessment of severance faces a number of key problems, philosophical, conceptual and in the choice of phenomena for examination.

What are the effects of changes in the urban environment on people and on the action which people take in response to such changes? The effects explored in the literature include: (a) changes in behaviour (e.g. trip making to facilities, friendship patterns); and (b) changes in attitudes and perception of neighbourhood, attitude to traffic.

What are the likely determinants of the nature and extent of effects of changes to the urban environment? The determinants examined in the literature include: (a) the psychological, social and demographic characteristics of those on whom the changed environment is imposed (e.g. personality traits, class, stage of life, friendship patterns); (b) the character of the social or physical change to the environment (e.g. traffic flows, class of new environment); and (c) the mode of implementation of the change to the environment (e.g. sensitivity of the authority implementing the changes to the environment). One of the most useful policy implications of analysis in this area is the development of an understanding of the circumstances under which particular groups are susceptible to social severance.

Two broad philosophical positions are available for the social analysis of severance: sociology of knowledge and the functionalist approach. A sociology of knowledge approach has been adopted herein (for discussion see Simmie, 1974, and Bottomore, 1971). Specific analysis of work based on the functionalist approach is discussed in the next section.

Functionalists operate from the position that society is analogous to an organism, where the various parts of the organism (e.g. professionals, the managers and the labourers) contribute functionally to the operation of the society as a whole. The norms, values, beliefs and patterns of interaction characteristic of people occupying various parts of the organic whole are functionally necessary for the maintenance of social order and the perpetuation of society (i.e. the organism).

This is fundamentally a consensus model of society which posits an overall 'social good', similar to the aggregate welfare approach of conventional cost-benefit analysis. The practitioner operating under this paradigm has two problems:

(1) to specify the overall aims of society or the social good (e.g. strict *laissez-faire* economic development);
(2) to determine how best functionally to achieve such aims.

Social bonds would be evaluated in terms of the functional importance of their contribution to the overall social good.

Sociology of knowledge (e.g. Berger and Luckmann, 1971) takes as its philosophical tenet that existence and consciousness are in a dialectical relationship. People take on beliefs, values and activities consistent with their relationship to the means of production. The means of production may be strictly defined (e.g. capital or labour) or considered in a more disaggregate way (e.g. professionals, scientists, students, labourers). Social intercourse both shapes and is shaped by its conditions of existence. In a given situation, the nature of social intercourse reflects basic productive forces. This acknowledges two levels of social reality, the basic means of production (second-order constructs) and the surface norms and values which overlie them (first-order constructs).

The means of production designates basic areas of conflicting interests (e.g. Marxist class interests). A value stance must be taken by the planner and cannot be avoided. The problems faced by the evaluator are quite distinct from those facing the functionalist. They are:

(1) to find out the needs or interests of the groups concerned;
(2) to resolve these issues in a plan or course of action which almost inevitably favours one group or a set of groups over another group or groups.

This philosophical stance is similar to a disaggregated approach to economic evaluation, stressing equity concerns (see Nash, Pearce and Stanley, 1975).

The nature of local communities is an important concept in the evaluation of social severance, both in understanding the importance of local social bonds and in understanding the literature on social severance. Two early writers in the field, Tönnies (1957) and Durkheim (1964), provide a significant contrast. Tönnies saw two polar types of human motivation, rational and natural will (*Gesellschaft* and *Gemeinschaft* respectively). *Gemeinschaft* was characterised by fellowship and kinship centred on the family and extended kin in a geographically constrained area. *Gesellschaft* was characterised by exchange and rational calculation, determined by money interests, with relationships geographically unconstrained. Durkheim similarly saw two polar types, mechanical and organic solidarity, basically corresponding to Tönnies' types. However, while Tönnies favoured the community embodied in *Gemeinschaft*, Durkheim saw the functional interdependence of the increasing division of labour giving rise to more worthwhile relationships based on functional interdependence rather than tradition. Both conceptions remain in the contemporary literature.

The creation of self-sufficient communities, with a coincidence of physical boundaries and social activities is a prevalent theme in planning literature (e.g. Stretton, 1970). Strong local communities, and the factors which create them, have received considerable attention (e.g. Gans, 1962; Young and Willmott, 1957; Hill, 1967). Others have argued that local communities or neighbourhoods generally have little importance by comparison with other social institutions (e.g. work, school and family):

> Neighbouring in dynamic urban areas is no longer part of a tight network of interdependent activities and obligations concentrated within a small physical and social space; it is simply one more segmentalised activity. (Keller, 1968, p. 119)

Another significant problem in the use of the community or neighbourhood concept is the wide range of meanings which have been attached to these terms (Stacey, 1969). Some of the most useful work concerning severance has rejected *a priori* notions of 'community' and 'neighbourhood'. Instead it has examined social bonds through the *networks* of interaction which exist, and attempted to identify the factors which create and sustain them. This applies to participant observation studies of specific areas, and to more formal analysis of social networks using social surveys.

SOCIAL BONDS

The greatest quantity of research into the nature of social bonds has been conducted using survey methods of data collection. Participant observation, in the few cases in which it has been used, has provided excellent insights. Group techniques have been little used but have significant potential use as a research and possibly a social evaluation tool.

The theoretical and philosophical basis of participant observation will not be pursued here (see Manis and Meltzer, 1972). The basic characteristic of this method is that the participant observer becomes part of the group being studied, attempting to build up an understanding of the patterns of social interaction through experience of them. The proponents of participant observation argue that behaviour and opinions depend on the situation, and participant observation places the observer in the real situation in which social activity is occurring.

It has been argued that in contrast to the social survey which encompasses only one highly specialised situation, participant observation allows the researcher access to all kinds of situations (Becker and Greer, 1972). This method seeks to understand the meaning of everyday life and social behaviour as it is actually carried out (e.g. Whyte, 1955).

The seminal work of Gans (1962) is reviewed in considerable detail because it offers insight into the effect of relocation on the group studied, and an understanding of the level of information provided by participant observation. Gans (1962) coined the term 'urban village' to characterise the nature of social relations in the West End of Boston, in contrast to a cohesive neighbourhood. The urban village was conceived in contrast, too, to the 'urban jungle', a term more in keeping with the pathological connotations of a slum suitable for renewal. Ten major groups were identified in the West End, each with distinctive characteristics which set them apart from their fellow residents. The urban village corresponded to the residents' conception of many sub-areas defined by the predominance of particular ethnic groups.

Particular attention was focused on second-generation Italian-Americans, the largest group in the West End. Social interaction beyond the surperficial level was almost entirely confined to the ethnic group. Most of the West Enders' relations were with peers, among people of the same sex, age and life-cycle status. Class was important, but behavioural attributes over which people were assumed to exercise some control supplemented class as a basis for compatibility.

> The major criteria for ranking, differentiating, and estimating compatibility are ingroup loyalty and conformity to established standards of personal behaviour as well as interpersonal relations. West Enders expect each other to maintain prevalent social practices and consumer styles to marry within the ethnic – or at least religious – groups, and to reject middle-class forms of status and culture. (Gans, 1962, p. 27)

Four major behaviour styles predominated among the group studied: routine seekers, action seekers, maladapted and middle-class mobiles. *Routine seekers* as the term suggests, strive to establish a stable way of living, for example through adherence to a weekly menu for meals, entertaining the same people on the same night of the week every week, and giving the same gifts every year. *Action seekers* have an episodic life, where periods between thrilling episodes are seen as killing time. Action seeking is a male prerogative, and is characteristic of adolescents who often become routine seekers when they marry. The *maladapted* are 'unable to control their behaviour because of alcoholism or other personal difficulties' (Gans, 1962, p. 31). The *middle-class mobiles* aspire to the middle class either for themselves or their children and have to model themselves on outsiders, detaching themselves from relatives and old friends who in turn often reject the middle-class aspirants. Each group (with the probable exception of the maladapted) regards its own mode of living as superior to each of the others.

Can this material provide an insight into the effects of relocation severance? Clearly an understanding of the social structure prior to relocation is a prerequisite to understanding the basis on which those relocated are severed. Within the Italian-American group each of the ideal types discussed could be expected to face different relocation experiences, though it is a matter of opinion to decide which group faces the most difficult relocation problems.

The routine seekers could be expected to suffer a shattering blow to their established pattern of life. Their reliance on group experience, what Gans terms an 'expanded' family, makes them vulnerable to severance from some or all of their regular friends or relatives. The routine seekers have middle-class aspirations and could be expected to seek similar accommodation elsewhere. They found accommodation through friends or relatives in nearby areas rather than the available public housing. Public housing apparently offered no solution to the severance effects which had been generated.

The impact of relocation on the action seekers is more difficult to estimate. The West End had action, which may not have been provided elsewhere. Action seekers were highly dependent on their male peers. They often held the most poorly paid and 'dirty' jobs which gave them little financial power over the selection of alternative accommodation.

The middle-class mobiles could be expected to be those least affected by relocation; they were already 'severed' in a sense from the West End. They could be expected to be the most capable of coping with the relocation problems. It is difficult to predict the effect of relocation on the maladapted as Gans makes little mention of them.

Gans's work also makes it clear that the social and political manner by which public projects become a reality can accentuate severance. The West Enders did not understand the legal and bureaucratic manoeuvres in the redevelopment of their area. '[They] had considerable difficulty in understanding the complicated parade of preliminary and final approvals, or the tortuous process by which plans moved back and forth between the Housing Authority, the City Council, the Mayor, the State Housing Board, and the federal Housing and Home Finance Agency' (Gans, 1962, p. 290). When final approval for redevelopment occurred, the West Enders perceived it as merely another irrelevant bureaucratic decision. Their scepticism about the likelihood of the area being demolished was turned to bitterness when apparent corruption was exposed in the contracts for renewal. More real to the residents were the rumours, and the installation of new facilities in the area by other agencies; facilities that would be torn down if renewal occurred.

As a result the West Enders could only cynically interpret the motives of those pressing for renewal. Their failure to appreciate the process by which renewal became a reality meant that they failed to adapt in advance to their impending relocation. The severance effects, it could be assumed, would be more bitter as a result of the perceived self-seeking, but unshakeable power, of those pushing for renewal. Furthermore, the severance effects remained relatively unreal until notices finally arrived explaining relocation procedures, six months after state and three months after federal approval. In this way West Enders failed to make the necessary adjustments and plans to cope with their impending relocation.

Even the policies adopted to assist rehousing were quite out of keeping with the needs of the residents. The agency predicted that the eligible 60 per cent of residents would move into welfare housing, but only 10 per cent did. The assistance given in finding housing for the 90 per cent who obtained private housing had several deficiencies. The professionals sought middle-class standards of 'decent, safe and sanitary' housing. The West Enders were equally if not more concerned with social considerations. The professionals thought in terms of the nuclear family unit while the residents wanted to maintain other ties. Finally the professionals recognised the need to move households but not institutions, contributing to severance on this basis as well. The agencies organising relocation failed to appreciate the social dimension of it. They saw replacement housing purely in physical terms. The only social criteria actually applied seemed to operate against the interests of the Italian West Enders at least, as they sought to break up the ethnic ghettos.

Group techniques have been little used in understanding how various groups interact with their social and physical environment. Their potential seems relatively untapped, judging from the application of group techniques to similar problems. Two main types of group technique have been employed: 'market research' and the 'search conference'. Market research small group techniques have primarily been developed in private sector product planning. Within the market segment to be explored, homogeneous groups are used to generate a supportive environment. The search conference (Emery *et al.*, 1975) and related approaches were developed as a technique for resolving organisational problems and instituting worker participation. Heterogeneous slightly larger groups are used for identifying and resolving organisational conflict.

Widespread interest in the development of participatory evaluation has encouraged the exploration of the use of the search conference in planning. Social disruption to towns, identified by the search conference technique, played a significant role in the evaluation of alternative routes for the Hume Highway in Australia (Commonwealth Bureau of Roads, 1975). The market research approach has been little used in severance assessment, but the supportive environment created in market research groups may provide a particularly suitable situation for developing an understanding of severance. Whilst it is clear that group techniques can provide an efficient means of identifying evaluative dimensions of particular problems, the full potential of such techniques in evaluation is still unexplored.

A variety of problems involving severance have been addressed using survey techniques from a range of theoretical perspectives. Fried (1967) and Holdsworth (1973) have examined the effects of forced relocation. Appleyard and Lintell (1970) have considered the effects of traffic flow on social interaction within the street environment in which the traffic flow occurs. Whyte (1957), Festinger *et al.* (1963), Carey and Mapes (1972), Lewis (1974) and Helmer *et al.* (1975) have examined the effects of physical layout and social planning policies. Lee *et al.* (1975) have documented some of the barrier effects of major roads in London. Burkhardt (1971), Hill (1967), McLean and Adkins (1971) and Ellis (1968) have attempted to assess social sensitivity of neighbourhoods to disruption caused by construction of major roads. These works are sufficiently different in approach, the problems they addressed and the type of findings produced, to preclude simultaneous discussion of them. The discussion centres on recent neighbourhood-based American work, the work of Appleyard and Lintell (1970) on the severance effects of traffic, and the work of Lee *et al.* (1975) on severance by major roads.

Much of the recent American work has been based on the neighbourhood concept. It has sought to identify neighbourhoods in terms of their sensitivity to disruption by freeways constructed through them or along their boundaries (see Burkhardt, 1971; Hill, 1967; McLean and Adkins, 1971; Ellis, 1968; Klein *et al.*, 1971). This school of writers could be termed functionalists, as they define neighbourhood function as the stable transmission of the social order (e.g. Hill and Frankland, 1967). According to this view, strong neighbourhoods are stable and homogeneous and weak neighbourhoods are unstable and heterogeneous (Hill and Frankland, 1967). Homogeneous stable neighbourhoods are considered desirable and the most susceptible to neighbourhood severance.

Hill and Frankland (1967) measured social stability in terms of residential mobility. Hill (1967) developed an index of social stability based on residential mobility, proportion of owner-occupied houses, and proportion of single-family residences. Attempts have been made by this school of writers to define neighbourhood boundaries with a view to constructing freeways along them. McLean and Adkins (1971) use architectural style as the criterion for defining neighbourhood boundaries. They confirm, using a comparison of constructed freeways, that residential mobility increases in unstable heterogeneous neighbourhoods through which freeways are constructed. However, without any direct measure of social interaction there seems little reason to believe either that residential stability is a direct proxy for social interaction, or that architectural style corresponds to boundaries of social interaction.

Burkhardt (1971) and Ellis (1968), while operating from the same general position, examined some of the social interaction variables which made up the neighbourhood concept. Burkhardt examined three behavioural social interaction variables (neighbouring, use of local facilities and participation in local organisations) and three perceptual variables (identification as belonging to a distinct community or area, commitment to continue in the area and evelution as a place to live). He used factor analysis on the six variables. Factor one correlated highly with commitment to continue in the area, participation in local organisations and evaluation of the area as a place to live. Factor two related to the presence of friends or kin (a proxy for neighbouring) and the use of local facilities.

Burkhardt added the two factors produced to compute a neighbourhood index. Predictors of this index were sought from census data. Mobility, percentage of residential land and housing units per acre were found to be significant. He concluded that: 'by using readily available data for mobility, percentage of residential land, and housing units per acre, the highway planner can easily obtain an estimate of the social interaction occurring within a particular neighbourhood' (Burkhardt, 1971, p. 90).

Burkhardt's claim to predict social interaction so simply should not be accepted uncritically. To add distinct factors produced by factor analysis is merely to confound two quite different variables. His own analysis indicates that at least two dimensions are involved in the way in which people relate to their local areas. For example, participation in local organisations is relatively independent of the use of local facilities. The attempt to build a single index of 'neighbourhood' strength, it appears, is too simplistic.

Appleyard and Lintell (1970) have studied the effect of traffic flow on perception of the street environment and social interaction in the street. They examine actual perceptions and actual social interaction in three street blocks in San Francisco rather than using a fixed neighbourhood concept. The microscopic nature of their study makes it a particularly neat one for analysis. The three adjacent parallel streets were of 'similar residential character' but carried markedly different traffic volumes. The 'heavy' street was one-way, carrying a peak volume of 900 vehicles per hour and more trucks and buses than the other streets. The 'moderate' street was two-way and carried a peak volume of 550 vehicles per hour. The 'light' street carried only 200 vehicles per hour at peak hour.

The interviews conducted covered five criteria developed by Appleyard and Lintell (1970).

(1) Traffic hazard. The heavy street traffic posed a forbidding environment, being 'unsafe for children, and even people washing their cars'. Even to leave the garage by car one had to negotiate the 'large number of cars speeding down the hill'. The continuous presence of strangers in the street gave rise to feelings of fear of being 'hassled from passing cars' and 'afraid to stop and chat'. Predictably, the light street suffered less perceived traffic hazard, but the hazard was relatively unpredictable, stemming from the 'hot-rodder'.

(2) Stress, noise and pollution. While the emphasis of this chapter is on social severance, the stress, noise and air pollution tended to sever people from the street in which they lived. Indeed in the heavy street people tended to live in the rear of their houses, effectively severed from their own rooms facing the road.

(3) Neighbouring and visiting. Light street inhabitants had three times as many local friends and twice as many local acquaints as those on the heavy street. Moreover, 'contact across the street was very much more rare' on the heavy than on the light street. In the heavy street there were only 0·9 local friends per respondent.

(4) Privacy and home territory. Perceived 'home territory' in the light street, for most respondents, extended to the ends of the street block. In the heavy street, home territory was either the apartment itself (or 'not even that') or the building in which the residence was housed, and in no case extended to more than the street frontage of the building itself. The moderate street stood intermediate between the other two. It is significant to note, however, that not all respondents disliked the atmosphere of the heavy street. For one respondent, though not for most, the heavy street was 'alive, busy and invigorating'.

(5) Identity and interest. On the heavy street people observed or remembered little of the street environment, while on the light street the responses were 'much richer in content'. Children in particular had an intricate knowledge of the street. It would appear logical to deduce that these difference perceptions of the environment imply a higher degree of connectivity with the street in the case of the light street.

The results found by Appleyard and Lintell, in quite a dramatic way, confirm intuitive expectations. But this work, and a good deal of other material on social severance, suffers from a basic defect. There has been little or no consideration of what factors other than the physical environment might contribute to social interaction. Appleyard and Lintell (1970) have mainly examined the effects of traffic on social interaction. Hill and Frankland (1967) and McLean and Adkins (1971) studied the effect of freeways on neighbourhood, where neighbourhood is measured in terms of mobility. Burkhardt (1971) and Ellis (1968), who considered a range of social interaction variables, do not seek the determinants of social interaction.

Helmer *et al.* (1975) questioned the apparently strong conclusions of the Appleyard and Lintell study on the grounds that intervening variables may explain much of the variation in the patterns of social interaction. That is, variables such as class and stage of life might explain a great deal of the variation in experience of the street environment and social interaction.

Appleyard and Lintell have documented some of the demographic characteristics of respondents, which show significant differences in family composition, ownership and length of residence in the three streets. The light street was predominantly a family street with many children. Half the households owned their dwelling. The average length of residence was over sixteen years. The heavy street had almost no children, most residents being single people over 20 years of age. There was a disproportionately large number of single elderly women. The average length of residence was about eight years, and most were renters. The moderate street stood generally in between.

While Appleyard and Lintell discuss principles of environmental self-selection and environmental adaption to explain why no public protests accompanied the steady degradation of the street environment over the previous ten years, they do not consider the relative importance of social and demographic factors compared to environmental factors (e.g. traffic). In the research implications section of their paper, no mention is made of the need to control for social and demographic variables. As pointed out by Helmer *et al.* (1975), this is a significant weakness in their study.

Their only mention of demographic variables which might influence the level of interaction is of interest, however. The middle aged (25–55 years) possessed a similar number of friends in their block, though those on the light street had more acquaintances. The young (under 25) and the elderly (over 55) had many less social contacts in their own block on the heavy street than on the light. This suggests, subject to the limitations of the study, that the middle aged are least susceptible to traffic severance.

Lee *et al.* (1975) examined some of the perceptual and behavioural responses to the presence of a major road. They conducted a comparison between the surrounding areas of major roads constructed five, ten and thirty years previous to the study. Levels of response, they argue, consist of perceptions of the barrier, cognitions which develop, structured organisation of cognitions as motives, feelings and attributes, and finally their manifestation in behaviour. These responses they see operating in a 'feed-back loop' continually adjusting to new situations. This they term a cognitive mapping approach. They predicted that the presence of major roads would impose a shrinkage of people's neighbourhood schemata with a reduction in their social activity and its spatial patterning. The effects were expected to reduce with distance from the road.

Much of the evidence they use concerns 'neighbourhood' maps drawn by respondents. They assume that perceptual variables of this type 'programme' behaviour, but there must be considerable doubt about this issue. Neighbourhood has a number of different meanings (cf. Stacey, 1969), any one of which might be the meaning perceived by the respondent. It could be defined in neighbouring terms; that is, where you know people socially. It could be defined in terms of where people habitually go. It could be defined as areas of architectural or social similarity. All one really knows is that respondents saw fit to draw their neighbourhood on a map, and to include some landmarks within and others outside that neighbourhood. Until the concept of neighbourhood is related to other perceptual and behavioural measures it cannot be interpreted usefully.

Based on their studies Lee *et al.* concluded that people living up to 1 kilometre from a major road respond to the road line as a barrier, reducing their commitment to but not knowledge of the other side. They enlarge their neighbourhood territory on their own side. These results do not confirm their initial hypotheses but, they argue, are consistent with a general trend that less barrier gives smaller neighbourhoods.

They found that people living on a 'major road' crossing the barrier being studied, who had easy access by car or foot to the other side, had smaller neighbourhoods. Yet it could readily be maintained (cf. Appleyard and Lintell, 1970) that living on a major crossing road was a source of severance itself. It will be recalled that Appleyard and Lintell found much smaller 'home territories' on streets with heavy traffic then those with light traffic. This points to other factors which might influence perceived neighbourhood size, such as traffic on the street in which the respondent lived.

Of particular significance is the *ceteris paribus* assumption of Lee *et al.* Severance is assumed to be an individual phenomenon in an otherwise unchanged environment. They do not consider that one of the responses to the barrier may be to leave, and this self-selection may have influenced the results they obtained. Similarly, activity locations may have differed between the sites and since the introduction of the new road. Householders, in responding to the barrier, redirected their trip making, which could possibly have led to greater self-sufficiency on each side of the barrier through adjustment and perhaps relocation of businesses or other centres of activity.

The field of variables considered by Lee and his colleagues is insufficiently wide. They neglect a number of potentially significant environmental factors (e.g. traffic in the respondent's street). Perhaps more important is their minimal consideration of social and demographic variables aside from class (e.g. stage of life). They do, however, examine severance by trip type, finding that no significant severance occurred for work, pub, church and club trips. It did occur for shop, school, library, social contact and doctor trips. This kind of work might eventually provide a basis for understanding the substitutability of various trip types.

According to Helmer *et al.* (1975) there is a need to examine a wider range of predictors of social interaction, including life-cycle, social class, female role, time allocation, residential mobility, residential density, ownership of dwelling, territoriality and environmental design. The relative importance of these factors in various situations has not been fully defined. However, some of the findings are discussed in the following section.

Most writers accept the importance of *environmental design* on severance though some argue it has been over-rated in importance with respect to social factors (Helmer *et al*, 1975; Gans 1968). It is widely accepted that such things as relocation, creation of a barrier or traffic on a street do sever people and induce a variety of changed perceptions and behaviour. Social and demographic variables appear in many cases to be very important in mediating the effects of environmental design on social relationships (Michelson, 1970; Gans, 1968).

Class is a particularly important variable. Booth and Camp (1974) found that blue collar families voluntarily relocated into higher status areas found some difficulty in adjusting. They experienced 'marital stress', the 'traditional reliance on kin' was intensified, their proportion of friendship ties with workmates increased and couples (particularly wives) maintained a higher level of contact with their neighbours. They concluded that relocation to higher status areas was more stressful than relocation to areas of similar status for blue collar families. The work of Gans (1962) similarly implies that most working-class Italian-Americans in the West End of Boston would suffer from a move to higher status neighbourhoods. There may, however, be less stress and more benefits to the 'middle-class mobiles' than other groups. Fried (1967) like Gans studied people from the West End of Boston. His study of those relocated also stressed the importance of status: 'the higher the status . . . the smaller the proportions of severe grief' (Fried, 1967, p. 366). Confirmation of this effect may be found elsewhere (Young and Willmott, 1957; Hall and Guseman, 1975; Klein *et al.*, 1971).

The effect of class in other situations is not clear. Lee *et al.* (1975) report uncertain results regarding the effect of class on the response to a barrier. They tentatively conclude that middle-class sites show more disturbance but greater adjustment than working-class sites. There is no evidence to indicate the effect of class on traffic severance. Helmer *et al.* (1975) argue that areas homogeneous with respect to class will generally be amenable to measures to increase social interaction e.g. street closures, pedestrian malls). However, in heterogeneous areas, in the 'urban cockpit', such measures are likely to promote inter-class conflict. Heterogeneity with respect to class may be mediated by other factors, especially stage of life (Lewis, 1975).

There is some evidence that *stage of life* is important in mediating the effects of severance. Not a great deal has been reported on the effects of relocation severance with respect to stage of life but that which has been reported seems to indicate special difficulties for the elderly (e.g. Holdsworth, 1973; Hall and Guseman, 1975). UMPT (1974) report, however, that dissatisfaction with relocation did not relate to age. Appleyard and Lintell (1970) found that the middle age-group (25–55 years) appeared least affected by traffic in their street, and had a similar number of friends within the street, independent of the level of traffic. The young (under 25) and the elderly (over 55) had many more social contacts in the presence of light traffic than of heavy traffic.

Ethnicity has been found of importance in social severance. Ethnicity may limit the choice of replacement housing for ethnic groups (Hall and Guseman, 1975; Gans, 1962). The disruption of ethnic bonds may impose significantly on patterns of interaction (Gans, 1962).

There is evidence that those who have a long *period of residence* suffer from relocation more severely than more mobile residents (Hall and Guseman, 1975; Holdsworth, 1972; Klein *et al.*, 1971). There is however some indirect but contradictory evidence on this point. Lewis (1975) found that neighbours who settled an area simultaneously were most important initially, but suggested that the importance of neighbours might be declining with the passage of time.

Disruption to one's sense of continuity or feelings of belonging to a locality has been reported as a significant factor in relocation severance (Fried, 1967; Gans, 1962). This factor may act in concert with class (Fried, 1967) and it is not clear from the literature whether it operates independently of class. The *sense of spatial identity* was found by Fried to relate closely to the experience of grief reaction by forced relocation. This seems to confirm the earlier conclusion that severance would be particularly severe for the 'routine seeker' (Gans, 1962).

Fried (1967) found the presence of *friends* in the West End and positive feelings towards *neighbours* were relatively good predictors of the severance grief reaction. Those with their five closest friends in the West End and those with very positive feelings towards neighbours more often suffered severe grief reactions than those who did not meet these criteria. These interpersonal factors and spatial orientation had relatively independent effects on the grief reaction. Fried concluded that if both spatial identity and interpersonal identity were localised, then the grief at relocation was greatest.

Personality traits may influence the nature of the response to severance but little has been reported on this subject. Fried (1967) noted that *depressive orientation* did influence the severity of grief in relocation but the relationship was not simple. It only applied to those who saw the West End as their real home. For them, depressive orientation and the proportion of those showing severe grief were positively related.

SEVERANCE EVALUATION

In this chapter limits to the application of the cost-benefit approach to severance evaluation have been identified. A range of alternative approaches to understanding the personal and social dimensions of severance have been presented. There has been little attempt, however, to illustrate how these distinct approaches to severance, cost benefit on the one hand and social analysis on the other hand, might coexist as part of an evaluation process.

The cost-benefit approach seeks a monetary yardstick for all benefits and costs. There is clear evidence that, for social severance in particular, monetary valuation has quite limited applicability. There may be some trading of social well-being for economic well-being, though there is no conclusive evidence on this point. Some people probably do have few local social bonds and for these people analysis of their local social bonds will be unnecessary. But for many people, bonds to local friends, places and institutions are important and cannot adequately be described in monetary terms. It is probably safe to argue that those to whom the cost-benefit approach is least applicable (particularly those who will not state a 'surplus') are those to whom social evaluation is most applicable.

The relationship between the two approaches is particularly important but as yet has not been fully defined. Economic and social evaluation could be seen as competing incommensurable paradigms (Kuhn, 1970). That is, they provide quite different bases on which to examine problems. It is possible that one or other paradigm will make adjustments and absorb the other. It is regarded as more likely and logical that both the social dimensions and the economic dimensions of project evaluation will be treated as distinctive approaches to specific problems (alongside other approaches, for example environmental evaluation). The two approaches are not mutually exclusive, merely providing different perspectives from which to understand human experience.

The precise means of evaluation of social severance cannot be made specific at this stage without further research, and in any event no formula for evaluating the social aspects of severance is likely to be appropriate. Further work in this field should examine the factors which create and influence bonds between people, between people and institutions and between people and particular localities. The factors will include: environmental design (e.g. introduction of a barrier); the social and political means of introduction of an environmental change (e.g. supply of information by bureaucracies); and the social characteristics of the affected people (e.g. class, ethnicity) and the host population in which they live or into which they move.

In all the cases in which severance has been discussed (relocation, traffic and barrier) the local orientation of residents has been a continuing theme. Local orientation, however, may be a multidimensional concept. There is evidence that orientation to the local place is distinct from the level of local social interaction (Fried, 1967). There may be other ways in which people relate to their area in local but different ways. There is a need to examine this concept further: to understand the different ways in which people react to local areas; to develop predictors of different kinds of local social interaction; to develop a framework in which sensitivity to disruption of different local bonds may be estimated; and to develop social policies and environmental design incorporating consideration of social bonds.

There are several methods which may be employed in understanding the importance and distribution of particular social bonds. Participant observation is regarded by some as of limited applicability in view of the unrepresentative nature of the information it provides. However, it is considered to be of singular value in developing an understanding of the importance of social bonds. Group techniques have special relevance in raising issues relevant to a planning problem by those who may be affected. They can provide a relatively low cost qualitative basis on which to define the nature of the perceptions of a group, and insight into the importance of social severance in a locality. They have currently unexplored potential for use in the evaluation process. Survey techniques are relatively flexible, being able to provide both qualitative and quantitative information. They are obviously of prime importance in developing quantitative data and relationships.

The introduction of social evaluation into the evaluation process inevitably created philosophical, conceptual and technical problems. There is no obvious way in which social analysis can be placed on the same basis as economic analysis. Value judgements will be, perhaps, more difficult to make. Ultimately social evaluation will rest on evidence concerning social bonds and value judgements regarding which group is to receive social benefits, comparable to the manner in which equity questions are addressed in economics. Life will become more complicated, but perhaps more realistic, for the evaluator.

REFERENCES

Appleyard, D., and Lintell, M., *Environmental Quality of City Streets, Working Paper No. 142* (Berkeley, California: Institute of Urban and Regional Development, University of California, 1970).

Becker, H. S., and Greer, B., 'Participant observation and interviewing: a comparison', in *Symbolic Interaction: A Reader in Social Psychology,* 2nd edn., ed. J. G. Manis and B. N. Meltzer (Boston: Allyn & Bacon, 1972), pp. 102–12.

Berger, P., and Luckman, T., *The Social Construction of Reality* (Harmondsworth: Penguin, 1971).

Booth, A. and Camp, H., 'Housing relocation and family social integration patterns', *American Institute of Planners Journal*, vol. 40, 1971, pp. 124–8.

Bottomore, T. B., *Sociology: A Guide to Problems and Literature*, 2nd edn (London: Allen & Unwin, 1971).

Burkhardt, J. E., 'Impact of highways on urban neighbourhoods: a model of social change', *Highway Research Record*, no. 356, 1971.

Carey, L., and Mapes, R., *The Sociology of Planning: A Study of Social Activity on New Housing Estates* (London: Batsford, 1972).

Commission on the Third London Airport: Further Research Team Work (1970), 'Consumer surplus in housing: report of survey work' (unpublished).

Commonwealth Bureau of Roads, *Hume Highway Corridor Study: Goulburn to Albury-Wodonga, First Report* (Melbourne: Commonwealth Bureau of Roads, 1975).

Cropsey, J., 'What is welfare economics?', *Ethics*, vol. LXV, 1975, pp. 116–25.

Downs, A., 'Uncompensated non-construction costs which urban highways and urban renewal impose upon residential households', in *The Analysis of Public Output,* ed. J. Margolis (New York: NBER, 1970), pp. 69–106.

Durkheim, E., *The Division of Labour in Society* (New York: Free Press, 1964).

Ellis, R. H., 'Toward measurement of community consequences of urban freeways', *Highway Research Record*, no. 229, 1968.

Emery, F. E., Emery, M., Caldwell, G., and Crombie, A., *Futures We're In,* 2nd edn (Canberra: Centre for Continuing Education, Australian National University, 1975).

Festinger, L., Schachter, S., and Back, K., *Social Pressures in Informal Groups* (Stanford, California: Stanford University Press, 1963).

Flowerdew, A. D. J., 'Choosing a site for the third London airport: the Roskill Commission's approach', in *Cost-Benefit Analysis,* ed. R. Layard (Harmondsworth: Penguin, 1972), pp. 431–51.

Fried, M., 'Grieving for a lost home: psychological costs of relocation', in *Urban Renewal: The Record and Controversy,* ed. J. Q. Wilson (Cambridge, Massachusetts: MIT Press, 1967), pp. 359–79.

Gans, H. J., *The Urban Villagers* (New York: Free Press, 1962).

Gans, H. J., *People and Plans: Essays on Urban Problems and Solutions* (New York: Basic Books, 1968).

Garfinkel, H., 'Common sense knowledge of social structures: the documentary method of interpretation', in *Symbolic Interaction: A Reader in Social Psychology,* 2nd edn, ed. J. G. Manis and B. N. Meltzer (Boston: Allyn & Bacon, 1972), pp. 356–78.

Glaser, B. G., and Strauss, A. L., 'Awareness contexts and social interaction', in *Symbolic Interaction: A Reader in Social Psychology,* 2nd edn, ed. J. G. Manis and B. N. Meltzer (Boston: Allyn & Bacon, 1972), pp. 447–62.

Goffman, E., *The Presentation of Self in Everyday Life* (New York: Doubleday Anchor Books, 1959).

Hall, J. M., and Guseman, P. K., 'Displaced persons: social impacts of relocation', *Texas Transportation Researcher,* vol. 11, no. 4, 1975, pp. 3–4.

Harrison, A. J., *The Economics of Transport Appraisal* (London: Croom Helm, 1974).

Healey, P., 'Social impact analysis on the planning process', Paper A95, Seventh Conference, Australian Road Research Board, Adelaide, 1974).

Helmer, J., Rockliffe, N., and Paterson, J., 'The sociology of residential streets', Paper delivered to the Annual Congress of the Australian and New Zealand Association for the Advancement of Science, Canberra, 1975.

Hicks, J. R., *A Revision of Demand Theory* (Oxford: Clarendon Press, 1956).

Hill, S. L., *The Effects of Freeways on Neighbourhood* (California: Right of Way Research and Development and US Department of Transportation, 1967).

Hill, S. L., and Frankland, B., 'Mobility as a measurement of neighbourhood', *Highway Research Record*, no. 187, 1967.

Holdsworth, J. H., *Residential Disruption Costs in Urban Areas* (Melbourne: Commonwealth Bureau of Roads, 1973).

Keller, S. I., *The Urban Neighbourhood: A Sociological Perspective* (New York: Random House, 1968).

Klein, G. E., Currey, D. A., Ellis, H. B., Fratessa, C. L., McGillivray, R. G., Moon, A. E., Thompson, G. I., and Tilton, P. D., *Methods of Evaluation of the Effects of Transportation Systems on Community Values* (California: Stanford Research Institute, 1971).

Kuhn, T. S., *The Structure of Scientific Revolutions*, 2nd edn (Chicago: University of Chicago Press, 1970).

Lee, T., Tagg, S. K., and Abbott, D. J., 'Social severance by urban roads and motorways', in Planning and Transport Research Advisory Council, *Symposium on Environmental Evaluation* (London: UK Department of the Environment, 1976).

Lewis, D. R. E., 'Primary social networks in Canberra', unpublished thesis, Australian National University, 1975.

Manis, J. G., and Meltzer, B. N., eds, *Symbolic Interaction: A Reader in Social Psychology*, 2nd edn (Boston: Allyn & Bacon, 1972).

McLean, E. L., and Adkins, W. G., 'Freeway effects on residential mobility in metropolitan neighbourhoods', *Highway Research Record*, no. 356, 1971.

Michelson, W., *Man and His Urban Environment: A Sociological Approach* (Don Mills, Ontario: Addison-Wesley, 1970).

Mishan, E. J., 'What is wrong with Roskill?', *Journal of Transport Economics and Policy*, vol. 4, 1970, pp. 221–34.

Nash, C. A., Pearce, D. W., and Stanley, J. K., 'An evaluation of cost-benefit analysis criteria', *Scottish Journal of Political Economy*, vol. 22, 1975, pp. 121–34.

Simmie, J. M., *Citizens in Conflict: The Sociology of Town Planning* (London; Hutchinson, 1975).

Stacey, M., 'The myth of community studies', *British Journal of Sociology*, vol. 20, 1969, pp. 134–47.

Stretton, H., *Ideas for Australian Cities* (North Adelaide: Hugh Stretton, 1970).

Tönnies, F., *Community and Society*, ed. and trans. C. P. Loomis (East Lansing: Michigan State University Press, 1957).

Urban Motorways Committee, *New Roads in Towns* (London: HMSO, 1957).

Urban Motorways Project Team (UMPT), *Report to the Urban Motorways Committee* (London: HMSO, 1973).

Urban Motorways Project Team, *Social Surveys*, techniques used in the case studies, Technical Paper No. 2 (London: UK Department of the Environment, 1974).

Whyte, W. F., *Street Corner Society* (Chicago: The University of Chicago Press, 1955).

Whyte, W. H., *The Organisation Man* (New York: Doubleday, 1957).

Young, M., and Willmott, P., *Family and Kinship in East London* (London: Routledge & Kegan Paul, 1957).

Chapter 8

Social Costs and the National Accounts

INTRODUCTION

A country's economic performance is conventionally summarised by its Gross National Product (GNP). Growth in GNP is a major objective of national policy. It is not so long ago that a prominent economist wrote, 'Growth is the grand objective, the aim of economic policy as a whole' (Harrod, 1964). Since then, however, this measure has come under vehement attack. For example, it has been rechristened by some environmentalists 'Gross National Pollution'. More fully reasoned critiques have been given by Mishan (1967) and Boulding (1970). The purport of these criticisms is that, at best, GNP measures the output of goods and services which are produced for sale, and neglects important goods and services which never reach the market. Moreover, many of these latter, for example pollution, waste heat, noise, congestion, want creation and, more debatedly, various social ills, are unwanted by-products or social costs of market production. The market production is faithfully recorded in GNP while the by-products are systematically ignored. As the world becomes increasingly crowded by man and his economic activities, these by-products become increasingly serious and according to some (e.g. Meadows *et al.*, 1972, MIT, 1970, Heilbronner, 1974) threaten the very survival of mankind. Accordingly, it is argued, GNP is not just a poor but a dangerously misleading guide to economic policy; certainly it is not a measure of a nation's 'welfare'.

These criticisms have provoked a variety of responses as follows:

(1) GNP was never intended to be a welfare measure;
(2) GNP is a partial measure of welfare, but there is a general presumption that differences in GNP will reflect differences in welfare;
(3) GNP is one among a variety of interesting components of welfare, which should be considered together;
(4) GNP can and should be modified to yield a similar but more comprehensive welfare measure.

Let us look at each of these responses in turn.

The first group insists that GNP has no normative significance; it is simply an interesting aggregate found useful in a variety of economic analyses and policy exercises, such as cyclical management. This view is well expressed by Jaszi of the US Bureau of Business Economics:

> The focus on the measurement of welfare is a snare and delusion to the national accountant. It is more fruitful to look upon his task in another way ... to construct a comprehensive description of the economic process that is disciplined and realistic and, as such, useful in the analysis of problems that call for decision making in our society. Obviously ouput must be in the centre of this picture, and the process that is depicted must be production, distribution, and use of that output, because that is what our economy is about. (Jaszi, 1973)

Archibald writes more generally:

> We need not encumber ourselves with metaphysical enquiries into the true meaning of 'happiness', 'satisfaction' or 'utility' ... there are many other reasons besides our own value judgement for finding an index interesting. (Archibald, 1959)

In other words, value judgements should be kept out of economics. The economist should confine himself to *positive* questions of means, leaving *normative* questions of ends to the 'policy maker'.

Unfortunately, a rigid separation of positive and normative cannot be achieved. Choices must be made as to which relationships are to be investigated and how; data must be grouped and summarised in aggregated statistics, such as GNP, and considerable discretion exists as to what aggregates should be selected (see, for example, Hicks, 1942). It is not realistic to suppose that such choices can be made exclusively by policy makers; they are too detailed and technical to be made by anyone but workers in the field. Beckerman (1974) is surely nearer the mark when he writes, 'The basic conventions that have been adopted for the purposes of GNP measurement are still founded on some notion of what measures of economic activity can best represent the contribution of that activity to welfare.'

Once selected, such measures are liable to have undue influence and qualifications tend to be ignored. For example, growth in GNP is an important objective, despite the protests of professional economists. In fact such protests until recently have been rather rare. Jaszi, in the passage quoted above, finesses most of the objections with the value-laden suggestion that 'the production, distribution and use of ... output ... is what our economy is about'. Heller (1972) writes : GNP 'is highly useful and constantly used by economists ... as a measure of the availability of output to meet changing national priorities'. But what is to be regarded as output? And what if the shift in priorities (e.g. dealing with pollution) results from the output increases?

The second group admits that GNP is only a partial indicator of welfare and even then, once subsistence needs have been met, many of the most important aspects of welfare are excluded. Nevertheless they maintain that, by and large, increases in GNP bring increases in welfare. Thus Denison (1971), defending the existing increase, writes: 'Whatever want, need or social problem engages our attention, we ordinarily can more easily find resources to deal with it when output is large and growing than when it is not.' Lipton (1968), Heller (1972), Beckerman (1974) and other apologists of growth write in similar vein. This seems to provide a rather strong justification for policies to raise GNP.

One might, following Pigou (1924), distinguish between 'economic welfare' and 'social (or overall) welfare' and represent the situation thus:

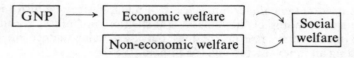

Economic welfare may be taken to relate to all those items covered by GNP, and non-economic welfare all other considerations, for example climate, natural beauty and quality of human relationships. Countries with the highest GNP might not have the highest social welfare because of variations in non-economic welfare; for example, very cold countries would have to devote a large proportion of their GNP to counteract the cold, an expenditure which would be unnecessary in a more temperate country. However, if the diagram tells the whole story, one could expect to find a positive correlation between GNP and social welfare; this is indeed Pigou's view ('there is a clear presumption that changes in economic welfare indicate changes in social welfare in the same direction') and also Denison's. More important, it is implied that increases in GNP would lead to increases in total welfare. Such conclusions depend, however, on the absence of any systematic link between GNP and non-economic welfare. If, for example, increases in GNP involve increases in pollution or in crime, then it cannot necessarily be concluded that social welfare is increased.

The third group seeks to supplement GNP with other indicators of social welfare; these might include indicators of distribution, of environmenal quality, of life expectancy, of the socio-political fabric (e.g. crime rates and illness); they might also include indicators of subjective 'happiness' obtained from surveys. It is then left to policy makers to decide what weight to attach to particular indicators. The idea clearly has merit but there are major difficulties. First, to be manageable, attention must be focused on a relatively small number of indicators; this gives rise to acute problems of selection and the danger that certain aspects of welfare may be neglected.

Then, to achieve reasonable coverage, heavy aggregation is inevitable. For example, how are murders and shoplifting to be combined in an index of crime? Should all crimes be given equal weight, or should minor crimes (how minor?) be omitted from the index? Or should a weighted index be constructed? If so, how should the weights be chosen? Again, an increase in life expectancy could arise from a decrease in infant mortality, or prolongation of the lives of old people, from increased longevity of the mentally subnormal or of people in acute pain. Should allowance be made for these distinctions and if so, how?

Indicators, unless chosen with great care, can be misleading. For example, crime rates inevitably reflect *reported* crime. Research has indicated that reporting crimes is encouraged by the probability of their solution. Hence an increase in the resources devoted to crime solving may result in opposite movements in crimes committed and crimes reported.

Finally, the coverage of indicators is liable to overlap. For example, reductions in air pollution will lead to increase in life expectancy. GNP is particularly liable to overlap with other indicators: increases in hospital facilities raise life expectancy, increases in pollution control lower air pollution; both will be picked up in GNP. In the light of such overlaps it is difficult for the policy maker to determine how much weight to attach to individual indices.

GNP, for all its faults, covers a well-defined area systematically, comprehensively, without duplication and according to clearly defined principles. The same can scarcely be said of social indicators.

The fourth group wishes to extend the coverage of GNP in a systematic way using, as far as possible, the same principles or natural extensions of those that are used in constituting GNP. The idea is certainly attractive and the next three sections will be devoted to an explanation of the principles by which such a measure might be constructed and a report on an attempt to construct such a measure.

GNP is in fact made up of two broad components, consumption (private and public) and investment. Consumption is an indicator of current welfare, while investment, by increasing productive potential, contributes to future welfare. In the following section we shall consider how the concept of consumption might be extended to provide a more complete measure of current welfare. The third section concerns similar extensions to investment.

Individual well-being depends not only on absolute GNP but on the number of people amongst whom this output must be spread. This point is generally met by using GNP *per head* as the welfare indicator.

In the fourth section the inadequacy of this procedure is demonstrated and alternatives examined. The fifth section assesses a pioneering attempt to attach figures to some of the proposed new concepts, and in the final section conclusions are drawn.

It must be stressed that a comprehensive appraisal of GNP is not attempted. Attention is focused on recent criticisms of GNP, mostly connected with environmental degradation, resource depletion, population increase and the social environment. Other issues are introduced only in as far as this is necessary to clarify the current controversies. A particularly notable omission concerns the failure of GNP to reflect the distribution of income. For the older controversies, the reader is recommended to consult a standard text on national income accounting (e.g. Hicks, 1942).

MEASURING CURRENT WELFARE

Before considering extensions, it is important to understand how consumption is measured at the moment. Our discussion will be brief and those with no knowledge of national accounting would be well advised to consult a text such as Beckerman (1968). Conversely those with a good knowledge of these matters may like to skim or skip this discussion and pick up the argument again at page 177.

In a one-good economy, consumption could be measured in physical units. When many goods are produced, their contributions must be expressed in a *common* unit, inevitably money. Consumption may be calculated as

$$C = p_1 q_1 + p_2 q_2 + \cdots + p_n q_n = \sum_i p_i q_i$$

where the qs are quantities and the ps prices. This total is of course simply the total value of consumption. But this must not obscure the fact that our basic concern is with *quantities*; prices are introduced solely to bring the qs to a common unit. This means that in comparing consumption with what it is at another time (or place, or what it would be under other policies) one must *hold prices constant*. Thus:

$$\frac{C_t}{C_s} = \frac{\sum_i p_i q_{it}}{\sum_i p_i q_{is}},$$

where s and t refer to the base time period and current time period respectively.

Consumption may be viewed as a weighted sum of quantities consumed, the weights being held constant over any comparison. Notice a certain arbitrariness over the choice of weights: they may for example be prices at time t or equally the prices at time s, or an average of the two, or indeed prices at some other time r. What of course matters is relative prices (or weights), the *overall* price change having been deliberately eliminated, and it is sometimes convenient to treat one good, say the first, as *numeraire*, choosing the (physical) unit of measurement such that $p_1 = 1$. Then

$$C_t = q_{it} + \sum_{i \neq 1} p_i q_{it}.$$

The p_i may now be taken to represent prices *relative* to p_t. The procedure is illustrated for the two-good case in Figure 8.1. Consumption is at P, and p_2/p_1 is given by the slope of ZPZ'. Total consumption is measured by OZ. Figure 8.1(b) shows how crucially consumption comparisons

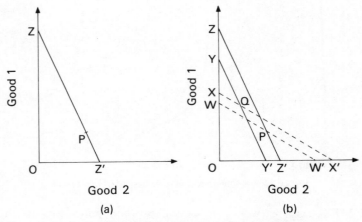

Figure 8.1   *The dependence of* consumption *on relative prices*

depend on the relative weights or prices. At relative weights given by ZPZ', consumption at P is OZ, that at Q lower at OY. But at relative weights given by WPW' (dotted lines) consumption at P is OW and that at Q is higher at OX.

It may seem 'natural' to use *market prices* as weights, but the logic of so doing depends on the claim of relative prices to measure relative (marginal) values, which depends in turn on perfect markets or some equivalent assumption. Figure 8.2 illustrates this. FF' is the production frontier, II' an indifference curve and ZZ' is the price line at the optimum point P. (We abstract from investment and international trade so that consumption equals production.) At P, relative prices measure both the marginal rate of transformation (relative marginal costs) and the marginal rate of substitution (relative marginal utilities). Using these prices as weights, we obtain the satisfactory result that consumption is maximised at P; however this is a result of limited significance, since these weights derive their justification from the prior choice of P.

As we move away from P, the marginal rate of transformation (MRT) and the marginal rate of substitution (MRS) both change. If resources were concentrated on producing Good 1, OF, not OZ, could be produced. And the amount of Good 1 which, on its own, would yield welfare equal to that attaining at P is not OZ but OI (possibly infinite). Only in the special cases where FF' and II' are linear do F and X, I and X coincide. This result is worth noting in view of subsequent discussion.

If markets are not perfect, the relevance of market prices is reduced. Figure 8.2 (b) illustrates a divergence between relative prices

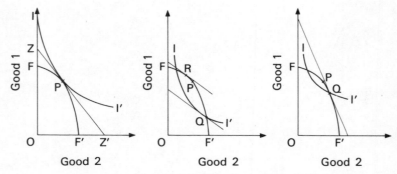

Figure 8.2   *Relative prices as a measure of relative values*

and MRT, such as would be caused by monopoly elements in the production of Good 2. Market prices still measure MRS correctly and north-west movements along the frontier increase 'consumption' and are correctly deemed improvements. However the optimum position at these relative prices is incorrectly deemed to be R rather than P.

Figure 8.2 (c) illustrates a divergence between relative prices and MRS, such as might arise from consumption externalities (e.g. congestion). Using weights given by market prices, 'consumption' will be maximised at Q, a misleading result.

These examples illustrate three propositions.

(1) Consumption comparisons are heavily dependent on the weights used to combine the components.
(2) Weights yielded by market prices are, even in ideal circumstances, only appropriate in evaluating small changes.
(3) The significance of the weights obtained by market prices depends on perfect markets.

National accounting is based on the idea that there are two classes of economic activity, namely, production and consumption. It is the function of the production sector (typically 'firms') to produce goods and services which (still neglecting investment and international trade) are sold to private households to consume. Consumption is the source of welfare, production is merely a means to this end. The total value of consumption is measured at the point of sale to consumers. This may be calculated from the production side but, if this approach is adopted, 'intermediate' goods, such as steel sold to the motor industry for incorporation in cars, must be excluded.

However, goods produced-sold-consumed in this way are not the sole source of welfare. This has long been recognised and certain imputations and other allowances have long been standard practice.

First, there is government non-market activity, for example defence or education. Most of these activities provide benefits to individuals and thus contribute to welfare. Some (e.g. education) could have been sold, and in some cases there are close private substitutes. If so, a value could be imputed from the prices paid for these substitutes (e.g. private school fees); however there may be systematic quality differences, which it would be difficult to allow for, and besides many government services (e.g. law courts) have no close private substitutes. The alternative, universally adopted, is to draw the production boundary one stage back, to regard the government itself as a consumer (on behalf of individuals), buying, for example, exercise books, chalk and the services of teachers.

Secondly, there is household activity. There are a wide range of goods and services which individuals provide for themselves, their families or their friends without payment: growing vegetables, putting up shelves, helping (tutoring) one's child in maths, cooking one's husband's dinner, taking a crippled neighbour for a drive. In all these cases marketed substitutes exist (bought vegetables and shelves, tuition, etc.), though the point does not really rest on the existence of such substitutes. Such items are generally excluded from GNP on the pragmatic ground that they are so difficult to trace and value. Also, as we shall see, there are often severe conceptual difficulties in separating consumption from production in this kind of activity. This neglect can lead to anomalies and (if great care is not taken) to misleading policy prescriptions. Consider, for example, the increase in the proportion of women who go out to work. The value of their market activity is faithfully recorded in GNP but no deduction is made for the loss of their services at home, which must now be done by charwomen or machines (both included in GNP) or not at all. Clearly policies on working women should not be judged by their impact on GNP.

In one case (only) the anomaly is judged so great that a correction is made – namely, for food consumed by the grower. This is a conceptually clear case and presents relatively few estimation problems. The matter is perhaps not of great importance in advanced countries (where most food is marketed) but in a developing country, subsistence agriculture accounts for a large proportion of all food consumption and a significant proportion of GNP. This case provides an interesting precedent.

A similar problem arises when a firm provides goods or services free to employees, customers or business associates. Examples include free offers, concessionary coal, use of petrol paid for by the firm but used for pleasure motoring, gifts to promote business deals and expense-account lunches. The firm will regard all these items as inputs (and it may be difficult for the national income accountant to separate them out). But their effect on welfare is much the same as if the firm had given cash with which these benefits could be bought. In practice imputations of this sort are rather rare. In Britain they are confined to food and clothing supplied to the armed forces. If, due to rising tax rates, perks to employees are increasing (or conversely due to tougher laws they are diminishing) trends in GNP will be misleading.

All the examples so far discussed concern goods or services similar to marketed goods or services which for some reason fail to pass through a market. The principles underlying such cases are pretty well accepted and a ready method of imputation exists (but see Jaszi, 1973, p. 87, for some difficulties).

We now pass to some other cases which do not fit nearly so closely into the production-consumption model. The first group concerns services provided by the physical environment – the climate, the landscape, air and water quality, and so on. Clearly these have a most important direct effect on human well-being (they may also affect production but this *is* reflected in GNP). Moreover they vary from time to time and place to place and are powerfully influenced by economic activity. Environmentalists suggest that increases in output have led both to a deterioration of environmental quality and to the diversion of resources to offsetting the damage.

Consider the pollution of a river by a chemical firm; such pollution is of course not picked up by the GNP, although it reduces the welfare of would-be swimmers. Now suppose a clean-up operation is mounted. If this is run by the firm, then the costs are treated as intermediate and do not appear in GNP. If however it is undertaken by the government, the costs are counted as final and are included in GNP. Clearly it is anomalous that the impact on GNP should depend on *who* performs the clean-up, and it is the treatment of the second case that appears to be wrong. The joint contribution to welfare of the chemical production and the clean-up is simply the chemicals produced. The clean-up simply cancels an adverse side-effect of the chemical production, and is said to be a *defensive expenditure*.

'Defensive' expenditures may also be incurred by individuals.

Suppose, for example, individuals buy pills which neutralise the effect of the pollutants or incur higher transport costs to swim farther upstream. Again these expenditures will normally be included in GNP and again the case for their exclusion is strong.

In one respect, allowance for defensive expenditures is straightforward. No imputations are necessary; items identified as defensive are simply omitted. Unfortunately the *identification* of defensive expenditures is not straightforward. Moreover it will be seen that to deduct defensive expenditures without at the same time allowing for associated changes in environmental quality can do more harm than good.

One problem is that environments can differ (e.g. from country to country), quite apart from differing impacts of human activity. To cite a favourite example, country A has a colder climate than country B. However, by appropriately large expenditure on energy, A could achieve an equally high indoor temperature. Should the additional expenditure be regarded as 'defensive' and then excluded from GNP? If our concern is with actual welfare then the answer must be yes: the expenditure simply nullifies an adverse endowment of nature. However if our aim is, more modestly, to measure the impact of human activity of welfare, then *provided the need for the additional expenditure is external to the system*, the expenditure should be included. Unfortunately, whether this is the case is not always clear. Suppose for example country A, though mainly cold, includes a region as warm as B. The need for heating could be reduced by moving all the inhabitants to this region. Ignoring possible disadvantages (e.g. congestion) associated with such a policy, should the need for heating then be regarded as exogenous or should it be regarded as the outcome of a gratuitous decision of a section of the population to live in the older parts of the country? Consider another classic case, defence. Many national accounts reformers (Nordhaus and Tobin, 1972; Juster, 1973) argue for its exclusion because they 'see no direct effect . . . on household economic welfare'. In itself, this argument is absurdly weak: defence reduces military risks just as dams may reduce flood risks or medical expenditure health risks. These must all be presumed gains to national welfare; for evidently this is the government's view and it is difficult to see how the national income account can challenge the government's valuation. However the need for defence (like heating) depends on an aspect of the external environment, in this case the strength and intentions of foreign powers. Provided these are exogenously given, defence must be included in GNP. If, however, defence expenditure influences the potential aggressor's military expenditure, the level of external threat becomes endogenous; defence expenditure is then 'defensive' and should be excluded. Thus the proper treatment of defence depends on what we believe to be the determinants of other countries' military expenditure.

In any case, *simply* omitting defensive expenditures from GNP is adequate only if these expenditures exactly counterbalance the impact of economic activity on environmental quality. Otherwise allowance must also be made for any residual change in environmental quality. Suppose, in the pollution example, the clean-up was only partial. The contribution of chemical-plus-clean-up to welfare comprises (1) the output of chemicals and (2) the net deterioration of the river. Thus defensive expenditures must be excluded *and* allowances made for any change in environmental quality. In other cases the 'defensive' expenditures do more than counterbalance the initial effect, for example if double-glazing installed to keep out airport noise provides heat insulation at the same time. In such a case a full deduction for defensive expenditure would be too much.

If deducting defensive expenditures is not enough, should it be regarded as a step in the right direction? Denison (1971) convincingly indicates how this adjustment on its own could be seriously misleading: 'to do this would mean that the more we diverted our resources and output from other uses to improve the environment, the smaller would be GNP ... It yields the false result that we are equally well-off whether in the same circumstances, we do or do not [undertake defensive expenditures].'

The issue of evaluating environment quality is particularly serious because of the conflict between the output of marketed goods and the preservation of environmental quality.[1] At any point of time one may represent the attainable combination of marketed goods (including perks, home production and similar 'might-have-been-marketed' goods) and environmental quality by a production frontier (Figure 8.3). The output of marketed goods is maximised at X, but environmental

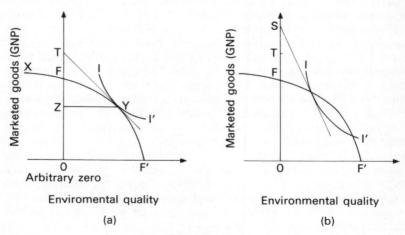

Figure 8.3   *GNP and environmental quality*

quality is very low. The optimal position, may (in principle) be determined by drawing in the indifference curve and finding the point Y, where the production frontier touches an indifference curve.

How can the GNP concept be extended to allow for environmental quality? It will be recalled that GNP is calculated by weighting together the outputs of various final goods and that market prices are generally used as weights. The reason for this procedure is that market prices represent the marginal valuations by consumers of the various goods. The principle is (conceptually speaking) quite readily extended to environmental quality. We need first to find the marginal valuation of (each component of) environmental quality and then to apply this to the difference between the level of environmental quality and the 'zero' level. The choice of this base level is essentially arbitrary but makes no difference[2] provided the level is adhered to consistently. The generalised GNP measure (GNP*) in Figure 8.3 (a) is OT (which is greater than OZ because the level of environmental quality is higher than the arbitrarily chosen zero level). Notice that this is *not*, as sometimes stated, 'what GNP would have been had environmental quality been maintained at its zero level'. This is OF, not OT. F and T coincide only if the frontier FF' is linear.

The measurement principle does not of course depend on the attainment of the optimum position. For example, at the sub-optimum W (Figure 8.3 (b)), the marginal valuation of environmental quality is given by the slope of the indifference curve at W and GNP* is given by OS. Of course in *comparing* positions, the weights must be held constant. It is irrelevant for example that OS > Ot. There are two reasonably valid ways of comparing GNP* at W and Y, one is to draw a line WT' parallel to YT, the other to draw WS' parallel to YS. Both correctly indicate the superiority of the optimal position.

Of course, the measurement of environmental quality, like the determination of environmental policy, requires a view on the indifference map. Since environmental quality attributes are not marked, this may be very difficult to determine. One well-known approach is to set a tax or price on environmental inputs such that the relative price equals the marginal rate of substitution. The tax then measures the marginal valuation of environmental quality and may be used to calculate GNP*. Of course, if the tax is wrongly set, not only will a sub-optimal point be reached but the tax will fail to measure the marginal valuation of environmental quality correctly and GNP* will be incorrectly estimated. If methods other than taxes (e.g. physical regulations) are used, this approach is anyway not available, and estimation is likely to be very difficult. However basically the problem is that discussed in the earlier chapters of finding willingness-to-pay.

The use of willingness-to-pay is of course subject to the same objections here as in cost-benefit analysis. Firstly it reflects not only preferences but *ability-to-pay*, i.e. greater weight is given to the preferences of the affluent. This defect may in both cases be corrected by the application of distributional weights (cf. Pearce, 1971; Feldstein, 1972).

Secondly, it incorporates all the limitations of market-based behaviour. It reflects failure to act in one's own best interests through ignorance or otherwise, possibly under the influence of advertising or other pressures. These failings (the importance of which is controversial) are in no way confined to imputed values for environmental quality, applying just as strongly to the most conventional components of GNP (Lecomber, 1974).

In some cases (as in cost-benefit analysis) it is possible to allow for imperfect knowledge by valuing an item at 'how people would value it if they were more knowledgeable'. Sometimes indeed this valuation procedure is used accidentally. For example, one method of valuing air pollution involves estimating and valuing the resultant effect on mortality (Ridker, 1967). This bears little relation to 'what people would pay to avoid pollution' if (as is usual) people are ignorant of the effects on health, but is, arguably, the more appropriate measure of this aspect of the costs of air pollution.

Of course one could depart from willingness-to-pay altogether and use 'planners' values'. The difficulties of this approach are analogous to, but perhaps more serious than, the difficulties surrounding the use of planners' values in cost-benefit analysis. How are these values to be derived?· Are they the values of the analyst or the government or 'the population' as somehow assessed through the ballot box or by opinion polls? If the government, may they not alter wildly with each change of government? If the population, may not the same irrationality and ignorance be manifested in the ballot box or opinion surveys as in the market? A cost-benefit analysis is at least a one-off job to illuminate a particular decision. The values of the government of the day are perhaps appropriate to such an analysis. But it would be inconvenient for GNP* to be so flimsily based, inconvenient indeed if the whole series had to be recalculated for each change of government. In short, there seems little alternative to willingness-to-pay, possibly corrected for ignorance (and distribution.)

Welfare is affected also by a wide group of factors which may be collectively categorised as the 'social environment'. It will be convenient first to return to some of our earlier examples. Consider the man who took his crippled neighbour for a drive in the country. It was suggested that he was providing the services of chauffeur, and that the price of this market-based substitute might be used in valuation. But in fact this approach misses the most important elements of the situation. First it is unlikely that, in the absence of the man's kind offer, the cripple (or substitute girlfriend – or wife!) would have hired the services of a chauffeur; by itself this suggests that the value is less, possibly far less than the price of chauffeuring. On the other hand it may be that she enjoys the drive with her neighbour (boyfriend, husband) rather more than a chauffered drive, so that the two are after all not very close substitutes. It is also possible that the kind neighbour enjoys the drive too – should this not also be taken into account? The production-consumption analogy is unhelpful in such a case and marked substitutes provide no guide to evaluation.

Next consider employee benefits. The cases so far considered all concern goods which might otherwise have been purchased from money income. But suppose the employer installs new machines which (probably incidentally to their main purpose of increasing efficiency) make conditions on the shopfloor less onerous, less noisy or less dangerous (or conversely less interesting). Here again, the product-consumption analogy is unhelpful. It is in fact inadequate to regard production simply as a means to consumption. The only meaningful way of looking at this is to note an improvement (or deterioration) in the work environment, and inquire how much the beneficiaries would be willing to pay.

The importance of this kind of factor is all-pervasive. Relationships between husband and wife, parent and child, neighbour and neighbour, casual acquaintance on the beach or in the supermarket, relationships between workers and management, workers and foremen, mates on the shopfloor, are a most important determinant of happiness, arguably more important than most of the goods and services sold on the market. Extreme manifestations of these phenomena are crime, strikes, street brawls, wife battering, etc. and results may include deaths, depressions, suicides and other worrying social phenomena.

The importance of these components of welfare is scarcely in dispute. What is more controversial is their relationship to conventional economic magnitudes. As with the physical environment, however, there must be some sort of trade-off between GNP and the social environment. GNP may be maximised by ignoring the social environment (except of course in as far as it feeds back on to production). If resources are devoted to maintaining the social environment above the minimal level, GNP will be reduced. Figure 8.3 applies. The same valuation procedures also apply although their application is even more difficult.

EXTENDING THE INVESTMENT MEASURE

Capital goods are no more than intermediate goods which outlive the period of account. Investment is simply a *means* to the end of higher consumption in the future. Why then should investment be included at all in a measure of welfare? A conventional or extended consumption measure at first sight seems more appropriate.

However current consumption is not (by itself) an appropriate objective of policy. For consumption may always be increased at the expense of investment, i.e. to the detriment of the future. If a consumption measure is to be used, it must be extended to embrace future as well as present consumption. Some writers (e.g. Weisbrod, 1962) indeed suggest using a measure of the form

$$W = \sum_{t=0}^{\infty} w_t C_t. \tag{1}$$

The weights, w_t, represent the relative marginal valuations of consumption in different time periods. The principle is illustrated for one good and two time periods in Figure 8.4. This figure is identical to

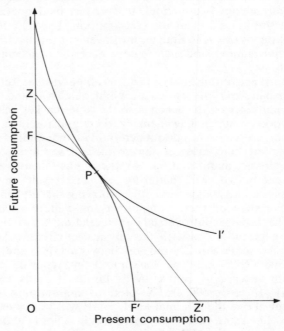

Figure 8.4   *Maximising consumption over time*

Figure 8.2 (a) with the axes relabelled. The relative price of present to future consumption is $(1+i)$ – where i is the interest rate. Equation 1 becomes

$$W = \sum_{t=0}^{\infty} (1+i)^{-t} C_t. \tag{2}$$

This is no more than an expression for wealth including not only

physical and financial capital but all determinants of future spending power.

To see this, consider an individual's wealth. This is normally regarded as comprising his physical and financial assets. Were the individual constrained to live solely off the wealth (W), his consumption stream would be constrained by Equation 2. In these circumstances, his wealth may be regarded as the (maximum) *present value of his consumption stream*. This concept may be generalised to the more usual cases where the individual (or group of individuals, such as the nation) possesses other 'assets', such as pension rights or the ability to contribute to productive activity and thus earn income. Indeed the former are frequently included in statistics of personal wealth, while the latter is referred to as 'human capital'. The extensions of consumption to include household production, environmental services and other

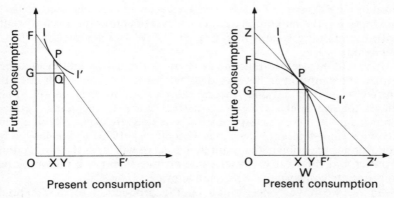

Figure 8.5 *Investment as a measure of future consumption*

imputations and to exclude defensive expenditures of course necessitates further extension to the concept of wealth. Thus defined, wealth is an appropriate maximand, an appropriate index of socioeconomic performance.

A major difficulty with this measure, however, is that it involves *explicitly* the prediction of future consumption levels and the selection of discount rates. These problems are apparently circumvented by using *investment* as a measure of the impact of current activity on the future consumption stream. The procedure is explained for the two-period case using Figure 8.5.

Figure 8.5(a) shows a linear production frontier. OF > OF' on account of technical progress and the greater efficiency of round-about production. The slope of FF' revalues future consumption in terms of present consumption foregone. Wealth equals present consumption plus discounted future consumption, i.e. $OX + XF' = OF'$.

This is in fact the maximum possible present consumption. But notice that its attainment involves not merely *not increasing* capital but actually *running it down* to the maximum possible extent.

Now consider investment explicitly: with perfect markets, the value of a marginal investment (in terms of present consumption foregone) must equal the value of the increment to future consumption discounted by the market rate of interest. If zero investment is defined as that level which keeps wealth intact (so that future consumption = maximum present consumption, OG = OF'), then the value of investment is XY and production (consumption plus investment) is OY. Thus wealth equals production plus maximum possible disinvestment.

Figure 8.5(b) shows a curvilinear production frontier. Now future consumption is valued at the operative marginal rate given by the slope of ZZ'. Wealth is OZ (not OF') investment XY (not XW) and production OY (not OW). It is not true (as sometimes stated) that production is the maximum attainable level of consumption consistent with maintaining wealth intact. That is OW (see Samuelson, 1961; Weitzman, 1976).

It should be stressed that the problem of predicting and evaluating future consumption is not avoided by this procedure – it is merely shifted from the national income accountant to the market. The diagrammatic analysis assumed perfect markets including perfect knowledge. If these assumptions fail – as they are especially likely to do with inter-temporal decisions (Lecomber, 1975) – the tangency conditions break down, the indifference curve will cross the production frontier and the relative social value of investment will no longer be appropriately measured by its relative price.

So far we have concentrated on the production of new capital goods. Investment represents a possible use for productive resources, an alternative use to consumption. This provides the basis for the method of valuation just outlined. In addition capital goods depreciate, through ageing and through use; they obsolesce, finally they are scrapped; year by year they lose economic value. It is universally recognised that investment, and hence production, should be measured net of some measure of depreciation.

The difficulties surrounding the measurement of depreciation are notorious and so great that most economists prefer to work with the theoretically inferior gross concepts. One difficulty stems from the fact that second-hand capital goods are not normally bought and sold and, when they are, they are generally sold at a price which greatly understates their value-in-use. Thus a machine may be of great value to the using firm, but have no more than scrap value to anyone else. The conventional procedure in valuing capital goods both for tax purposes and for national income accounts is accordingly to assume an economic life for the good, to assume that the initial value of the asset is equal to its cost, that its final value is its scrap value and to obtain values at intermediate date by interpolation.

The length-of-life assumption is particularly crucial and is very arbitrary. The difficulty stems from the fact that the life of most assets is determined less by physical ageing than by obsolescence, caused especially by the development of more efficient alternative machines. Hence the important point that the length of life and hence the proper allowance to be made for depreciation (by the firm, the tax man and the national income accountant) depends on expected technical developments which can only be guessed at. A related problem is how to treat an *un*anticipated technical development which reduces the value of existing assets. Is this to be regarded as depreciation or as a capital loss and, if the latter, how should this be treated in the accounts? This issue is of theoretical importance and will recur in our discussion of natural resource depletion. In practice the problem is entirely obscured by the arbitrary conventions adopted to measure depreciation.

Depreciation of man-made assets is an ancient problem of national accounting and has been extensively discussed. It has been introduced here because the problems encountered closely parallel those of measuring depletion of natural resources.

Natural resources, oil, minerals, agricultural land, etc., are an important input to production and an important component of our wealth. Their use frequently involves their destruction or impairment for future use and may therefore have an adverse effect on future consumption. If so, resource use must be regarded as disinvestment and a deduction should be made from the welfare measure. If resource pessimists are right in their view that resource depletion presents a grave threat to future prosperity and perhaps even human survival, the deduction should presumably be a large one.

Unfortunately the valuation of resource depletion presents all the problems encountered in valuing depreciation and some additional ones. Let us look at possible approaches.

First, notice that the procedures used for depreciation are not available, because there are no production-cost values to use as starting values. However the non-availability of such unsatisfactory procedures should not perhaps be regretted too much.

Conceptually the most satisfactory way is to estimate the impact of reducing the resource stock on the future consumption stream. The present value of this impact provides an estimate of depletion. Of course this approach involves an assessment of future development in technology and tastes as well as future resource discoveries. It also involves the choice of a discount rate. At one extreme, with few new discoveries or technical developments, the impact on future consumption is considerable and should be given a high weight on account of the respective poverty of future generations. A correspondingly large figure should be entered for resource depletion. At the other, technical developments greatly reduce the future value of conserved resources and a low or zero figure should be entered. Alternatively, if we (who?) do not care much about future generations' welfare, a high discount rate should be used and again the present value of the impact is small. It was precisely this desire to avoid predicting future developments and choosing a discount rate that led us to prefer output to wealth as a welfare measure.

A second approach is to use the prices of resource products. Of course these will reflect market views of future resource scarcity, which may be erroneous, but to rely on market views of the future accords with the general methodology of national income accounting. These prices will include the costs of extraction and transport and these latter will have to be deducted to arrive at the value of resources *in situ*. With constant costs of extraction this approach would be relatively straightforward. However the extraction cost function is, typically, extremely complex and in particular immediate costs depend on the amount of ore or fuel *previously extracted*. Thus extraction of a unit now raises the cost of subsequent extraction and this effect must be regarded as a cost of extraction. The full expression for marginal extraction cost is quite complex, even assuming the cost function to be known and constant. If these assumptions are abandoned, not only does marginal cost become even more involved but, more fundamentally, depends on developments in technology, etc. The national income statistician is once again forced back on his own predictions of the future.

This may sometimes be avoided by measuring the values of resources *in situ* directly. But this approach too is surrounded by difficulties. First, transactions in oil wells or mines are comparatively rare (and typically involve plant and 'goodwill' as well as the natural resources). This is the more serious in that the value of one mine cannot be inferred from the selling price of another due to differences in ore quality or accessibility. Moreover we need to know not merely the value of a mine at a particular date, but the change in value due to extraction. As explained above, this could not be simply inferred from the proportion of ore extracted, due to the complexity of the cost function. Nor could the change in the value of the land be used, as this would incorporate inflation in prices of such land. In particular if, as pessimists fear, oil becomes increasingly scarce, the price of oil-bearing land will increase and, since oil is inelastic, so will its value; clearly it would be nonsensical in these circumstances to say that oil stocks are growing. The situation is familiar enough to national income accountants: the increase in the value of stocks must be purged of stock appreciation. In the case of material stocks, the stock appreciation element is relatively easy to disentangle, in the case of resource stocks it would be extremely difficult.

Many writers (e.g. Barnett and Morse, 1963) have emphasised that resource scarcity is mitigated by new discoveries and improvements in extraction techniques. Historically, as optimists emphasise, 'known' reserves of most mineral and fuel resources have risen over time due to these factors. How these factors should be treated in the national accounts is not altogether clear and depends partly on the origin of such discoveries. If they are accidental, then, although the present value of the welfare stream has increased, it may be argued that this is not as a result of economic activity – it represents an exogenous change (like a change in climate or in the aggressiveness of neighbour countries) and should therefore not figure in GNP.

On the other hand, discoveries and technical improvements are largely the result of systematic exploration and research, no doubt particularly stimulated by incipient scarcity. If so, given suitably perfect markets, the cost of the marginal unit of exploration or research will equal the value of the expected return. Provided these activities are treated as investment, GNP already includes an appropriate allowance for exploration and research. Of course the above applies only to marginal exploration (or research) and there will be supramarginal exploration with apparently higher returns. But this difficulty applies equally to other forms of investment. The principle underlying national income accounts is measurement at the margin. In practice most exploration activity is appropriately treated as investment, but much research activity is regarded as current and hence intermediate expenditure and excluded from GNP. This difficulty, which has often been noted (e.g. Juster, 1974), is common to all R&D expenditure, not solely that related to extraction technology.

So far only *non-renewable* productive resources have been considered. In the case of *renewable* resources, such as forests, fisheries and agricultural land, no adjustment is required provided they are in fact renewed, that is, provided their quality is maintained. But of course this cannot always be assumed. Forests may be felled, fisheries overfished, land fertility reduced by, for example, erosion or leaching of nutrients. The future productive potential of these resources is thereby reduced and disinvestment has clearly occurred. Effectively the resources are being 'mined' and the above discussion of non-renewable resources, the same principles and the same difficulties apply.

Certain productive resources are more intangible, for example climate and crop resistance to pests. If human activity (e.g. fuel consumption, pollution, diversion of rivers, felling of forests) leads to climatic change and this change affects crop fertility, then clearly this change represents an investment (positive or negative) just as much as if fertility is changed by erosion or drainage or similar impact on the land. Similarly, if application of pesticides leads to the destruction of natural predators or the development of more virulent pests, this should be regarded as a disinvestment.

It may perhaps be thought that we have concentrated excessively on *adverse* effects on natural resources. It is certainly true that man can augment the productivity of renewable resources. However most deliberate augmentation (e.g. tree planting, land drainage, etc.) is already appropriately classified as investment. There is one exception to this, probably a rare one, namely, abstinence. If man refrains from fishing from a depleted stock, the stock will build up, and this should indeed be regarded as investment. (This case closely parallels the depreciation of physical capital.) Accidental impacts on the environment are almost invariably adverse.

Extending the consumption concept necessitates a parallel extension to investment. Any change affecting the future welfare stream must be regarded as investment or disinvestment. Suppose, for example, a new factory spoils a beautiful view. The future welfare stream is favourably affected by the goods produced, an effect measured more or less correctly by the cost of the investment. The stream is at the same time adversely affected by the impact on the view. This impact, currently ignored, is clearly a disinvestment. Its value is the net present value of the deterioration of the view. This is of course notoriously difficult to estimate, so difficult indeed that it has not even been considered in the earlier chapters of this book.

Consider another case, the building of a new airport. In this case, the main disamenity arises not from the airport itself but the noise of aircraft landing and taking off. It might be thought that no disinvestment arises in respect of the former. But this would be erroneous. The noise effects could be avoided only by not using the airport, but if this were done, there would be no benefits from the airport, and the conventional value of the investment should be excluded too. The investment is undertaken and hence valued on certain assumptions about its future operation. Whatever disbenefits arise from such operations must be regarded as disinvestment.

Notice that, in the absence of noise controls, the mode of operations of the airport will be sub-optimal. If optimal noise controls were introduced, both the marketed benefits and the noise disbenefits would be reduced and the value of the investment would rise. This indicates that the valuation of an investment depends on the level of environmental controls in the future. Should the national income statistician assume 'optional' controls, or should he attempt to predict the control regime likely to operate in practice? Welfare is also affected by the quality of human relationships and hence any persistent change in this important aspect of life must also be regarded as (dis)investment. Juster (1973) labels such investment 'changes in the stock of socio-political' wealth. Though important this would seem to present almost insuperable measurement problems.

POPULATION

A few writers advocate GNP itself as a welfare measure. The general view however is that it is not the size of the cake (GNP) that matters so much as the size of the individual slice. The size of the average slice may be obtained by dividing GNP by the number of individuals. If desired, some correction may be made for variations in needs between different demographic groups, for example children or pensioners, population being re-expressed in terms of equivalent adults. This issue of possible variations in needs however opens a Pandora's Box and is considered in more detail later.

Focusing on income per head does involve certain paradoxes. For example it is easy to show (e.g. Lecomber, 1974) that if a man migrates from a poor country to a rich country, income per head may fall in both countries as a result and yet everyone be better off. The paradox illustrates well the conceptual difficulties involved in comparing the welfare of different-sized groups. In the case of migration, this may be avoided by considering separately the welfare of three unchanging groups; (1) migrants, (2) other residents of the host country and (3) other residents of the other country. If the welfare of all three groups moves in the same direction, clear conclusions may be drawn; if not, then distributional issues arise which simple aggregates cannot hope to resolve.

But how should population changes through births (or deaths) be evaluated? One might ask how the welfare of the *previously existing* population changed (this should include an allowance for parental satisfaction incidentally), but how to deal with the welfare of the new arrivals is more difficult since it seems to involve comparison with the state of 'non-existence'. This is of course the same difficulty that arises in the evaluation (e.g. by cost-benefit analysis) of birth control programmes (Blandy, 1974).

Public consumption is customarily valued by the expenditure incurred. This approach is particularly inadequate when population changes. In the case of a pure public good the benefits to existing consumers are unaffected by additional consumers resulting from population increase. Thus for a constant level of benefits, expenditure *per head* falls. Pure public goods represent an extreme example of economies of scale which are inadequately reflected in a cost-based measure of benefits.

Where public goods (e.g. roads) are subject to congestion, the situation is more complex. While uncongested, the above argument applies. But as congestion sets in, the average benefits from any given road system begin to fall, slowly at first and then rapidly. Congestion may be overcome by expanding the system. If expansion takes place *pro rata* with population increase and with constant returns to scale, expenditure per head will be an adequate indicator of benefit per head. But if there are diminishing returns to road construction or if, e.g. on account of external costs of roads, congestion is allowed to increase, then the rise in *per capita* expenditure on roads will overstate the average level of benefits. This kind of phenomenon is perhaps becoming increasingly common as population densities increase.

The remedy to these problems is to measure the benefits rather than the costs of public expenditure. This is doubtless difficult, but perhaps no more difficult than, for example, attempting systematically to measure environmental quality.

So far we have considered the effects of population size. In addition, population *growth* has implications for welfare in that, in the absence of *disembodied* technical change, investment is required simply to maintain existing welfare. This effect is indeed well known in the population literature. It has accordingly been suggested, e.g. by Nordhaus and Tobin (1972), that investment be measured net not only of depreciation but of the increase in the capital stock required to match the increase in population. (If there is disembodied technical progress then 'a given level of consumption could be sustained with a steady decline in the capital-output ratio' (Nordhaus and Tobin, 1972, p. 7). It is not altogether clear whether zero investment is that level which keeps consumption per head constant or that which allows it to grow at the rate of technical progress.)

A PIONEERING ATTEMPT AT REFORM

The extensions proposed in the preceding sections raise formidable problems of concept and measurement. Not surprisingly, hard-pressed official statisticians have been reluctant to initiate reforms, while outsiders have lacked the resources to collect and process the required information. Virtually all the work on the subject has been at a conceptual level. One notable and interesting exception is a paper by Nordhaus and Tobin (1972) (hereafter NT) which attempts to derive an extended 'measure of economic welfare' (MEW) for the United States in selected years. This study is quoted extensively (especially as evidence against the anti-growth position) and therefore merits especially careful scrutiny.

We shall first consider NT's corrections one by one in the order in which they were introduced in the last two sections. We shall then put the results together and attempt an overall assessment.

Home production   NT do not attempt a direct valuation of home production – the necessary data are just not available. Instead they estimate the time devoted to home production and infer a value from this. They divide non-work time into three components. The first comprises a standard seven hours for sleep, plus commuting and other time associated with work and personal care – these they regard as 'instrumental maintenance items' conferring no final benefit. The second is an item in a survey of living habits as 'housework' – this would appear to include cleaning, washing, preparation of meals, etc., as well as gardening, redecorating the house or do-it-yourself. The third group comprises pure leisure including 'time at restaurant, tavern; at friends' or relatives' home; in games, sports, church; recreation at home; reading; and sleep' in excess of the allotted seven hours.

In the general calculations (variants are also presented) home production is valued at the current value of the real wage; thus it is assumed that home production shares in the productivity increases of the market sector (also that the real wage measures productivity and that technical progress is labour augmenting). This is perhaps not unreasonable in view of the major innovations in labour-saving appliances.

Perhaps the greatest difficulty with this approach is the assignment of time to household production. For example, it is difficult to see why cleaning one's face should be regarded as instrumental while cleaning one's house is assumed to confer final value. In both cases what matters is whether extra cleaning activity confers cleanliness or whether it is simply offsetting some by-product of socioeconomic activity, e.g. air pollution. Time spent digging one's own garden is apparently classified as leisure. Some of these problems could certainly be resolved by more comprehensive surveys, especially if designed specifically to estimate MEW, but many conceptual difficulties would remain.

Leisure NT's definition of leisure time has just been given. It is valued at base-year wage rates throughout and thus its value is assumed not to be augmented by technical progress. Arguably, with improved leisure equipment, this assumption is conservative and alternative figures are also presented.

Particular difficulties arise with the valuation of the time of the non-employed. NT credit the unemployed with a zero price during normal working hours, but note that this is too low where unemployment is frictional or voluntary (one might however suggest a negative valuation to represent the social distress associated with involuntary unemployment). The time of housewives and those in full-time education is rather arbitrarily valued at the wages of similar groups within the workforce. It should also be noted that transportation studies suggest that the value of leisure time is a small fraction of the wage rate. This finding is partly explained by income tax and in this connection it is not stated whether the wages are reckoned gross or net of tax. Finally, certain uses of leisure time could be regarded as 'defensive' as when journeys to friends or recreation are lengthened by congestion.

Defensive expenditures   These are referred to by NT as 'instrumental expenditures' or 'regrettable necessities'. They distinguish under this head (1) commuting and private business expenses and (2) defence. These are two obvious items, but a small fraction of the items that might have been considered. Conspicuous omissions are expenditures to prevent any deterioration of physical or social environment. Notice that investment as well as current items can be regarded as defensive and that defensive investment may be undertaken by firms as well as by government. On the other hand, as explained earlier, the recognition of defensive expenditure is not easy, and the automatic assignment of 'defence' to this category is questionable.

Government intermediate expenditures   Conventionally all government expenditures are assumed to confer final benefit. Clearly some expenditures (e.g. advice to industry) are more appropriately regarded as intermediate. NT assign to this category a large class of government expenditures including 'general government', sanitation and 'civilian safety'. This assignment seems very dubious as many of the benefits accrue to individuals rather than firms. Current expenditure on roads presents at least as good a case for inclusion in this head. On the other hand 'civilian safety' might possibly be excluded on the alternative ground that it is defensive.

Environmental quality   NT confine their attention to one aspect of environmental quality, namely, that an increasing percentage of the population live in high-density, urbanised areas. The relative disutility of urban living is assessed from wage differentials. Wages are regressed against population size and density, percentage of the population urbanised and other variables, using cross-section data for US districts in 1960. Then, assuming no change in the *relative* disutility of varying degrees of urbanisation, the effect of demographic changes on amenity can be calculated. A small though rapidly growing item results.

This approach is subject to numerous difficulties as discussed in Lecomber (1975). But perhaps the main points to be made are the following: on the one hand it is a very comprehensive measure in that it picks up *all* differences between the urban and rural environment, not only noise, pollution, visual effects, etc., but also violence, crime and the quality of social relationships. On the other hand it makes no attempt to pick up the extent to which the quality of either urban or rural environment has changed over time, and according to many of the social critics these changes are large and adverse. NT's estimates lend no support whatever to the following statement made by Juster in his foreword: 'Their calculations suggest that the extensively discussed and debated gaps in the accounts data relating to the growth in environmental disamenities (pollution, urban crises, racial disharmony etc.) while sizeable in absolute terms play a relatively modest role in the total picture when compared with other gaps.' Other commentators too seem unduly impressed by the small size of these estimates of disamenity.

As similar data for a number of years become available, it would be possible to examine the secular change in the urban wage premium. If it could be assumed that the quality of rural life is unchanged, the change in the quality of urban life could be estimated. However this assumption is very questionable and in any case the whole method lays excessive weight on the perfection of labour markets.

Additional categories of capital NT recognise the following non-orthodox categories of capital: (1) cars and other consumer durables, (2) government infrastructure (excluding military) and (3) human capital (health and education). Expenditure on these items is transferred from current expenditure to investment. This has no effect on GNP but certain consequentials do.

These additional assets provide services, some final, some intermediate. No adjustment is required in respect of the latter whose value is already adequately reflected in the output of final goods. However estimates for the final services provided must be added into MEW. Thus NT treat purchase of cars (analogously to the standard treatment of housing) as extensions to the capital stock subject to depreciation and yielding 'motoring services' just as they would if the cars were rented from a hire firm instead of being bought outright. The required distinction between final and intermediate services is not easy to make and NT make some very arbitrary assumptions. In particular, the 'admittedly extreme' assumption is made 'that no direct gains in satisfaction are produced by health and education, whose sole benefit is assumed to lie in increases in productivity'. In fact they may provide both immediate and deferred final benefits and a strong case could be made for regarding these as more important than the productivity benefits.

The growth requirement NT assume technical progress to be labour augmenting and calculate the growth requirement as the level of investment required to keep consumption per head not constant but rising in line with the growth in technical progress. The dependence of the estimate on a specific assumption about the form of the production function should be noted.

The results of NT calculations are summarised in Table 8.1.

Column 1 gives the values of the various items in the base year (1958), column 2 expresses these as a percentage of GNP. It will be seen how the adjustments (rows 3–9) are dominated by leisure and home production. Since leisure grows much more slowly than GNP the effect of the adjustment is to reduce growth as measured in the conventional percentage way (column 4). NT comment: *'Per capita* MEW has been growing more slowly than per capita NNP (or GNP). 1·1 per cent for MEW as against 1·7 per cent for NNP.' But it must again be stressed (cf. p. 175) that the zero benchmarks for many of the items, including the dominant leisure item, are essentially arbitrary and so therefore are rates of growth. Absolute changes, shown in column 3, do not suffer from this defect.

Table 8.1   *From GNP to MEW*

	\$ thousand million, 1958 prices and %				
	1958	% GNP	Change 1929–65	% Change 1929–65	Error assess- ment
1 GNP	447·3	100	414·2	204	low
2 NNP	408·4	91	379·5	207	—
3 Home production	239·7	54	209·7	244	v. high
4 Leisure	554·9	124	287·4	84	v. high
5 Defensive expenditures	−76·3	17	−77·1	454	medium
6 Environmental quality (disamenities of urbanisation)	−27·6	6	−22·1	171	v. high
7 Additional capital services	54·8	12	49·2	166	high
8 Additional capital consumption	−27·3	6	−73·4	380	high
9 Growth requirement	−78·9	18	−55·7	121	high
10 Sustainable MEW	1,047·7	234	697·5	128	high
11 GNP/head (\$)	2,500		1,503	90	low
12 Sustainable MEW/ head (\$)	5,991		1,916	43	high

Source: Nordhaus and Tobin (1972), Tables A16, A17, A19.

Column 5 shows NT's assessment of reliability. 'Medium', 'high' and 'v. high' percentage errors are about two, five and ten times the percentage errors associated with GNP. Errors both of concept and data are taken into account. The very high errors associated with home production, leisure and disamenities or urbanisation should especially be noted.

In assessing the study, it should be stressed that no adjustments have been made for the following items;

(1) goods or services provided free to employers, customers or business associates;
(2) working conditions;
(3) the wider aspects of the quality of the physical environment;

(4) the quality of the social environment;
(5) the depletion of natural productive resources;
(6) the depletion of resources providing environmental services;
(7) changes in socio-political wealth;
(8) changes in welfare associated with changing wants, some of these arising as a by-product of economic activity.

It will be recognised that these are very important aspects of welfare and at the same time ones which are very difficult to measure. One of these, resource depletion, is in fact considered explicitly by NT and merits further comment. In the section headed 'Extending the Investment Measure' it was suggested that the appropriate value of resource depletion depends on the prospects for technical progress, substitutions and discoveries in the distant future. In as far as these factors are effective in alleviating resource scarcity, resource depletion is near costless and a small or zero item is correct. NT construct and estimate a three-factor neo-classical production function. They find that the elasticity of substitution between labour-capital and resources is high and that technical progress has been resource augmenting. Very similar conclusions have in fact been reached by Barnett and Morse (1963) and others who have made a historical study of resources. In fact, the significance of these results is negligible, for a variety of reasons. (1) It is *assumed* that the quantity of resource inputs is constant. Their model indeed applies only to renewable resources. In the case of non-renewable resources, resource inputs have been increasing, this arguably hastening the date of eventual exhaustion (NT in fact admit this limitation, but thereafter ignore it). (2) The past history of resources provides virtually no guide as to whether future resource scarcities will be overcome (NT remark on p. 15: 'Of course it is always possible that the future will be discontinuously different from the past', but clearly consider entertainment of such a possibility to be the height of perversity). (3) The model applies only to resources that are marketed, and excludes common resources (e.g. fisheries) as well as externality effects (e.g. from the felling of forests). Altogether NT's work provides little guide as to the future cost of current resource depletion and hence to the appropriate entries to be made in the national accounts. For a fuller discussion see Lecomber (1975, appendix).

CONCLUSIONS

Nordhaus and Tobin's Measure of Economic Welfare is deficient in many important respects. Of course, such deficiencies are to be expected in a pioneering study of this sort. Without doubt MEW could be greatly improved by further conceptual and empirical work, especially in conjunction with a major data-gathering effort by the official statistical services. Nordhaus and Tobin had to rely on fragmentary data collected for other purposes. If the Measure of Economic Welfare is to occupy the central place currently occupied by GNP, special surveys should be mounted to fill the main statistical gaps.

But while much could be done to improve MEW, the cost not only to government but to the individuals and firms asked to supply the information would be very great. In statistical conferences, respondents often admit to taking very little trouble to provide accurate data; they complain that the burden of form filling is large, increasing and unreasonable, that they receive no private gain and can perceive little social gain from their efforts. This suggests both that the frequently ignored cost to respondents of data collection is high and also a possible relationship between the quantity of data collected and its quality. Not only may further data be inaccurate but its collection may impair the accuracy of existing series. In short, the costs of constructing a more adequate MEW are great and the proposed measure requires a correspondingly strong justification.

It must also be recognised that a perfect MEW is an impossibility: in the first place, data requirements are heavy and prospects are not improved by the considerations of the last paragraph. It is inconceivable that all the data gaps could be plugged and probable that much of the data collected would be inaccurate and, worse, systematically biased. Moreover our discussions indicated how much any MEW depends on predictions of the future and on value judgements.

Most fundamentally, MEW (like GNP) makes no attempt to measure satisfaction directly. Rather it is inferred from willingness to pay. The relevance of such inferences depends on two critical but dubious assumptions: (1) that consumers are successful maximisers of their own welfare and (2) that consumer preferences are given exogenously, that is, independently of the socioeconomic system. In fact consumers often act in ignorance and may also exhibit weakness of will or inconsistency. This is indicated by the regret that people often express over past choices and the restrictions they place on their own future choices, to avoid falling victims to temptation (compulsive eating and addictions to drink or tobacco are extreme examples). Such 'irrationality' is given official recognition in laws on drugs, drink, product quality and the wearing of seat belts and in the heavy (regressive) taxation of tobacco. Many social critics (e.g. Galbraith, 1958; Mishan, 1967; Tsuru, 1972) provide lists of goods which (they claim) add little to or even subtract from human welfare.

Changing preferences creates an even more serious problem in that the theories of Duesenberry (1947) and Galbraith (1958) imply a systematic bias to GNP of a type that could seriously mislead policy makers. Deusenberry suggests that an individual's welfare is determined not by his *absolute* income but by his income *relative* to that of his reference group. Galbraith suggests that 'wants are increasingly created by the process by which they are satisfied . . . passively . . . by suggestion or emulation . . . or . . . actively . . . through advertising and salesmanship'. Both these suggestions mean that a rise in GNP or any measure based on willingness-to-pay shifts individual preference curves in such a way that individuals become less satisfied with a given bundle of goods. This makes the rise partly or even entirely or more-than-entirely self-defeating. Such is indeed an important strand of the anti-growth case.

No one but an economist would attempt to deny the reality and significance of these phenomena. Refreshingly, Nordhaus and Tobin readily admit that 'consumers are susceptible to influence by the examples and tastes of other consumers and by the sales of producers' but add 'the philosophical problems raised by the malleability of consumer wants are too deep to be resolved in economic accounting'. If willingness-to-pay can be accepted as a criterion of value, then national income accounting and indeed applied welfare economics is reduced to the (difficult enough) empirical problem of determining willingness-to-pay. If willingness-to-pay is abandoned, an alternative source of value must be found. That the individual is a poor judge of his own welfare does not imply that anyone could do any better. This is why, except in extreme cases, governments are reluctant to restrict or bias consumer choice. If it is sometimes the business of government to make value judgements, it is surely the business of the national income accountant to avoid them. As Okun (1971) puts it: 'There is no room for philosopher kings.'

In short, NT's judgement that no allowance can be made for changing preferences is surely justified. But the fact remains that a measure which includes no such allowances cannot seriously claim to be a Measure of Economic Welfare and cannot therefore be used as a policy maximand.

A possible alternative approach is to measure welfare according to individual's own subjective assessments. Numerous surveys have been conducted and an interesting cross-country analysis is reported by Easterlin (1974). (One finding was little correlation between GNP and avowed happiness and a mildly inverse correlation between growth and happiness.) There are obvious difficulties to this approach. (1) Are avowals of happiness necessarily well correlated with inner feelings of happiness? (2) Is happiness an appropriate goal? What about the lotus-eating or Brave New World brands of happiness? Perhaps we should be more concerned with the full development of personality – at any event these deep questions about the ultimate goals of human life must be answered explicitly. (3) How can the investment of socioeconomic activity be handled? Despite these limitations, these researches are perhaps worth pursuing; it is surely at least as useful to find out what makes people say they are happy as what makes for a large GNP (or MEW).

But this raises an even more fundamental question. Do we really need an aggregate measure of welfare? A good starting point is to consider the uses currently made of GNP.

(1) *As a short-term indicator of economic activity used in demand management.*

(2) *As an explanatory variable in various economic and social analysis (e.g. a determinant of the birth rate or the level of public expenditure).*

In both these uses, especially the former, MEW seems likely to perform markedly less well than GNP. A welfare measure is after all not particularly appropriate to these exercises. One implication of this is that if MEW were to be constructed, it should be in addition to, not instead of, GNP.

(3) *As a summary of general historical interest.*

(4) *As a figure for politicians and others to bandy about as measures of achievement.*

These are essentially subsidiary uses, and little need be said about them. The historical interest stems partly from uses (1) and (2) above for which GNP is appropriate enough; partly because GNP is regarded as a measure of achievement. Clearly, in this latter aspect, GNP is deficient and MEW would seem preferable. However one should consider the more fundamental question as to whether summary statistics of achievement are required. After all, the obvious and cheapest remedy to the use of a misleading measure is to use no measure at all. Indeed the social critics have achieved some success in dethroning GNP. To substitute an extended, improved, but still very inadequate MEW could be a retrograde step.

(5) *As a maximand of economic policy*

There have been a number of investigations of the causes in variations in economic growth (e.g. Denison). The causes once found can be operated on, thus increasing the growth rate. More generally, policies could be, and sometimes are, assessed by evaluating their impact on GNP. The legitimacy of such procedures depends entirely on the claim of GNP to measure welfare and to the extent that this claim fails, such procedures are extremely pernicious. It is in this connection that the need for an extended MEW seems strongest.

However, closer investigation suggests that impact on MEW could play but a minor and then often misleading role in the evaluation of most policies. Suppose that somehow a perfect MEW had been constructed, perfect in that it values all components of welfare at the appropriate marginal valuations of the base year. Consider a project. Its impact on MEW is somewhere near the net present value as evaluated by standard cost-benefit techniques. However there is one major difference. Cost-benefit takes account of consumer surplus, an aspect of welfare that is almost impossible to incorporate in our economy-wide MEW. Hence a standard cost-benefit evaluation is in most respects identical and in one respect superior to an evaluation of the impact of the project on even an ideal MEW. In practice also it will be possible to take account of all kinds of factors (including income distribution) in the context of a specific cost-benefit analysis that are difficult to accommodate systematically in MEW.

A standard objection to cost-benefit analysis is that it is a partial equilibrium technique, not appropriate to evaluating major structural shifts in the economy involving widespread changes in relative prices. A model embracing the whole economy is needed and it might be thought that an economy-wide welfare measure is appropriate. However, here too we run into the difficulty that MEW, by employing constant weights, takes no account of shifts in relative prices. Such shifts can readily be allowed for in the context of any particular investigation, but are difficult to incorporate in an overall index, which therefore obstructs rather than assists analysis.

It is only in empirical investigation of the causes of economic welfare (in the Denison manner) that use of MEW seems to offer any real assistance. But once again, the inevitable deficiencies in MEW will tend to invalidate the conclusions. In any case MEW includes so many diverse conditions that a more disaggregated approach is likely to be more illuminating.

In short it is difficult to see that MEW has any useful part to play in the formulation of policy.

(6) *As a basis for assessing contributions to (or receipts of) international funds.*

There is certainly a case for basing such contributions on a more comprehensive welfare measure. However ideally the criterion should be a measure of welfare itself, rather than the contribution of the socieconomic system to welfare. Those with a superior climate or a more beautiful environment should contribute more, as should those whose populations are naturally healthy or contented. The difficulties of constructing such an all-embracing welfare measure are even greater than those already considered. However, even if the ideal is unattainable, a movement towards a more comprehensive measure of welfare represents an improvement, though one which it is surely not worth a great expenditure of resources to secure.

Work on extending GNP has had a useful effect in clarifying the

196   *The Valuation of Social Cost*

determinants of welfare and highlighting the deficiencies in GNP itself. It also reveals clearly the enormous conceptual difficulties and costs involved in obtaining a more comprehensive welfare measure which scarcely seems to justify the slight and questionable benefits such a measure would confer.

NOTES

1 It is sometimes suggested that increasing output enhances environmental quality, e.g. Beckerman (1974). The fallacies underlying this view are exposed by Mishan (1972) and Lecomber (1975).
2 To comparisons in absolute terms. Growth rates are however affected. Suppose our generalised GNP measure, for some zero, changes from a_0 to a_1. the growth rate is then $(a_1 - a_0)/a_0$. If the zero is shifted by d units, the absolute change $(a_1 - a_0)$ is unaffected but the growth rate changes to $(a_1 - a_0)/(a_0 - d)$. The impossibility of devising a satisfactory 'natural zero' is discussed in Lecomber (1975, pp. 18–24). A similar point arises in the correction of GNP to allow for leisure (see Usher, 1973).

REFERENCES

Archibald, G. C., 'Welfare economics, ethnics and essentialism', *Economica*, vol. XXVI, 1959, pp. 316–27.
Barnett, H. J., and Morse, C., *Scarcity and Growth* (Baltimore: Johns Hopkins Press, 1963).
Beckerman, W., *An Introduction to National Income Analysis* (London: Weidenfeld & Nicolson, 1968).
Beckerman, W., *In Defence of Economic Growth* (London: Jonathan Cape, 1974).
Blandy, R., 'The welfare analysis of fertility reduction', *Economic Journal*, vol. 81, 1974, pp. 109–29.
Boulding, K. E., 'Fun and games with the GNP – the role of misleading calculations in social policy', in *The Environmental Crisis*, ed. H. W. Helfrich (Yale: University Press, 1970), pp. 157–70.
Denison, E. F., *Why Growth Rates Differ* (Washington DC: The Brookings Institute 1968).
Denison. E. F., 'Welfare measurement and the GNP', *Survey of Current Business*, vol. 51, no. 1, 1971, pp. 13–16.
Duesenberry, J. S., *Income, Saving and the Theory of Consumer Behaviour* (Harvard: Harvard University Press, 1947).
Easterlin, R. A., 'Does economic growth improve the human lot? Some empirical evidence', in *Nations and Households in Economic Growth: Essays in Honor of Moses Abramovitz*, ed. P. A. David and M. W. Reder (New York: Academic Press, 1974).
Feldstein, M. S., 'Distributional preferences in public expenditure analysis', in *Redistribution Through Public Choice*, ed. H. Hochman and G. E. Paterson (Columbia: Columbia University Press, 1972), pp. 136–261.
Galbraith, J. M., *The Affluent Society* (London: Hamilton, 1958).
Harrod, Sir R., *Reforming the World's Money* (London: Macmillan, 1965).
Heilbroner, R. L. *An Enquiry into the Human Prospect* (New York: Norton, 1974).
Heller, W., 'Coming to terms with growth and the environment', in *Energy, Economic Growth and the Environment*, ed. S. H. Schurr (Baltimore: Johns Hopkins Press, 1972), pp. 3–19.
Hicks, J. R., *The Social Framework* (Oxford: Clarendon Press, 1942).
Jaszi, G., 'Comment', in *The Measurement of Economic and Social Performance*, ed. M. Moss (New York: National Bureau of Economic Research, 1973), pp. 25–84.

Juster, F. T., 'A framework for the measurement of economic and social peformance', in *The Measurement of Economic and Social Performance,* ed. M. Moss (New York. National Bureau of Economic Research, 1973), pp. 84–99.

Lecomber, J. R. C., *The Growth Objective,* International Institute for Social Economics, Monograph No. 3 (Humberside: Emmasglen, 1974).

Lescomber, J. R. C., *Economic Growth versus the Environment* (London: Macmillan, 1975).

Lipton, M., *Assessing Economic Performances* (London: Staples, 1968).

Massachusetts Institute of Technology, *Man's Impact on the Global Environment: Assessment and Recommendations for Policy* (Cambridge, Massachusetts: MIT Press, 1970).

Meadows, D. H., *et al., The Limits to Growth* (London: Earth Islands, 1972).

Mishan, E. J., *The Costs of Economic Growth* (London: Staples, 1967).

Nordhaus, W. D., and Tobin, J., 'Is growth obsolete?', in *Economic Growth,* National Bureau of Economic Research (Columbia: Columbia University Press, 1972).

Okun, A. M., 'Social welfare has no price tag', in *The Economic Accounts of the United States: Retrospect and Prospect,* anniversary issue of *Survey of Current Business,* vol. 51, no. 7, pt 11, 1971, pp. 129–33.

Pearce, D. W., *Cost Benefit Analysis* (London: Macmillan, 1971).

Pigou, A. G., *The Economics of Welfare* (London: Macmillan, 1924).

Ridker, R. G., *Economic Costs of Air Pollution* (New York: Praeger, 1967).

Samuelson, P. A., 'The evaluation of social income, capital formation and wealth', in *Theory of Capital,* ed. F. A. Lutz and D. C. Hague (London: Macmillan, 1961), pp. 32–57.

Tsuru, S., 'In place of GNP', in *Political Economy of Environment Problems of Method* (Paris: Mouton: 1972), pp. 11–25.

Usher, D., 'An imputation to the measure of economic growth for changes in life expectancy', in *The Measurement of Economic and Social Performance,* ed. M. Moss (New York: National Bureau of Economic Research, 1973), pp. 193–236.

Weisbrod, B., 'An expenditure measure of welfare', *Journal of Political Economy,* vol. 70, 1962, pp. 353–67.

Weitzman, M. L., 'On the welfare significance of national produce in a dynamic economy', *Quarterly Journal of Economics,* vol. XCI, 1976.

Index